T0329974

CURRENT ISSUES IN OPEN ECONOMY MACROECONOMICS

The only generalization that can be made about economics is that in economics no generalization can be made.

J.L.F.

Current Issues in Open Economy Macroeconomics

Paradoxes, Policies and Problems

J. L. Ford
University of Birmingham

Edward Elgar

Published by
Edward Elgar Publishing Limited
Gower House
Croft Road
Aldershot
Hants GU11 3HR
England

Gower Publishing Company
Old Post Road
Brookfield
Vermont 05036
USA

British Library Cataloguing in Publication Data
Ford, J. L. (James Lorne) *1939–*
    Current issues in open economy macroeconomics: paradoxes,
    policies and problems.
    1. Macroeconomics
    I. Title
    339

ISBN 978 1 85278 185 8

Contents

v

Contents

Preface

This volume is a collection of essays which I have written with colleagues and some of my doctoral students at the University of Birmingham during the past 18 months. The majority were completed in the Spring Term of 1989, whilst I had the luxury of Study Leave.

We like to think that there are several main areas of the subject in which we have been researching in the Department of Economics at Birmingham, and we have tried to encourage our (many) doctoral students to research in one of them. My own interests in recent times have embraced Uncertainty in Economics, Financial Models, Monetary Theory and Policy and Open Economy macro; but the research attempted has frequently involved all areas and arbitrage between the various techniques they utilize. Work on the topic of open economy macro per macroeconomic theory, which constitutes the essence of this Collection, began in 1984 when, together with my colleague Somnath Sen, research was started to expound the role of commercial policy, by means of a general tariff or quotas, in a macro, as opposed to a micro, context. Commercial policy had been severely neglected in analytical research, despite the fact that much had been written and said about such policy, especially in regard to the attempt by the Protectionist Lobby to re-assert itself consequent upon the declining fortunes of the world economy and the reluctance of some Western economies to indulge in the kind of expansionary, locomotive, policies which others in the world demanded. Discussion on commercial policy in the microeconomic literature, in what is referred to as the pure theory of international trade is, by contrast, voluminous. The open economy macro literature is still absolutely, and not just relatively, small. It was also our opinion that the literature which did exist at the time (up to the early 1980s) was not devoid of misunderstanding. So, we endeavoured to write a monograph on the subject, setting commercial policy alongside conventional stabilization policies, bearing in mind the forms of labour market structure which might exist in the world economies.

That book was the springboard for several critical appraisals and extensions of the open economy macro literature. These were taken up either by ourselves or by some of our doctoral students: Mansoob Murshed (now a colleague on the lecturing staff); Georgios P. Kouretas; Jassodra Maharaj; and King-Long Yang. The essays in this volume draw on that work.

Essays 2, 3 and 4 are co-authored with Dr Somnath Sen. Essay 5 is co-authored with Dr Kouretas, and is developed from one of the key chapters in his thesis. Essay 6, likewise, is based upon one of the central theoretical chapters of Dr Yang's thesis, though it also incorporates a summary of relevant econometric findings: it is co-authored with him and his principal supervisor, Dr David Dickinson. My collaborators for Essay 7 are (mainly) Dr Murshed and Dr Maharaj. The final essay in the Collection draws its inspiration from Dr Murshed's outstanding theoretical thesis on models of North-South macro interaction; even though the thesis *per se* does not contain an East-West model of the kind formulated in Essay 8.

In compiling this 'symposium', as would be anticipated, I owe a clear debt to my colleague Somnath Sen for the tireless way in which he has argued over key issues, provided ideas and insight. Mansoob Murshed has also been a source of inspiration and an invaluable foil against which ideas and analyses could be assessed. His own wide interests, embracing as they do the field of development economics, have been especially valuable. The general contribution of David Dickinson, with his particular expertise in monetary/financial theory, must also be mentioned. But special thanks must be extended to colleagues elsewhere who have kindly read these essays: Professor Bob Baldwin (whose principal interest is protectionism, even though his own many seminal contributions have tended to focus on its microeconomic aspects); Professor David Peel (whose focus is primarily on the theoretical aspects of stabilization policies in open-economy macro); and, particularly, to Professor Stephen Turnovsky (whose interests embrace all the issues covered in this collection), who also offered perceptive, general, comments on the composition of the collection and the design of some of the essays.

Finally, the list of acknowledgements would not be complete without a particular thanks to Mrs Linda Williamson, who typed the various editions of the manuscript. Despite the familiar problem of having to grapple with handwriting (I am still old-fashioned and averse to preparing even first drafts on a word processor!), she has had to handle a large quantity of highly technical material, more than is even apparent from this final manuscript. She has accomplished this task with efficiency and equanimity, and produced a manuscript whose high quality was commented upon by all who read it. To her, then, I proffer an inadequate 'thank you'.

J.L. Ford

1 Introduction

I have recently had the pleasure of reviewing Professor Charles Kindleberger's (1987) latest book, *International Capital Movements* (Ford 1989). In several respects this is a splendid volume, not the least of its best features being Kindleberger's exceptional facility to model complex features of the international economy by relying on fairly simple theoretical structures, but from which the maximum of insights are extracted; and his willingness to switch from one paradigm to another as he believes the situation requires. In that latter regard, he puts his position succinctly:

> In part . . . I have come to believe that in order successfully to interpret what goes on in the real world it is necessary to change models continuously: . . . and the analyst that relies on a single model is led deceptively into blind alleys. (Kindleberger 1987, p2).

For my own part, I happen to share Kindleberger's sentiments that there is no such thing as a universal model suitable for the analysis of international macroeconomics; and, equally, I have a natural affinity with his opinion that, as far as possible, the models we use should be as straightforward as we can make them. Even though there are senses in which Harry Johnson's famous *obiter dictum*, that an ideal economic model is one which 'produces much from little', is inadequate, perhaps as a guideline it has much to commend it. Yet, even the smallest model which is germane to the investigation of many central issues in international macroeconomics is often complex in its solution; for it is frequently impossible to limit, or to reduce, the model to one which amounts to no more than a second-order system.

As a consequence, formal, rigorous, analysis does require the use of formal, mathematical, models. In that respect, we have to depart in this Collection of Essays, from the 'descriptive theory' approach which Kindleberger pursues. Nevertheless, we endeavour, without destroying the purpose of our theoretical constructs, to keep their scale within bounds; and we have also adhered to frameworks which contain basic, fundamental, notions. We have tried to avoid the temptation to fill out our models with features which will not add substantially to their properties and to our conclusions. Hopefully, we have indeed eschewed the appendage of ostentatious attributes.

Again, in the spirit of Kindleberger, these essays seek to consider important issues, which in some ways, direct or tangential, are relevant, indeed, maybe crucial, to aspects of the international macroeconomy. *Ergo,* the conclusions obtained in the essays should be of direct or indirect value in the assessment of national and *inter*national economic policies; including implications for international co-operation in and, perhaps, co-ordination of, the conduct of economic policies by the various national government agencies (e.g. Central Banks, Treasuries).

Within the compass of government policies, some of the essays investigate the role of commercial policy, instead of, or as well as, the role of the more conventional forms of monetary and fiscal policy. That investigation is invariably undertaken in a world of flexible exchange rates. All but two of the essays are founded on a regime of floating exchange rates; those are: that concerned with the problems with which the open economy presents the small oil-exporting LDC; and that devoted to the development of a model for considering East-West dependence.

Some of the essays provide a challenge to current orthodoxy. The first contribution, for example, considers the Mundellian 'theorem' that under flexible exchange rates, commercial policy (ostensibly tariffs, but also quotas) if adopted by a small open economy in a venture to remove unemployment (to increase output) will inevitably be doomed to failure. This must be the outcome, almost *ex definitione*, the followers of the Mundellian tradition would argue: freely adjusting exchange rates negate (not just neutralize) the on-impact beneficial home-employment effects of the change in relative prices induced by the tariff. The Mundellian result is still almost sacrosanct in the literature and is frequently cited by the international economists seeking to offer policy prescriptions for the current ills of the world economy as providing an incontrovertible case against the adoption of any kind of protectionist stance by small open economies and by all LDCs. We have challenged that position in a comprehensive fashion in a previous monograph (see Ford and Sen 1985). It is true that some of what we have demonstrated there is infiltrating the literature and is being accepted as casting reasonable doubt at least on the Mundellian proposition. It seems to be of no import that as soon as the real sector framework utilized by Mundell *et al.* is extended to incorporate some kind of money/financial sector based on a portfolio of assets, the proposition no longer holds necessarily. The predominant opinion appears to be that the money/financial sector will be so primitive that the real sector effects within and across trading countries are paramount. The inevitable consequence is the tendency to accept with alacrity (especially if interventionism is regarded as an anathema) the application of the Mundellian theorem to a variety of economic experiences.

We make a plea, as it were, on the frontispiece of our monograph: *audi partem alteram.* Well, we have been successful in some small measure, as we have noted! However, we feel it necessary here to make a further attempt to set out the basic Mundellian framework and to analyse rigorously the Mundellian theorem. The exposition of the model (and its problems) is similar to that presented in Chapter 2 of Ford and Sen (1985); but it is not identical with it. We also provide yet *another* means by mathematical methods (to complement those in Ford-Sen 1985) of proving that the Mundellian proposition is *not* one which is universally valid, even in the confines of its own economic model of the home country and of the Rest of the World. Despite the fact that we do not make any attempt in Essay 2 to extend the model to encompass a money/financial sector, *et cetera*, as we have done previously, we regard the findings in the paper of some importance; this is not because of their own intrinsic nature but is due to the overwhelming acceptance of the Mundellian proposition as the orthodoxy.

Having said that, it is important for us to remark that we have omitted discussion of several aspects of tariffs in Essay 2: including the relevance for our findings of permanent versus temporary tariffs. These have been fully expored in Ford and Sen (1985); as has the (non) equivalence of tariffs and quotas. Those issues, however, played no part in the Mundellian schema. Additionally, we have not considered the role of tariffs through the new micro-economics literature on industrial organization and international trade (for a summary see Krugman 1987). That literature has provided extra reasons for the notion that free trade might not always be the optimum policy to pursue. Yet, Krugman's overall evaluation of that new literature, which he was so instrumental in developing, is that, on balance, it does not provide sufficient weight of argument against a policy of free trade, essentially though for reasons of political economy. On balance the new theory argues that 'free trade is passé: the implementation of interventionist policies (and their possible provocation of trade wars) is the drawback.

The role of commercial policy is also touched upon in Essay 3 which develops the Ford–Sen effect and condition; both of which overturn the Laursen–Metzler effect and its concomitant condition, in respect of the impact of the terms of trade on total expenditure. In this essay, we draw out the implication of the Ford–Sen effect and condition for major propositions in the open economy macro-literature. *Inter alia,* we cast doubt on the alleged universality of propositions concerned with: the comparative advantage under flexible exchange rates of monetary and fiscal policy in stimulating domestic economic activity; the assignment of stabilization policies under floating exchange rates; and the extent of economic dependency between nations, again in a regime of flexible exchange rates.

Essay 4 is devoted to consideration of another key concept in the literature, namely, (what we have labelled) the Niehans' paradox (1975). In developing the Mundell–Fleming model, under flexible exchange rates, Niehans demonstrated that provided particular (rather restrictive) conditions obtained, expansionary monetary policy in the domestic economy would *reduce* its aggregate output. The Mundell–Fleming conclusion was that it would automatically increase output, even with perfect capital mobility. In Essay 3 we have challenged that notion, as we have just intimated. But, in Essay 4 we do so by considering the role played by the Niehans' paradox itself in the establishment of his anti-orthodox conclusion.

Except for a section of Essay 3 devoted to the spill-over effects from country to country of economic expansion, or demand/supply shocks, to the other country, the first three essays have focused on models of small open economies. The second country is cast merely somewhat anonymously as The Rest of the World. Essay 5 moves away from that paradigm and introduces a second country with economic features which are as fully specified as are those of the domestic economy, so the rather faceless nature of the second economy has been repaired. The essay analyses stabilization policies in terms of how they affect the home and the foreign country's economic activity and 'economic welfare' (at least it discusses the impact on changes in those concepts). It does so by including an added ingredient: the nature of the labour market in each country. Accordingly, it is able to embody the presence of nominal or real wage rigidity in either or both countries. It also endeavours to analyse the issues of co-operation in, and co-ordination of, economic policy making between the two economies. This, together with the prior investigation of monetary, fiscal and commercial policies under the varying wage regimes, is of some relevance to the real world; wherein we see the policy conflict that has arisen, perhaps needlessly in recent times, between the Western economies (including here the Japanese economy) and the American. The former have, essentially, real wage resistance, while the latter economy exhibits money wage rigidity. The Western economies have been reluctant, as a consequence, to answer the repeated calls from the American policy makers, for fiscal expansion to be intiated in the Western bloc. The apprehension on the part of the Western economies has been that such an expansion would benefit economic activity in the USA but would emerge as a profligate policy for the Western bloc, because it would merely lead to stagflation. It is issues such as this to which we address ourselves in Essay 5.

The subject of the ensuing essay is the impact on asset and foreign exchange markets of Central Bank policy, including capital controls:

together with an inquiry into the effects on those markets of disturbances emanating from the domestic economy or from abroad. The model is somewhat between the small open economy and the two-country paradigm: and it is essentially a monetary model. The real sectors in the home and foreign countries play no overt role in the determination of equilibrium, hence of excess demand, in the various asset and exchange rate markets in the model. The framework we develop includes a domestic (UK) and foreign (US) money/financial market, a Euro-currency market (Euro sterling and Euro-dollars) together with a spot and forward exchange market for dollars (or sterling).

So, in further contrast to the previous essays, Essay 6 includes several financial assets/liabilities. It is also, as a consequence, a more disaggregated construct: we have several economic agents or sectors in the model. These include domestic banks, Euro-banks, the household sectors and the domestic Central Bank. The theoretical analysis permits several empirical propositions to be deduced; and the (limited) empirical evidence on these for West Germany and Japan is noted, together with a *summary* of econometric results we have found for the UK.

'A macroeconomic model of a mineral exporting LDC', Essay 7, reverts to the introduction of an essentially real sector framework; and it is very much a model of a small open economy. It is to be envisaged as an endeavour to capture the essence of an economy such as that of Trinidad and Tobago; an economy which relies heavily on the export of oil. The analytical structure is less aggregative than most of the models we have employed in this collection. It is essential to recognize that there are other key features of such small open economies which must be embodied in any worthwhile macro-model. They contain modern industrial sectors, (producing goods which are predominantly consumed domestically) which, furthermore, depend for their existence upon imported capital inputs. The non-tradeables sector and its need for capital inputs must be accommodated in the model: we assume that the prices of non-tradeables are determined by cost-plus considerations, for the fix-price principle seems to be prominent in such economies. Whilst several of the properties of our model are contained in the previous short-run models of Dornbusch (1980) and of Taylor (1983), our model is not identical with theirs; and the long-run version of our model and its dynamics differ markedly from theirs. Essay 7 examines, *inter alia,* the short-run and long-run effects of supply shocks (e.g. productivity changes), in both the tradeable (oil) and non-tradeable (import substitution) sector, on domestic output, prices and economic welfare.

The final essay returns to a two-country paradigm similar, but by no means identical, to that used in Essay 5. Its subject is East-West macro-interaction. The model embraces both monetary and real phenomena; though, by the policy strategies assumed, and by virtue of the fact that the money supply process in the Eastern bloc is monopolized (meeting only the needs of trade), the model telescopes into a real one. The model, of course, is highly aggregative, with each economic bloc only producing a composite commodity; it also, inevitably, ignores many important attributes of inter-bloc inter-dependence. Nevertheless, it is advanced as a first endeavour to model schematically the crucial elements in East-West interaction, using a macro-framework which encapsulates the essence of aggregate demand and supply in each bloc. The consequent comparative statics analysis of the 'general equilibrium' model provides us with some insights into the impact on the Eastern terms of trade and economic welfare of policy actions taken by the Western policy makers; those actions include fiscal expansion, monetary expansion, commercial policy in the form of relaxing the balance of payments constraint on the East, and the provision of technological aid or expertise to the East, along lines reminiscent of Marshall Aid (1948–1950) to Europe. Accordingly, we are able to evaluate the relevance of co-operation over and co-ordination of, economic policies by the West and the East. One of the general conclusions to emerge, which in a sense is contained in the constraint we have formulated for the Eastern regime, is that the West can indulge in commercial policy and a Marshall Aid type policy, which will be welfare improving for its own economy and not just for that of the East. This is more likely to be so under *perestroika;* and in the essay we do try to model a regime switch in the Eastern bloc as it moves away from being centrally planned along Soviet-type lines.

So, whilst there are distinct common threads in these essays, there is also a considerable amount of divergence, by model construct, by solution techniques used, and by coverage of topics. All things considered, the essays concern themselves with: Paradoxes, Policies and Problems, as our sub-title intimates. However, we have resisted the temptation to try to sub-divide the essays into three such parts. The discerning will also note that we have used paradoxes rather than the correct word paradoxa: this was to avoid even the remote possibility that this volume might be mistakenly regarded as one devoted to philosophical ideas!

Naturally, it is our hope that there will be aspects of these essays which provide interesting results, of relevance to policy and not just pedagogy; which suggest extensions to other lines of enquiry, whilst making some mildly original contributions to the literature. Even those who do not accept our basic premise that different circumstances require different models might share that view. But, all that we can say to the reader is: *utrum horum mavis accipe.*

References

Ford, J.L. (1989) Review of Kindleberger: *International Capital Movements, Journal of Economics, (Zeitschrift für Nationalökonomie)*, No.2.

Kindleberger, C. P. (1987) *International Capital Movements,* Cambridge University Press,- Cambridge.

Krugman, P. R. (1987) 'Is free trade passé?', *Economic Perspectives,* Vol.1, no.2, pp 131–144.

2. Output, tariffs, the optimum tariff and flexible exchange rates: a critical exegesis and extension of the Mundellian analysis

1 Introduction

The economic, especially the 'microeconomic', effects of general tariffs have been a source of debate, cyclical in its manifestation depending upon events of the moment, ever since the serious study of political economy began. Emphasis on the macroeconomic implications of general restrictions on imports by tariffs (or by quotas) has tended to be much less; but the British General Tariff of 1932 and the subsequent events of the Depression of the 1930s provoked a wider examination of protectionist policies. However, it is only when those policies are set in a framework of flexible exchange rates (whether that framework be limited to 'a small open-economy, rest of the world' paradigm or embraces models where the countries are completely inter-dependent) that the investigation of the macro-economic consequences of protectionism provides interesting challenges, with possibly problematical results. In a world economy where there is a fixed exchange rate system, the gold standard which tended to colour events in the 1930s being, of course, the example *par excellence* of such a system, a general tariff imposed by a country on its imports will tend to exhibit effects similar to 'Keynesian' interventionist stabilization policies. A *ceteris paribus* tariff will increase the tariff-imposing country's output: but at the expense of the level of economic activity in the rest of the world economy. In short, a general tariff will be beggar-thy-neighbour in character: it will more than likely lead to the kind of retaliatory, self-defeating, tariff policies witnessed in the 1930s.

The world economic scene has changed radically over the last 50 years: that is a platitude. There have been three major changes, out of the many that have occurred, which are germane to this paper: these are essentially interwoven. The first is the move towards freely floating exchange rates: that move seems now to have become permanent for the developed countries, after some faltering episodes, and despite periods of massive joint Central Bank intervention on foreign exchange markets. So we experience a system of 'managed floating' to flexible exchange rates. The second change is the integration of world capital markets and the trend in the increasing economic inter-dependence which has also developed. The integration of capital markets has arisen partly because flexible exchange rate regimes have been permitted by monetary authorities (and foreign exchange restrictions removed), but for a variety of reasons concerned with the spread of multi-national corporations, the technological transformation in the transmission of information, and so on (see Kindleberger 1987). That financial integration has tended to lead to 'perfect capital mobility' across major countries. The third development in the international economy has been the attempt by some 'third world' countries to exploit the growing economic interdependence between them and the industrial countries, by forming economic clubs, the classic example being, of course, OPEC, to reduce the economic hegemony of the richer nations, and to extract from them a larger share of the world's income and wealth. The consequence of such a strategy by OPEC is now history: the world was subjected to two radical hikes in the price of oil, which created equally radical supply side shocks for western economies to absorb. The consequent effect upon them, on their growth and balance of payments, frequently led in political circles to demands for import controls. The protectionist lobby has always been particularly strong in the USA; and it has become more vociferous in recent times. In a small open economy such as the UK the protectionist threat is always there.

Of course, many changes on the international political economy front have also occurred in the 1980s. It seems apparent that via the Group of 7, OECD, IMF, and GATT, there is a growing awareness that world economic integration does require world co-ordination of economic policies by governments: that despite attempts by major Western governments to run their economies by a minimum of interventionist policies (and at least by their stated intensions to do so: in the UK case we have seen as much intervention by the policy-making bodies since 1979 as prior to that date; it has merely assumed a different form), a consensus does now seem to be emerging, that international policy-making, and on a co-operative basis, is necessary.

Having said all that, however, it has to be conceded that it is always a possibility that a small open economy, developed or under-developed, seen as a country or an 'economic bloc' might invoke a protectionist position to attempt to countervail the impact of supply side shocks, even if it is operating in a regime of floating exchange rates. If we make the supposition that the supply side shock reduces the domestic economy's output, the question is, then, the Mundellian one (1961): can that country increase its domestically-produced output (so, in principle, to recoup the loss) by imposing a *general tariff* on its imports from the Rest of the World?

Mundell's (1961) paper, diminutive as it is, provides the seminal answer to this question, under flexible exchange rates. That paper abstracts from capital mobility: though as in Mundell's later papers this can be readily included, via an assumption of perfect capital mobility, to characterize current world trends, if we wished to do so (see Ford and Sen 1985). Neither does it address the question of the macro-economic effects of general tariffs as an antidote to supply shocks emanating from the rest of the world. That is of no major substance, because the model could be adopted to incorporate such effects; and quite straightforwardly, it can encompass shocks to the domestic economy via demand, which will suffice for our purposes, by means of a shift in the autonomous component of world demand for domestically-produced goods. We do not need, in fact, to consider such a possibility explicitly, since only the qualitative answer to the question raised at the end of the previous paragraph is apposite to this (and to Mundell's) paper.

In terms of a 'real' model, a 'Keynesian' model, of a small open economy, operating under flexible exchange rates, the Mundellian result stated in his 1961 paper has been taken to be both definitive and sacrosanct. However, we here challenge the result, entirely within the Mundell framework used by him and by his followers (see also Ford and Sen 1985).

Mundell's conclusion is stated, with limited analysis and exposition, in the brief Section V of his paper. His conclusion was that commercial policy (defined as 'any policy which restricts imports or promotes exports without directly affecting the level of saving or investment' (Mundell 1961, p514), and hence a non-retaliatory tariff, will have adverse consequences for output and employment, in a world of flexible exchange rates. The argument was (deceptively) simple: tariffs lead to a current account surplus, an appreciation of the exchange rate, a lowering of the domestic price level and a *reduction* of output and employment in long run equilibrium.

In spite of some early scepticism regarding Mundell's results (Sohmen 1969), recent analysis has come full swing in accepting his conclusions even with a large number of extensions to the basic model. Chan (1978), Eichengreen (1981) and Krugman (1982) all demonstrate formally that a non-retaliatory general tariff is contractionary from a macroeconomic point of view, in the sense that it reduces aggregate output and increases unemployment. Eichengreen (1981) shows that there might be short term beneficial effects of tariffs but even these are counterbalanced by long term adverse effects.

The main purpose of this paper is to demonstrate that when the Mundellian model is examined in detail, and analysed formally, it is *not universally* the case that a general tariff will be contractionary for the home country. It can be expansionary; and, simultaneously, it can also be beneficial to the Rest of the World. The general tariff is not invariably a beggar-thy-neighbour policy instrument. We demonstrate, *inter alia*, that: (i) the Laursen–Metzler (1950) effect, which relates the terms of trade to domestic absorption, has either not been utilized by Mundell *et al.* when they thought that they were doing so, or it has been used in a specific form which is not universally valid; (ii) even if that particular representation of the Laursen–Metzler effect is adopted, whilst it might be true that a small, once-and-for-all-tariff, might be contractionary, this does not permit us to deduce that the optimum tariff is also zero; indeed, *the optimum tariff is not zero*, and in one simple case a general form is obtained for it, which has features similar to the Bickerdike–Edgeworth optimum tariff in the pure theory of international trade; (iii) and if we do allow the Laursen–Metzler effect to have the structure that is required to generate the Mundellian outcome, we make the point that the contractionary effect can depend upon invoking the Slutsky conditions on the home country's import demand, which are only useable in extreme situations. [That condition was used by Tower (1973).]

Having mentioned Tower (1973), we should note that although his findings are largely in keeping with the Mundellian results, he does offer conditions which are partly at variance with the conventional wisdom and give support to our contention, under (ii), that the optimum tariff need not be zero, even if the sudden imposition of a tariff reduces output. One of our models in respect of expenditure or absorption functions is similar to Tower's: but he uses a more general function in that, for example, the home country's (real) expenditure on imports is dependent upon its (nominal) total absorption, rather than on its income. Additionally, Tower works through versions of his model: the one assumes that *output is fixed* and investigates the impact of a general tariff on (real) absorption (the surrogate for real economic welfare); the other analyses the impact of a general tariff on both domestic output and real absorption. His conclusions which are germane to this paper are:

> . . . (c) if tariff revenues are . . . distributed as a neutral income subsidy . . ., then assuming that the absorption function is fixed in units of domestic output, increased protection will be deflationary, if and only if the initial tariff is below the maximum revenue tariff (d). If . . . the absorption function is fixed in real terms, then under flexible exchange rates (when increased protection improves the terms of trade) increased protection will be deflationary if and only if the initial-tariff is below the 'optimum' level. (Tower 1973, p453).

The maximum revenue tariff is taken to be the tariff which maximizes revenue when *output is fixed*; and the 'optimum tariff', as far as can be discerned, is taken to be the tariff that maximizes real absorption, when *output is fixed*. In a sense then, applying these two tariffs as reference points for the model where both output and real absorption can, in principle, vary as a tariff is imposed/increased makes little sense: its only merit is that the two tariff levels are easy to compute and have an easy interpretation (the optimum tariff is, in fact, the Bickerdike–Edgeworth tariff).

As we see, Tower essentially obtains Mundellian results in a Mundellian construct; for the essence of the Mundellian findings, remember, was that starting from a position of free trade, the imposition by the domestic economy of merely a tiny tariff (e.g. of 1 per cent) would necessarily reduce its own output. It is highly improbable that a maximum revenue tariff would be as low as that. Yet Tower's conclusions do point to a situation wherein increases in the (*ad valorem*) tariff will ultimately engender an increase in output; output will cease to fall (at Tower's optimum tariff) and gradually attain a peak at some output-optimum tariff (which will not be the Tower optimum tariff). However, whilst Tower's findings do support the important contention that the optimum level of tariff is not zero, just because the initial move from free trade to protectionism could provoke contraction, it is not always the case that either the latter will occur or that output will continue to fall for a range of tariffs below some level (e.g. such as Tower's optimum tariff) before climbing to a peak, which exceeds output at a zero tariff level. Tower refers to two alternative absorption functions. In essence, what they amount to is this; with the domestic price of (the composite) output fixed and normalized at unity, in one case, absorption, in terms of domestic output, depends upon domestic disposable income, also in domestic units; and in the other case, absorption also depends upon the (tariff-adjusted) domestic terms of trade. These correspond to the two forms of the absorption functions referred to by Tower in (c) and (d) above. When using either function, however, import demand, within absorption, is posited to be dependent upon disposable income in domestic units deflated by the (domestic) terms of trade; since the price of each composite good is fixed in terms of own currency, the terms of trade (dependent only upon the exchange rate and the tariff), amount to the cost of foreign goods, and the absorption function becomes effectively defined in terms of purchasing power over foreign goods.

We will remind ourselves of some of these issues later when we have set up the Mundellian model and have begun to consider 'the' question we are attempting to answer, illustrating the importance of points (i) – (iii) listed previously.

We proceed, in fact, as follows. A critical exegesis of Mundell's celebrated paper is essential to put the analysis in proper perspective, and might be of value *per se* given the dominance the paper has. This is provided in the next section. Section 3 analyses the conditions under which aggregate output (and thus employment) may increase within the simple framework of internal and external balance. Section 4 sets out a consistently specified model and shows how previous discussions have often misspecified the aggregate demand functions of economic agents and have utilized special forms of them and of the general or consumer price index: it is in that section that we draw out observations related to points (i) – (iii) we noted above; and we also refer to Tower's conclusions. Section 4 sets out some main findings.

2 The Mundellian model: exposition and critical exegesis

The model utilized in Mundell's (1961) classic paper is based upon the earlier work of Laursen and Metzler (1950) and Harberger (1950). It now figures as the most basic model of an open economy in most macroeconomic texts. But with (effectively) only minor changes it has been the framework in which the macroeconomic implications of commercial policy have been examined.

In essence the model is as follows. The government is assumed to perform no specific role in the economy; and its activities only need to be considered when commercial policy is implemented, say, via the imposition of an *ad valorem* tariff on the price of imports. Then the government's budget constraint is of the simplest kind, since it is hypothesized that it collects the tariff revenue and distributes all of the revenue to the private sector by means of transfer payments. For alternative assumptions about revenue disbursement see Tower (1973) and Ford–Sen (1985). It is assumed that there are no capital flows in the model; so the balance of payments is equated with the balance of trade. Since expenditure on domestic and foreign goods by the economy is assumed to be independent of a rate of interest, the role of the money market is ignored. It is also assumed that the model is fixed price; and so the domestic level and the import level are normalized at unity (in the respective domestic currencies). Equilibrium in the model is then attained when expenditure equals income (internal balance: IS schedule) and the value of exports equals the value of imports (external balance: BP schedule). *The exchange rate (r) is freely floating* and is determined, along with domestic output, by these two schedules.

In a situation where the government imposes an *ad valorem* tariff (*t*) we have internal balance represented by the equality of income and spending:

$$V = A + X - rI \qquad (2.1)$$

Here, V is output (equivalent to nominal income since the domestic price level, P_d, is set at one); A represents absorption, so it is the sum of expenditure by domestic residents on consumption (C) and investment (I^h) of *both home and foreign goods*, with G set at zero; X denotes the quantity (and here also the value) of domestic goods imported; and I is the foreign currency value of imports, which again since the price of imports, P_m, is set at one, is synonymous with the quantity of imports. As previously noted, r is the rate of exchange, defined as the units of domestic currency required to purchase a unit of foreign currency.

Balance of payments equilibrium obtains when:

$$X = rI \qquad\qquad (2.2)$$

Here both exports and imports should be expressed in nominal units of domestic currency, but P_d is omitted since it is set at one. The original Mundell (1961) paper is very loosely structured and it is only in the Appendix to it that anything approaching a formal specification of the IS and BP schedules is attempted. The statement is that equation (2.1) produces a relationship between V and r; the implicit supposition seems to be that I depends upon V and r (via the terms of trade) and that A depends upon real disposable income, namely V, deflated by a consumer price index (P) which is some function of the domestic price level and of the (tariff-ridden) import price level measured in domestic currency. It is then argued that the internal balance schedule must be positively sloped in (V, r) space:

> [The internal balance] schedule has a positive slope because an increase in output creates an excess supply of goods and services, while an increase in the price of foreign exchange creates an excess demand for goods and services; consequently, an increase in output must be associated with an increase in the price of foreign exchange for excess demand to return to zero. Similarly the [external balance] schedule traces the locus of exchange rates and output along which the balance of payments is in equilibrium. This curve also has a positive slope because an increase in the price of foreign exchange improves the balance of payments while an increase in income worsens it, and this means that increases in the price of foreign exchange must be accompanied by increases in output if the balance of payments is to remain constant. (Mundell 1961, p510).

This is the argument that is repeated in all of the literature and is incorporated in Krugman's (1982) excellent survey of the area.

However, the introduction of a general tariff into the Mundellian analysis is not as straightforward as Mundell and his followers, including Krugman, have assumed. Let us consider the explicit form of the Mundellian model when a tariff has been imposed on the price of imports. On the assumption made that the tariff revenue is merely redistributed to the

personal sector as an income transfer, *disposable* income in nominal terms
(y) now becomes:

$$y = V + trI \tag{2.3}$$

rather than just V; trI, naturally, being the tariff revenue. Real disposable
income (Y) is now:

$$Y = \frac{V + trI}{P} \tag{2.4}$$

P is the consumer price index mentioned previously; it is the price of the
basket of goods, consisting as the basket does, of home and foreign
produce. It is the only relevant price index in an open economy for
measuring the cost of living and consequent levels of economic welfare.
Now, the literature which has sought to formalize Mundell's model and to
prove his conjecture, such as Krugman (1982), has adopted a specific form
for P which helps, along with other considerations as we shall see, to
generate the Mundellian result. This specific form was also used by Tower
(1973), to obtain his results on the 'maximum revenue raising' and the
'optimum' tariffs (because, in effect, he cannot derive the simple expressions he uses for the change in real absorption consequent upon the tariff
unless he uses the following form of P). To be precise, this structure has
been assumed for the price index:

$$P = P_{\text{d}}^{(1 - \delta)} P_{\text{m}}^{\delta} \tag{2.5}$$

and

$$P_{\text{m}} = r^{\delta}(1 + t)^{\delta} P_{\text{f}}^{\delta} = r^{\delta}(1 + t)^{\delta} \tag{2.6}$$

In equation (2.5) P is the 'consumer price index' mentioned previously;
P_{d} is the domestic price level in terms of domestic currency; P_{m} is the
domestic currency price of imports; δ is the share of imports in expenditure. According to Samuelson and Swamy (1974), this will be a true, ideal
cost of living index; but only if we can assume that the expenditure
functions (for home and imported goods) are of the Cobb–Douglas type,
i.e. they are derivable from 'a' utility function of that type. We return to
that point later on: it is one crucial element in the alleged proof of the
Mundellian proposition. For the moment, we accept the Tower–Krugman
specification; and we have, since $P_{\text{d}} = P_{\text{f}} = 1$, by normalization:

$$P = r^{\delta}(1 + t)^{\delta} \tag{2.7}$$

Let:

$$X = X(r) \tag{2.8}$$

In other words, exports depend upon the terms of trade, *given world income*. Also assume, following Mundell–Krugman, that:

$$I = I(V, r(1 + t)) \tag{2.9}$$

$$A = A(Y) \tag{2.10}$$

Thus, imports depend upon output and upon the effective (tariff-ridden) terms of trade; if we assume that investment is fixed, with the additional assumption that the government plays no direct role in the economy, then A, as stated earlier, is equal to the demand for domestic output by domestic residents *plus* their demand for imports. Note that in $I(\cdot)$, there is no tariff revenue; so that equation (2.9) differs from that of Tower; whilst $A(\cdot)$ defines the second ('fixed' in real terms) absorption function used by Tower.

If we use the equality of income and expenditure to denote the attainment of domestic equilibrium, that equilibrium is epitomized in this internal balance line:

$$V = A(Y) + X(r) - rI(V, r(1 + t)) - rIt \tag{2.11}$$

External equilibrium is given by this external balance line:

$$(X(r) = rI(V, r(1 + t)) \tag{2.12}$$

Exclusive of the tariff these relationships are:

$$V = A \left[\frac{V}{P} \right] + X(r) - rI(V, r) \tag{2.13}$$

and

$$X(r) = rI(V, r) \tag{2.14}$$

From (2.13) we deduce that:

$$\frac{dV}{dr} = \frac{X_1 - I_2 r - I}{1 - A_1 + I_1 r} \tag{2.15}$$

The accepted convention is that: $X_1 > 0;\ I_2 < 0;\ I_1 > 0;\ 0 < A_1 < 1$.

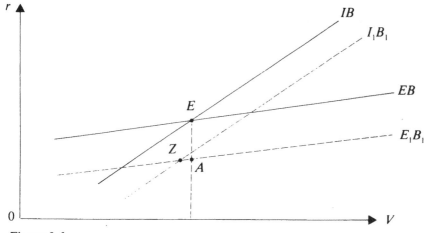

Figure 2.1

Here we have adopted the standard practice of denoting the partial derivatives of the functions by subscripts which take their number from the order of the relevant arguments in the functions. Given the signs of the partial derivatives we deduce from equation (2.15) that:

$$\frac{dV}{dr} > 0 \ iff \ X_1 - I_2 r - I > 0 \tag{2.16}$$

This is seen to be the *Marshall–Lerner* condition in this model. Thus from equation (2.14), with B defined as the balance of payments:

$$\frac{\partial B}{\partial r} > 0 \ iff \ X_1 - I_2 r - I > 0 \tag{2.17}$$

It follows further from equation (2.14) that the slope of the internal balance line, dV/dr, will be positive *iff* the Marshall-Lerner condition obtains, given the positive sign of I_1. In terms of equations (2.13) and (2.14), given the underlying assumptions in the model, it can be represented in Mundellian fashion by Figure 2.1.

Since the slope of the external balance line (*EB*) is:

$$\frac{dr}{dV} = \frac{rI_1}{X_1 - I_2 r - I} \tag{2.18}$$

it is smaller than that of the internal balance line (IB) as drawn in Figure 2.1.

Now suppose that the government imposes a tariff, which we may imagine it does in an attempt to increase domestic output by inducing expenditure switching by domestic residents from imports to domestic goods. The usual interpretation of the consequences of the tariff for the *IB* and *EB* schedules and hence for output (*V*), is that provided by Krugman (1982), namely:

> Now suppose the tariff rate is increased, starting from zero. Clearly, this shifts the external balance schedule down by improving the trade balance at any *r*. It also shifts the internal balance schedule down, which we can demonstrate by the following argument: at an unchanged rate of exchange, the effects of the tariff in raising the price level and the revenue cancel out, leaving real income and hence hoarding unchanged. Since the trade balance is improved, there is an excess demand for domestic output at that point, showing that the internal balance line must have shifted down.
>
> But it will not shift down by as much as the external balance line. Consider point A [in Figure 1]. At that point output and the trade balance are the same as at the initial position [E]. *But real income, and hence real hoarding, are higher* than originally because the terms of trade have improved. There is an excess of domestic output, showing that the internal balance line lies somewhere to the left.
>
> The result then is that output drops.
>
> (Krugman 1982, pp.144–146, *italics added*)

Thus, for Krugman the final equilibrium position will be a point such as *Z* on the new (dotted) *IB* and *EB* schedules. The argument Krugman has used is a paraphrase of that contained in Mundell's (1961) seminal paper, which has been used ever since then to demonstrate that output falls when a (small) tariff is imposed, or when there is a further small increase in an already-existing tariff.

We note that in his 'proof' that output does fall Krugman has set out the conditions for internal balance by transposing equation (2.13) so that it reads, in real terms:

$$\frac{V - A}{P} = H = \frac{B}{P} \tag{2.19}$$

where *B* denotes the Balance of Payments (equals current account balance) and *H* is 'hoarding'. The latter is a familiar quantity, of course, in the literature on the theory of the balance of payments, but it has no unique economic meaning in the way that hoarding does in monetary theory *per se*. In the standard literature, beginning with the path-breaking paper by Laursen and Metzler (1950), it is not referred to as hoarding: that concept is left for *saving* proper.

Suppose that the *IB* schedule does shift to the right in Figure 2.1 (it will, in fact, do so, as Section 3 shows). Let *IB* move to I_1B_1 and the external balance schedule shift to E_1B_1. Consider then, point *A* relative to point *E*.

It is correct, as Krugman maintains, that at point *A*, the balance of payments is identical with that at *E*, being at a value of zero. Output (*V*), is always the same at the two points. The Krugman argument is then that *H*, real hoarding, increases at *A*, compared with *E*, because of the improvement in the terms of trade. Hence there is an excess supply of output; to permit balance to be re-established in the market for domestic goods, output must fall. Therefore, equilibrium output must lie to the left of *A* along the new *EB* line.

In essence this conclusion depends upon the proposition that real disposable income does rise unequivocably at given *V* after the tariff has been introduced; and hence the terms of trade improve. That is not necessarily the case. By assumption:

$$Y = \frac{y}{P} = \frac{V + trI}{P} \qquad (2.20)$$

where $trI = R$, the tariff revenue. From equation (2.7):

$$\frac{dP}{dt} = \delta r^{\delta - 1}(1 + t)^{\delta}\frac{dr}{dt} + \delta r^{\delta}(1 + t)^{\delta - 1} \qquad (2.21)$$

Furthermore, from equation (2.12):

$$\frac{dr}{dt}\bigg|_V = r^2 I_2[X_1 - I - I_2 r(1 + t)]^{-1} \qquad (2.22)$$

This expression is negative by the Marshall–Lerner condition.

Hence, equations (2.21) and (2.22) imply that:

$$\frac{dP}{dt}\bigg|_V \gtreqless 0 \text{ iff } X_1 \gtreqless I \qquad (2.23)$$

Effectively, at the initial equilibrium (here $X \equiv rI$), the conditions stipulated in (2.23) amount to conditions on whether the 'price elasticity of demand' of exports is less than, equal to, or greater than unity.

Should d*P*/d*t* be negative then, naturally, *Y* must increase at any *V*, when a tariff is imposed. But if d*P*/d*t* should happen to be positive, then real disposable income may rise, fall or stay constant, for a pre-assigned level of output. This is an especially important result, despite the simplicity with which it is derived, because it informs us that *there is not an* *automatic improvement in the domestic country's terms of trade, at given output*, after it has imposed a tariff. Thus, in this model the terms of trade, σ, are defined as:

$$\sigma = r(1 + t) \tag{2.24}$$

Hence:

$$\sigma = P^{1/\delta} \tag{2.25}$$

An improvement in the terms of trade requires σ to fall as t increases. Mundell's (1961) own explanation of the fall in output from point A in a diagram equivalent to Figure 2.1 above (Mundell 1961, Figure 5, p515) rests explicitly upon there being an improvement in the terms of trade.

If we do suppose that there is a reduction in P, and a concomitant improvement in the terms of trade (σ), the fact that H will increase, if it is postulated to depend positively upon real disposable income, does permit us to deduce that the domestic demand for domestically-produced output has fallen, at *a given level of output*. Then, take the import function used by Krugman, namely, equation (2.12). Equilibrium along the internal balance schedule requires that the change in hoarding be zero. When we consider the possible movements in *IB*, we have, with V fixed, that:

$$d\left[\frac{V + trI}{P}\right] \equiv d\left[\frac{A}{P}\right] \tag{2.26}$$

Recalling that:

$$A = C^d + Ir(1 + t) \tag{2.27}$$

with C^d being real (equals nominal, here) consumption by domestic residents of domestic output, we discover that equation (2.26) will be satisfied when:

$$0 = \frac{dC^d}{dt} + I_2 r\left[r + \frac{dr}{dt}\right] \tag{2.28}$$

where we have assumed that the initial tariff is zero. The expression in square brackets in that case is the derivative of the terms of trade (σ) with respect to the tariff. If σ improves its value falls when the *ad valorem* tariff is imposed; and, *ex hypothesi*, $I_2 < 0$. Hence dC^d/dt must be negative.

What ultimately happens to the internal and external balance schedules, and hence what happens to the terms of trade and output, cannot be discerned from such a 'partial' analysis. The solution can only be deduced from a formal, general equilibrium, study: but at least the above indicates that the Mundellian answer is *not* the only outcome. The diagrammatic analysis which he and Krugman adopted tells only part of the story; and it is not a straightforward matter to analyse the impact of a 'jump' variable, which also strictly affects the slopes of the *IB* and *EB* schedules. Hence, we now turn to a simple formal analysis of the Mundellian model.

3   Increases in output in the Mundellian model and the optimum tariff

We use the two equilibrium equations given by equations (2.9) and (2.10), for internal and external balance, respectively, except that we adopt the general form of the absorption function introduced by Laursen–Metzler (1950), whereby absorption in terms of domestic goods, depends upon nominal income and the terms of trade, separately. This will enable us to draw out some of the points we made in the introductory section of this essay relating to the findings of Mundell, Krugman and Tower. So we shall later on translate our absorption function into the alternatives they utilized. To simplify the algebraic expression we shall omit the tariff revenue from the import schedule as Krugman (1982) did, even though Laursen–Metzler (1950) and Tower (1973) include it, and we ourselves have done so elsewhere (Ford and Sen 1985). Our main concern is the (total) absorption function, its properties and the measure of the consumer price index.

Hence:

Internal balance:
$$A(V + R, r(1 + t)) + X(r) - rI(V, r(1 + t)) - R - V = 0 \quad (2.29)$$

External Balance: $rI(V, r(1 + t)) - X(r) = 0$ $\qquad$ (2.30)

where these equations have been written in excess demand form (with $dV > 0$ when $A + X - rI$ exceeds income; and $dr > 0$ when there is excess demand for foreign currency) and:

$$R \equiv rtI \qquad (2.31)$$

Upon differentiation of (2.29) – (2.30), using (2.31) we discover that:

$$J\,dy = dx \qquad (2.32)$$

where J (the Jacobian of the system, of course) is:

$$J = \begin{bmatrix} [(A_1 - 1)(1 + trI_1) - rI_1] & [(A_1 - 1)(tI + tI_2 r(1 + t)) + A_2(1 + t) + \alpha] \\ rI_1 & -\alpha \end{bmatrix}$$

(2.33)

where:

$$\alpha = X_1 - rI_2(1 + t) - I$$

(2.34)

and is the Marshall-Lerner condition, assumed to be positive:

$$dy = \begin{bmatrix} dV \\ dr \end{bmatrix}; \quad dx = \begin{bmatrix} (1 - A_1)[rI + r^2 tI_2] - A_2 r + r^2 I_2 \\ -I_2 r^2 \end{bmatrix} dt$$

(2.35)

Here:

$$|J| = (1 - A_1)[\alpha + X_1 trI_1] - rI_1 A_2(1 + t)$$

(2.36)

The value of this determinant must be positive to guarantee stability. The *Laursen-Metzler effect* is captured explicitly by our specification and it is that A_2 *must be positive*: with $(1 - A_1) > 0$, $\alpha > 0$ and $X_1 trI_1 > 0$, it is likely that |J| will be positive.

Now, let us suppose that the initial tariff was zero, as stipulated in all of the Mundellian literature save for part of Tower's (1973) paper. Then we can discover by simple application of Cramer's rule that:

$$\frac{\partial V}{\partial t} = \frac{\alpha r(A_1 - 1)I + A_2 r(X_1 - I)}{\alpha(1 - A_1) - rI_1 A_2}$$

(2.37)

Assume that $|J| > 0$, then:

$$\text{sign } \frac{\partial V}{\partial t} = \text{sign } [\alpha r(A_1 - 1)I + A_2 r(X_1 - I)]$$

(2.38)

It follows immediately that a *necessary* condition for a newly-imposed general tariff to be expansionary in the home country is:

$$X_1 - I > 0$$

(2.39)

if the Laursen-Metzler (1950) effect does hold. At the point of (initial) equilibrium $X \equiv rI$ and so condition (2.39) translates into the requirement that the 'price elasticity' of export demand (ϵ) exceed unity; the condition we recall which we obtained hitherto for the terms of trade to worsen for the home country. When σ does rise we showed that home demand for home goods (*ceteris paribus!*) would also strengthen, and produce a concomitant increase in domestic output (V). The sufficient condition for $\partial V/\partial t$ to be positive:

$$\alpha(A_1 - 1) + A_2(\epsilon - 1) > 0 \tag{2.40}$$

will be met, naturally, if the Marshall–Lerner condition is only just satisfied.

How has the orthodox literature managed to produce a result whereby output falls uniquely after a small tariff is imposed on a previously free trade world? The answer is not hard to discover. It is that the consumer price index (P) has been specified in the Cobb–Douglas form given in equation (5). This has been used, explicitly or implicitly, to produce what we call *the Laursen–Metzler condition*, to distinguish it from the prior, and more economically meaningful, concept of the Laursen–Metzler *effect*, which states, as we have constantly reiterated, merely that $A_2 > 0$: the *ceteris paribus* impact of a deterioration in the (domestic) terms of trade, $\sigma(= r(1 + t))$, is to reduce domestic residents' absorption measured in terms of domestic output.

What is this Laursen–Metzler condition to which we have alluded? It can be stated baldly as follows, at the initial equilibrium, where income must equal absorption, with the balance of trade being zero:

$$A_2 \equiv I(1 - A_1) \tag{2.41}$$

Ex definitione:

$$PdA(\cdot) \equiv P\hat{A}(\cdot); \quad A = A(V + R, \sigma) \tag{2.42}$$

where Pd is the domestic price of the domestic output, set at unity in our model, and $\hat{A}$ is absorption in terms of the basket of goods.

The Mundellian absorption function, ostensibly following Laursen–Metzler, for the basket of goods, is:

$$\hat{A} = \hat{A}(y) \tag{2.43}$$

where y is real income, being disposable money income, deflated by P, the consumer (basket of goods) price index.

We deduce that:

$$A_2 = \frac{\partial P}{\partial \sigma} \hat{A}(y) (1 - \hat{A}_1) \equiv \frac{\partial P}{\partial \sigma} \hat{A}(y) (1 - A_1) \tag{2.44}$$

From the Cobb–Douglas price index:

$$\frac{\partial P}{\partial \sigma} = \delta \sigma^{\delta-1} = \frac{rI}{\sigma \hat{A}(y)} \tag{2.45}$$

Hence, combining (2.44) and (2.45), with the initial tariff in σ set at zero:

$$A_2 = I(1 - A_1) \tag{2.46}$$

However, such a specification for A_2 means that even if $\epsilon > 1$, the positive effect on output exerted by A_2 is not sufficient to outweigh the negative effect induced by the Marshall–Lerner condition and the (negative of the) propensity to save; in essence, there is no role for ϵ to play.

Thus, upon substitution of equation (2.46) into equation (2.37):

$$\frac{\partial V}{\partial t} = \frac{II_2 r^2}{[\alpha - rI_1 I]} < 0 \tag{2.47}$$

There is no need, in principle, for the income and price partial derivatives of $A(\cdot)$ to be tied together in the way required by expression (2.46). Even if we wish to retain the Laursen–Metzler effect, A_2 could be greater than $I(1 - A_1)$; with a CES price index, not only is that possible, but it is also likely that A_2 has to be negative. We have discussed these possibilities and their consequences for open-economy macroeconomies in another paper (see Ford and Sen 1988). If $A_2 > I(1 - A_1)$ and $\epsilon > 1$, $\delta V / \delta t$ can be positive.

What, meanwhile, is happening to the exchange rate and to the terms of trade (σ)? If the initial tariff is taken to be zero:

$$\frac{\partial r}{\partial t} = \frac{(1 - A_1)r^2[I_2 - I_1 I] + r^2 I_1 A_2}{\alpha(1 - A_1) - rI_1 I} \tag{2.48}$$

$$\frac{\partial \sigma}{\partial t} = r + \frac{\delta r}{\delta t} \tag{2.49}$$

again, the strength of A_2 could be sufficient to generate an increase in r and, hence, in the terms of trade (i.e. could cause the latter to deteriorate for the home country). Should this happen it is not the export price elasticity of demand that has played a central role, as might be thought, misleadingly, from the Mundell–Krugman partial, graphical, analysis. We note that it is easy to prove that output could rise, whilst r falls; and, hence, whilst σ falls. These are the antithesis of the Mundellian findings.

The allegedly unique relationship, via the presence of the Laursen–Metzler effect, between domestic output and the terms of trade, only necessarily materializes if we invoke the Laursen–Metzler condition; in that situation:

$$\frac{\partial r}{\partial t} = \frac{r^2 I_2}{[\alpha - rI_1 I]} < 0 \tag{2.50}$$

If I equals unity, initially, V and r change by the same amount and in the same direction. σ will also fall if the absolute value of (2.50) exceeds the initial value of r.

We now digress for a moment to enable us to draw into focus a point to which we referred in our earlier summary critique of the Mundellian story. This was that in some versions of it, the *Slutsky condition* has been relied upon to prove that the Mundellian model demonstrates that a tariff will cause output to contract. That condition enters the model once the tariff revenue is permitted to influence the demand for imports, so that the nominal variable in the import function is $V + R$, rather than just V. This enables us to deduce that, for an initial tariff of zero:

$$\frac{\partial V}{\partial t} = \frac{\alpha rI(A_1 - 1) + A_2 r[(I_2 + I_1 I)r + \alpha]}{\alpha(1 - A_1) - rI_1 A_2} \tag{2.51}$$

If we use the Laursen–Metzler condition:

$$\frac{\partial V}{\partial t} = \frac{Ir[I_2 + I_1 I]}{(\alpha - rI_1 I)} \tag{2.52}$$

Clearly, the sign of response of domestic output to the tariff depends upon the sign of the term in square brackets in equation (2.52). It is that which has been termed the Slutsky condition and signed, uniquely, as negative. Naturally, if we could say that all imports were solely for consumption, none being for production, it would be valid to utilize the Slutsky equation; and that requires us to sign $I_2 + I_1 I$ as negative. Despite the fact that the Mundellian schema is Keynesian in spirit, the supposition that the supply side of the domestic economy responds automatically to changes in demand does not mean that we must exclude from the model goods that are imported for production purposes. It cannot be disputed that it would be better to construct the model in such a fashion as to allow for that fact: but that is not our concern in this particular paper.

So, even if we use the highly specific Laursen–Metzler condition, tariffs need not be contractionary if $I_2 + I_1 I$ can be signed as positive. A small tariff newly imposed on a hitherto free trade world economy can be beneficial to the tariff-levying country, if its imports depend upon its total disposable income and are not used wholly for consumption purposes.

Let us move on to consider the *optimum tariff*, in relationship to output. When the initial tariff is not taken to be zero, the expression for $\delta V/\delta t$ reduces to:

$$\frac{\partial V}{\partial t} = \frac{(A_1 - 1)\,[X_1(rI + r^2 I_2 t) - rI^2 - II_2 r^2(1 + t)] + A_2(X_1 - I)r}{(1 - A_1)\,[\alpha + X_1 rI_1 t] - rI_1 A_2(1 + t)} \qquad (2.53)$$

When the expression is set to zero, the optimum tariff, t^*, is the solution for t from:

$$(X_1 - I)(A_1 - 1)(rI + r^2 I_2 t) + (X_1 - I)A_2 r + (1 - A_1)r^2 II_2 = 0 \qquad (2.54)$$

Hence:

$$t^* = \frac{(1 - A_1)\,[I(\epsilon - 1) - I_2 r] + A_2(1 - \epsilon)}{(1 - A_1)(1 - \epsilon)I_2 r} \qquad (2.55)$$

and we can further deduce that for an optimum tariff to exist at all, $\epsilon \neq 1$.

The second-order conditions for a maximum level of output to be attained at t^* require that:

$$(1 - A_1)I_2 r^2(1 - \epsilon)I < 0 \qquad (2.56)$$

This further requires ϵ to be less than unity.

Strictly speaking, the value of ϵ in equations (2.53–2.55) should be its value at a tariff level close to the 'optimum' tariff. When the sign of $\delta V/\delta t$ was being investigated by means of equations (2.37–2.39), the value of ϵ was to be the price elasticity of export demand in the free-trade state, prior to the imposition of the small tariff. Naturally, in the special case where the world demand function for the home country's exports is a logarithmic one, the two ϵ-values will be identical.

We can have two cases for which we investigate the optimum tariff. The first is where only the Laursen–Metzler effect holds and the second is where the Laursen–Metzler condition is present. In the first case t^* *can* be positive, whilst, simultaneously, V is at a maximum. If $\epsilon < 1$ then the latter condition is met; and provided the following inequality is satisfied in respect of the denominator of equation (2.55), $t^* > 0$:

$$\epsilon - 1 < \frac{(\epsilon - 1)A_2}{I(1 - A_1)} + \frac{I_2 r}{I} \qquad (2.57)$$

At a tariff (t) almost imperceptibly different from the optimum tariff (t^*), the terms of trade elasticity of import demand will be:

$$\eta \equiv \frac{I_2 r(1 + t)}{I} < 0 \tag{2.58}$$

Therefore, inequality (2.57) can be re-written as:

$$\epsilon + \frac{|\eta|}{1 + t} < \frac{(\epsilon - 1)A_2}{I(1 - A_1)} + 1 \tag{2.59}$$

If the Marshall–Lerner condition is to be fulfilled (α greater than zero in equation (2.53)) it follows that, in the traditional way of expressing it:

$$\epsilon + |\eta| > 1 \tag{2.60}$$

Both equations (2.60) and (2.59) can be satisfied when $\epsilon < 1$ for some t around the optimum tariff. It is feasible for $A_2/I(1 - A_1)$ to be greater than or less than unity if the Laursen–Metzler condition is not a feature of the small open economy. Of course, the likelihood of both (2.59) and (2.60) being satisfied simultaneously is that much higher if $A_2/I(1 - A_1)$ is less than unity.

Now, *ceteris paribus*, the values of the partial derivative of the absorption function will probably alter as the size of the tariff and the consequent macro-economic configuration of the economy change. However, if we were to suppose that those partial derivatives remained constant we can appreciate that we have arrived at this situation: starting from a position of free trade, if a small tariff is levied on the price of imported goods by the home economy, unless the rest of the world's price elasticity for home produce and $A_2/I(1 - A_1)$ both exceed unity, the impact of the tariff on domestic output will be to cause it to contract. Nevertheless, once that initial tariff is exceeded output will stop falling at some level of the tariff and begin to rise up to a maximum at t^*. So, if we do suppose that all partial derivatives and the concomitant elasticities are all constant, the situation can be portrayed in Figure 2.2.

When we consider the derivation of the optimum tariff when the Laursen–Metzler *condition* is also satisfied we can see, almost immediately, that the optimum tariff is, in fact, a *subsidy*, because t^* calculated from equation (2.55) provides a *minimum* level of output.

In this eventuality, t^* emerges as the solution to:

$$(\epsilon - 1)t - 1 = 0 \tag{2.61}$$

That is:

$$t^* = \frac{1}{\epsilon - 1} \tag{2.62}$$

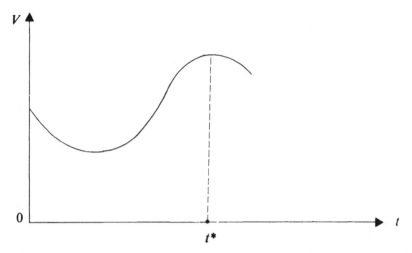

Figure 2.2

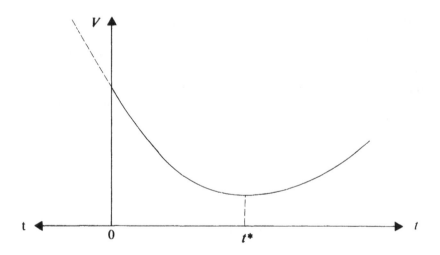

Figure 2.3

and *iff*, $\epsilon > 1$ now, can there be a positive optimum tariff. But the second-order condition for a 'maximum' level of output now informs us that output is at a minimum. The true optimum tariff will be a subsidy. The situation is illustrated in Figure 2.3.

t^* is the tariff which, in effect, minimizes output, and it is identical to the Bickerdike–Edgeworth optimum tariff, but it does not necessarily have the same implication for the home country's economic welfare (i.e. it does not automatically produce a maximum level of $\hat{A}$, absorption, in terms of the basket of goods).

The absorption function we have utilized is similar to that which Tower described as one wherein absorption is fixed in real terms (i.e. in his case A depends separately upon nominal disposable income and the (domestic) terms of trade, this latter, of course, being proportional to the price of the basket of goods). The situation illustrated in Figure 2.3 mirrors his conclusions: the only difference is that t^* for him is the 'optimum tariff' in the sense that that value of t^* would maximize (real) absorption when output is fixed and when the initial tariff is zero, we recall. However, we can now appreciate that even the initial contractionary effect of a general tariff depends not necessarily on its size (or size of income) but upon the special use of the Laursen-Metzler condition. Tower does use the Cobb-Douglas price function and this affects his earlier results on his two tariffs, the maximum revenue tariff and the optimum tariffs when output is assumed to be stabilized by conventional macroeconomic policies. Nevertheless, it is not obvious that he has made explicit use of the Laursen-Metzler condition in the section of his paper where he derives the conclusions (c) and (d) that we quoted from him previously and which are summarized generally by Figure 2.3.

4 Conclusions

The intuitive and graphical analysis of the simple Keynesian-Mundellian model suggested that under flexible exchange rates tariffs were always counterproductive. Even if a country were to impose a small tariff on its general imports from the Rest of the World it could not increase its own output. The adjustment in the exchange rate by the market, consequent upon the tariff would blunt the import substitution effects of the tariff; exports would fall, with the alleged improvement in the terms of trade (not just the fall in r *per se*), the income effect provided by tariff revenue would be dominated by the real income effect engineered by the price effect emanating from the improvement in the consumer price index (as a result of the improvement in the terms of trade), by the so-called Laursen-Metzler effect. The net result was supposedly demonstrated to be a fall in domestic demand by domestic residents to accompany that from the Rest of the World.

As it happens, the net effect that was alleged to follow from the Laursen-Metzler condition was a particularly potent one. Yet, there is no requirement that the income and price effects in absorption be limited in a unique fashion that will guarantee the Mundellian conclusion. Formal analysis confirms that the 'general equilibrium' results do not necessarily fully match up with the partial, graphical, internal/external balance analysis, which purports to demonstrate that the final equilibrium configuration after the tariff must, once the Laursen–Metzler *effect* is recognized, lead to a fall in output and to a lower exchange rate (it being also alleged, but never proved in any way, that the terms of trade would also fall, i.e. improve for the tariff-levying country).

We have endeavoured to show that the Mundellian result is not inevitable, and hence is not robust. Within the Mundellian paradigm it was proved that even a small, one-off, tariff could be expansionary for the home country; but even if this is not so, we conveyed the view that this does not mean that the optimum tariff is also zero. In general, when only the Laursen–Metzler *effect* is used, tariffs will be expansionary up to some optimum level if such a level will depend, as we would expect, upon the value of the export price elasticity of demand. It must be less than unity; and the optimum tariff itself will depend upon that elasticity and the elasticities of the absorption and import functions.[1] In the situation where the Laursen–Metzler condition is used, we do discover that the import effect of a small tariff is zero; but provided the tariff is further increased until it attains some 'optimum' level, output will thereafter begin to rise: *ceteris paribus*, for all tariff levels about the 'minimum optimum'. That finding is consistent with the most extensive formal analysis of the Mundellian model which was conducted by Tower: though, as we have mentioned, his overall conclusions are Mundellian ones.[2]

Notes

1.   It is not possible to convert the formula for t^* (equation 2.55) into anything meaningful in elasticities because this has to be evaluated, naturally, at the economic variables implied by t^* to be definitive.

2.   Krugman (1982) presents some mathematical analysis of the Mundellian model as we have indicated at the outset of this paper, and we have tried as far as possible to keep within his (and partly) Tower's formulation. However, Krugman operates with the hoarding function as we noted in the text. This can be a cumbersome procedure which masks the essentials of the Laursen–Metzler effect and it is not useful in larger scale models (see Ford and Sen 1988).

Krugman uses these two equations for internal and external balance:

$$d \left[\frac{B}{P} \right] - dH = 0 \tag{1}$$

$$d(rI - X) = 0 \tag{2}$$

where:

$$B = X - rI \tag{3}$$

$$H = \frac{(V + R) - A}{P} = H \left[\frac{Y}{P} \right] = H(y) \tag{4}$$

P and $X(\cdot)$ are as defined in the main text. In Krugman $I(\cdot)$ is postulated to be the same as the specification we have used. Here, initially, let us include R in the import demand function.

When t is initially zero:

$$\frac{\partial V}{\partial t} = \frac{\left| \begin{array}{cc} (rI_1 + H_1) \, rI + r^2 I_2 - H_1 Y\delta \left[\dfrac{H_1 Y\delta}{r} + \alpha \right] \\ -r^2 I_2 \qquad\qquad -\alpha \end{array} \right|}{H_1[\alpha - rI_1I]} \tag{5}$$

where α is again the Marshall–Lerner condition and δ is the share of expenditure on imports by the domestic economy, which is the exponent on the terms of trade in the consumer price index, P.

Therefore:

$$\frac{\partial V}{\partial t} = \frac{\alpha H_1[Y\delta - rI] + H_1 Y\delta r(I_2 + I_1I)}{H[\alpha - rI_1I]} \tag{6}$$

Should $I = I(V, \sigma)$ then the term rI_1 disappears from the first element in the numerator of equation (5) to transform equation (6) into:

$$\frac{\partial V}{\partial t} = \frac{\alpha H_1[Y\delta - rI] + H_1 Y\delta rI_2}{H[\alpha - rI_1I]} \tag{7}$$

By stability requirements, the denominator of these expressions must be positive to guarantee (local) stability generally rather than just, say, saddle-path stability. The supposition is made that $H_1 > 0$ (the Laursen–Metzler saving propensity is positive); and so the stability requirement is the same as working directly with the absorption function.

Take equation (7) first of all. It appears, in principle, that output could increase when the tariff is levied, since $Y\delta - rI$ could be positive, and sufficiently so, to dominate $H_1 Y\delta rI_2(<0)$. The term $(Y\delta - rI)$ is eliminated, however, by the use of the identity:

$$\delta = \frac{rI + R}{V + R} \tag{8}$$

by valuing δ at the pre-tariff values:

$$\delta = \frac{rI}{V} \tag{9}$$

At the pre-tariff equilibrium:
$$Y = V \tag{10}$$

and so $Y\delta = rI = 0$. Since $H_1 \equiv 1 - \hat{A}_1 \equiv 1 - A_1$, expressions (6) and (7) reduce to the results obtained by the absorption function approach *and* by using the Laursen–Metzler condition.

How can we reconcile these results with those in the text? They make no explicit reliance on the Laursen–Metzler effect. Krugman intimates that that effect is captured by the supposition that $H_1 > 0$. That is not the Laursen–Metzler effect; it is the saving (or 'hoarding') hypothesis of Laursen–Metzler, Harberger, and all who have written since: it states a standard proposition only, that as real income rises, saving will rise, but so too will expenditure, with $0 < H_1 < 1$. Furthermore, H_1 makes no impact on the sign of $\partial V/\partial t$ in either equation (6) or (7). If the parameter H_1 is meant to capture the Laursen–Metzler effect, then that effect, upon which total reliance was placed by Mundell and Krugman, to determine the impotence of tariffs under flexible exchange rates, in fact has no role to play in the evaluation of the macroeconomic consequences of tariffs.

In essence, what has happened is that the Laursen–Metzler effect has been used and also the Laursen–Metzler condition, by implication. Note that in the absorption models, $(1 - A_1)$ and A_2 both occur, essentially, in the tariff-output multiplier formula. The Laursen–Metzler condition results in the one term, $(1 - A_1)$, appearing, and multiplicatively, in both the numerator and denominator. That term, therefore, disappears, and it is H_1. It is the specification of P, which has been used in the derivation of internal balance, with the constancy which it assumes for δ which, essentially, produces the Mundellian answer. The hoarding approach is, with the use of the Cobb–Douglas structure for P, a short-hand method, as it were; it conceals the relevance, indeed, the central importance, of both the Laursen–Metzler effect and condition.

Thus, from the fact that:

$$d \left[\frac{V + R}{P} \right] - d \left[\frac{A}{P} \right] \equiv H_1 d(y) \tag{11}$$

with $A = A(\cdot)$ specified as in the main text, we have:

$$IH_1 = A_2 \tag{12}$$

References

Chan, K. S. (1978) 'The employment effects of tariffs under a free exchange rate regime', *Journal of International Economics*, vol.8, pp 414–424.

Dornbusch, R. (1980) *Open Economy Macroeconomics*, Basic Books.

Eichengreen, B. J. (1981), 'A dynamic model of tariffs, output and employment under flexible exchange rates', *Journal of International Economics*, vol.11, pp.341–359.

Ford, J. L. and Sen, S. (1985) *Protectionism, Exchange Rates and the Macro-economy*, Basil Blackwell, Oxford.

Ford, J. L. and Sen, S. (1988) 'The negation of the Laursen–Metzler effect (the Ford–Sen effect) and some standard propositions in open-economy macro–economics', Essay 3, this volume.

Harberger, A. C. (1950) 'Currency depreciation, income and the balance of trade', *Journal of Political Economy*, February, pp 47–60.

Keynes, J. M. (1936) *The General Theory of Employment, Interest and Money*, Macmillan, London.

Kindleberger, C. P. (1987) *International Capital Movements*, Cambridge University Press, Cambridge.

Krugman, P. (1982) 'The macroeconomics of protection with a floating exchange rate', in *Carnegie-Rochester Conference Series on Public Policy*, vol.16 North-Holland, Amsterdam, pp141–182.

Laursen, S. and Metzler, L. A. (1950) 'Flexible exchange rates and the theory of employment', *Review of Economics and Statistics*, November, pp281–299.

Mundell, R. A. (1961) 'Flexible exchange rates and employment policy', *Canadian Journal of Economics and Political Science*, vol.27, no.4, pp509–517.

Samuelson, P. A. and Swamy, S. (1974) 'Invariant economic index numbers and canonical duality: survey and synthesis', *American Economic Review*, vol.65, pp566–593.

Sohmen, E. J. (1969) *Flexible Exchange Rates*, University of Chicago, Chicago.

3 Negation of the Laursen–Metzler effect and its implications for standard propositions in open-economy macro models

The Laursen–Metzler effect, which depicts the impact on absorption of a change in a country's terms of trade, has been a key feature in the investigations into the role and impact of various forms of macro-stabilization policies in open economies; and on the macro-economic properties of flexible, as opposed to fixed, exchange rates. Indeed, the *locus classicus* for the Laursen–Metzler effect is their paper of 1950 in *The Review of Economics and Statistics*, which was especially concerned with a comparison of flexible and fixed exchange rate regimes in protecting employment (output) in the one country from random shocks (say a downward pressure on demand/output) in the other. The Laursen–Metzler effect, as we shall recapitulate later on in this paper, turns out to be the ultimate determinant of the presence of international interdependence under flexible exchange rates.

The Laursen–Metzler effect is, in fact, this postulate: as a country's terms of trade improve its absorption, measured in terms of domestic output, will fall, so that domestic output will have to fall to accommodate the reduced demand. This is because, under perfectly flexible exchange rates, the balance of payments must always be zero. If there is no capital mobility or 'perfect' capital mobility, the balance of trade must also be zero at every instant. As a consequence, *internal balance* is given at the point where domestic output equals domestic absorption. *External* balance obtains, for cases where the value of exports equals the value of imports: such a relationship determines the exchange rate. That alters, becomes 'flexible', if there is a random disturbance or even the pre-determined or policy variables alter. So, if, as an example, a general tariff is imposed by the domestic economy on its imports from the foreign country or from 'the rest of the world', as the model specification determines, the impact effect will be to worsen the domestic economy's terms of trade: *ceteris paribus*, to generate a unit value of imports more exports have to be exported than was the case before the tariff was levied. Such an impact would produce an increase in absorption; according to the Laursen–Metzler effect, this would increase the demand for domestic goods (with the worsening of the terms of trade having engendered a fall in imports: the increase in absorption must mean, *ex definitione*, that expenditure on domestic goods by domestic residents has increased). But, even under fixed exchange rates, that would not be the end of the story, since income has changed on impact and so will affect imports; it is certainly not the end of the story under flexible exhange rates, since the switch from importables to domestic goods, consequent upon the imposition of the tariff, must affect the exchange rate itself. The general view in the literature is that the Mundellian (Mundell 1961) result is correct (which Mundell based upon the existence of the Laursen–Metzler effect), that tariffs can only be 'deflationary' under flexible exchange rates. The reason for this is that it is argued — though not proved rigorously — that the final effect on the exchange rate will be an appreciation, but a percentage appreciation which is less than that of the (increase in the) tariff. The consequent improvement in the equilibrium terms of trade causes domestic absorption in domestic units to fall and hence domestic output falls.

In developing their framework for analysing the interdependency of economics under flexible exchange rates, Laursen and Metzler wrote:

> The argument in favor of flexible exchange rates as a means of isolating price movements is extremely simple, for it is based entirely upon the familiar purchasing-power parity theory of exchange rates. The view that flexible exchanges also isolate movements of output and employment, however, is based upon less obvious reasoning.
>
> . . . The accepted opinion seems to be that under a system of flexible exchange rates the *total* monetary demand for a given country's output will be unaffected by a contraction abroad . . .
>
> Since American exports may either rise or fall when output is expanded in the United Kingdom, it is apparent that output as a whole in the United States will not remain at its original level unless the change in exports is exactly offset by a change in the opposite direction in some other component of output. What are the reasons, in the traditional view, for believing that this will actually occur? . . . For the most part, it seems to be accepted as self-evident that if a country's exports and imports change by the same amount, as they would under a system of flexible exchange rates, the demand for the country's total output necessarily remains at a constant level. [This] . . . implicitly assumes that, when the domestic prices of imports rise or fall, any consequent change in a country's total domestic-currency expenditure on imports is exactly offset by a change in the opposite direction in expenditure on home goods . . . (Laursen and Metzler 1950, pp 284–285: *italics in original*).

It is that assumption which they challenge, and in so doing advance the Laursen–Metzler effect:

> Suppose, now, that import prices fall as a result of currency appreciation. How will this price change affect the expenditure schedule? The *composition* of

expenditure will, of course, be changed since the relatively cheaper imports will be substituted for home goods. But, . . . , we believe that a change will also occur in the total expenditure schedule itself. With given prices at home, a decline in import prices increases the real income corresponding to any given level of money income. Now the statistical evidence for the United States shows rather conclusively that the proportion of income saved tends to rise with a rise in real income . . . We therefore believe there is a strong presumption that, as import prices fall and the real income corresponding to a given money income increases, the amount spent on goods and services out of a given money income will fall . . . In short, our basic premise is that, other things being the same, the expenditure schedule of any given country rises when import prices rise and falls when import prices fall. (*op.cit.,* p 286; *italics in original*).

As we have remarked, this Laursen–Metzler proposition has been a cornerstone of most of the literature on open economy macroeconomics, and of almost the whole of that stratum of it which has studied the effects of tariffs under flexible exchange rates. In many instances, it is the Laursen–Metzler effect which has determined the analytical conclusions obtained in the literature.

Some of those central conclusions, which are now taken to be the orthodoxy in the literature, are considered in this paper. These are concerned with these issues: tariffs under flexible exchange rates; devaluation, output and fixed exchange rates; the comparative advantage of monetary and fiscal policy under flexible exchange rates; assignment of stabilization policies under flexible exchange rates; and economic dependency under flexible exchange rates. Essentially, our conclusions simply reverse those of the standard paradigms; for example, tariffs can be expansionary under flexible exchange rates. These reversals are achieved (even if, indirectly rather than immediately) as a consequence of merely reversing the Laursen–Metzler effect. In essence, the impact on domestic absorption of a change in the terms of trade is the opposite to that posited by Laursen–Metzler. However, we hope that what we provide in the following pages is a little more substantial than just altering a few mathematical signs in algebraic manipulations. The analyses themselves are, indeed, not as straightforward as that; but more important, we first of all set the background to our models, by a formal presentation of the Laursen–Metzler effect, and of even more importance we trust, by a formal demonstration based on utility considerations that domestic absorption falls when import prices rise and vice versa. That negation of the Laursen–Metzler effect we have rather boldly labelled the Ford–Sen effect: to it, in the investigation of the impact of tariffs on output under flexible exchange rates, we add a Ford–Sen condition.

The Laursen–Metzler effect has come under scrutiny of late, and it has been challenged in a model of consumer optimization of utility over time (see Obstfeld 1982, and Svensson and Razin 1983). We have also ourselves extended the analysis of such a model in Ford and Sen (1985) to demonstrate that the Laursen–Metzler effect might not hold. However, the current proof of the Ford–Sen effect is developed in the context of the overwhelming majority of open-economy models, which are timeless or even if pseudo-dynamic are (at best) implicitly founded on a static optimizing framework of aggregate consumer behaviour.

1   The Laursen–Metzler effect and its negation

We adopt the following notation:

A = real absorption measured in domestic currency units;
$\hat{A}$ = real absorption measured in terms of the consumer price index;
P_1 = the price of the home good in home currency units;
P_2 = the foreign price of the foreign (imported) goods in units of foreign currency;
r = the rate of exchange; defined as the units of domestic currency required for the purchase of a unit of foreign currency;
y = real income in terms of the domestic good;
V = the level of real output in the domestic economy;
p = the consumer price index;
δ = the share of expenditure on the foreign (imported) good in terms of total expenditure by domestic residents (which equals absorption);
and
σ = the domestic terms of trade.

Then *ex definitione:*

$$y = \frac{P_1 V}{P} \tag{3.1}$$

$$\sigma = \frac{P_2 r}{P_1} \tag{3.2}$$

$$P = F(P_1, P_2, r\,\delta) = f(\sigma, \delta) \tag{3.3}$$

P is then the price of 'the basket' of goods (home and foreign) that is purchased by the domestic economy;

$$P_1 A = P\hat{A}(\cdot) \tag{3.4}$$

The standard hypothesis is that:

$$\hat{A} = \hat{A}(y) \tag{3.5}$$

We can now proceed to our recapitulation of the Laursen–Metzler effect; and we can do so without loss of generality by making one further standard assumption, namely, that P_1 is normalized at unity. Then, from (3.5), we can deduce that:

$$\frac{\partial A}{\partial \sigma} = P\hat{A}'(y) \frac{\partial y}{\partial \sigma} + \hat{A}(y) \frac{\partial P}{\partial \sigma} \tag{3.6}$$

Making use of equation (3.1) this expression can be re-written as:

$$\frac{\partial A}{\partial \sigma} = \frac{\partial P}{\partial \sigma} \hat{A}(y) [1-\epsilon] \tag{3.7}$$

where ϵ is the elasticity of $\hat{A}$ with respect to real income.
Now:

$$A = A(V,\sigma) \tag{3.8}$$

Therefore:

$$dA = A_1 dV + A_2 d\sigma \tag{3.9}$$

It follows from (3.1) and (3.4) that:

$$A_1 \equiv \hat{A}_1 \tag{3.10}$$

and since at equilibrium in the Mundellian short-run open economy macro model 'hoarding' must be zero, $\hat{A}(y) \equiv y$, it also follows that:

$$\epsilon \equiv \hat{A}_1 = A_1 \tag{3.11}$$

Since $\partial A/\partial \sigma \equiv A_2$ we can, therefore, write equation (3.7) as:

$$A_2 = \frac{\partial P}{\partial \sigma} \hat{A}(y) [1 - A_1] \tag{3.12}$$

The normal supposition is $\partial P/\partial \sigma > 0$ and since, *ex hypothesi*, $0 < A_1 < 1$, A_2 *is taken to be positive*. That is the Laursen–Metzler *effect*: it leads to what we might label the Laursen–Metzler *condition* in the formalization, through the use of a specific form for P, of the Mundellian model. A *condition* which can be written, at the point of equilibrium, as:

$$A_2 = I[1 - A_1] \tag{3.13}$$

It is this relationship, coupled with the positive sign for A_2, which produces the classic Mundell (1961) result that a general tariff can never be expansionary, only contractionary, under flexible exchange rates.

Thus, if the Cobb–Douglas form is used for P:

$$P = P_1^{(1-\delta)}(P_2 r)^\delta \tag{3.14}$$

and if we let $P_1 = 1$, we deduce that:

$$\frac{\partial P}{\partial \sigma} = \delta \sigma^{\delta - 1} = \frac{rI}{\sigma \hat{A}(y)} \tag{3.15}$$

where we have used the definition of δ and have let I represent the quantity of imports. Hence, if the initial value of P_2 is also normalized at unity (as is again the case in the orthodox literature), the substitution of (3.15) into (3.12) does produce equation (3.13).

But suppose that the 'ideal' cost of living index (see Samuelson and Swamy 1974) is of the CES form; where δ must change as σ changes:

$$P = (P_1^{\Omega} + (P_2 r)^{\Omega})^{\frac{1}{\Omega}} \tag{3.16}$$

Hence:

$$P = \sigma \delta^{-\frac{1}{\Omega}} \tag{3.17}$$

where, as previously, we use the normalization $\sigma = r$, and the fact that:

$$\delta = (\sigma^{-\Omega} + 1)^{-1} \text{ [see Appendix]} \tag{3.18}$$

Therefore:

$$\frac{\partial P}{\partial \sigma} = \delta^{-\frac{1}{\Omega}} [1 - \delta \sigma^{-\Omega}] \tag{3.19}$$

Hence, using equation (3.12) we deduce that:

$$\frac{\partial A}{\partial \sigma} = A_2 \gtreqless 0 \text{ as:}$$

$$1 \gtreqless \delta \sigma^{-\Omega} \tag{3.20}$$

Hence, unless initially, $r = \sigma = 1$, A_2 *can be negative*. The latter situation we shall (rather egotistically!) label the Ford–Sen effect. So the normalization of the initial terms of trade does not have neutral effects for the analysis of the economy; *except* when the Cobb–Douglas price index is used. For the CES:

$$A_2 = \delta^z[1 - \delta\sigma^{-\Omega}] \quad I[1 - A_1]; \; z \equiv -\left[\frac{1}{\Omega} + 1\right]$$

(3.21)

where we have used the identity:

$$\delta \equiv \frac{rP_2I}{P\hat{A}(y)} = \frac{I}{\hat{A}(y)}$$

(3.22)

when A_2 is negative, as σ increases, the switch to domestic goods from foreign goods (i.e., $\partial I/\partial < 0$), will not be sufficient to prevent (total) expenditure measured in domestic goods from falling.

2. Expansionary tariffs under flexible exchange rates

The traditional literature in open economy macroeconomics is firmly wedded to the view first stated in anything approaching a formal way by Mundell (1961) that for a small open economy, the imposition of a general tariff on imports can lead only to a contraction of its national output (as more recent examples, see Tower 1973, Krugman 1982). We have demonstrated that this is *not* a robust result (Ford and Sen 1985) even if the Laursen–Metzler effect does hold. We produce here the result, that, if the Lauren–Metzler effect is violated, within the Mundell–Krugman Keynesian version of the open economy, tariffs can also be expansionary. In essence, if the Ford–Sen effect and condition both hold such an outcome can materialize; the presence of the Niehans (1975) paradox is not required for its generation.

The model we shall utilize to establish the proof of our proposition is that used in the Mundellian literature. In essence, we have only two markets that are of direct concern to us: the market for the domestic commodity and the market for foreign exchange. We assume, therefore, that there is no domestic economy and no international capital flows. The two countries in the world are assumed each to produce a composite commodity. The domestic currency price of home and foreign goods is fixed at unity. The rate of exchange, r (defined, we recall, as the number of domestic currency units which are needed to purchase a unit of foreign currency), is determined, via exports and imports, by the demand for and supply of domestic (foreign) currency. The domestic economy's level of output is labelled V, and this is demand determined: the quantity of the home country's exports are denoted by X and its imports by I.

Internal balance is given by the equality of *ex ante* demand for and supply of the domestic commodity; which in excess demand form is:

$$A(y,\ r(1+t)) + X(r) - rI(y,\ r(1+t)) - V - R = 0 \qquad (3.23)$$

where: A is absorption, measured in terms of the domestic commodity, which is equal to nominal absorption, of course, given our hypothesis that the home currency price of the domestic commodity is unity; y is the real income measured in terms of the domestic good (equal, again here, to nominal income); and t is the tariff rate, and so $r(1+t)$ becomes the domestic terms of trade.

Real income is composed of domestic output (V) and the real value (equals, nominal value, here) of the tariff revenue (R), where $R = rtI$:

$$y = R + V \qquad (3.24)$$

External balance is achieved when the balance of payments (the balance of trade) is zero; in excess demand terms for foreign currency this occurs when:

$$rI(\cdot) - X(r) = 0 \qquad (3.25)$$

If we differentiate equation (3.23) and (3.25), making use of (3.24), and letting the *initial* value of the *ad valorem* tariff be zero, for expositional convenience, we find that:

$$\begin{bmatrix} (A_1 - rI_1 - 1) & [X_1 - rI_2 - I + A_2] \\ rI_1 & [I_2 r + I - X_1] \end{bmatrix} \begin{bmatrix} dV \\ dr \end{bmatrix} = \begin{bmatrix} r^2(I_1 I + I_2) + rI(I - A_1) - rA_2 \\ -r^2(I_1 I + I_2) \end{bmatrix} dt \qquad (3.26)$$

The slope of the external balance (EB) line is:

$$\left. \frac{dV}{dr} \right|_t = \frac{X_1 - I_2 r - I}{rI_1} \qquad (3.26)(a)$$

The slope of the internal balance (IB) is:

$$\left. \frac{dV}{dr} \right|_t = \frac{X_1 - I_2 r - I + A_2}{I + rI_1 - A_1} \qquad (3.26)(b)$$

All partial derivatives are delineated by the order of the relevant arguments in the relevant functions. So that:

$$X_1 - rI_2 - I > 0 \tag{3.27}$$

is the Marshall-Lerner condition, in this model, for a depreciation of the home country's currency to improve its balance of payments. With $rI = X$ at the initial equilibrium, (3.27) can readily be translated into the conventional price-elasticities version of the Marshall-Lerner condition.

Since $I + rI_1 > A_1$, the slope of the *IB* line will be positive in (r, V) space, provided the Marshall-Lerner condition is satisfied; and the Laursen-Metzler effect holds $(A_2 > 0)$, or the Ford-Sen effect $(A_2 < 0)$ is not dominant. The Marshall-Lerner condition will result in the *EB* line also being positively sloped. Stability requires the trace of the Jacobian in equation (3.26) to be negative and its determinant $|J|$ to be positive. The trace condition is met by the Marshall-Lerner condition. The determinantal requirement is satisfied if:

$$(A_1 - 1)(I_2 r + I - X_1) - rI_1 A_2 > 0 \tag{3.28}$$

If the Marshall-Lerner condition holds, and if the Ford-Sen effect holds, so that $A_2 < 0$, or the Laursen-Metzler effect is weak, the Jacobian has a positive determinant.

From equation 3.26 we deduce that:

$$\frac{dV}{dt} = [(I_2 r + I - X_1)\ [I(I - A_1) - A_2]r + r^2[I_1 I + I_2]A_2]\ |J|^{-1} \tag{3.29}$$

If the Laursen-Metzler effect is present, as we have seen previously:

$$I(1 - A_1) = A_2 \tag{3.30}$$

and so,

$$A_2 > 0 \tag{3.31}$$

Thus, dV/dt reduces to this expression:

$$\frac{dV}{dt} = \frac{r^2[I_1 I + I_2]A_2}{|J|} \tag{3.32}$$

If, furthermore, the *Slutsky condition* (for this condition in trade models see Bhagwati and Johnson 1961) is used, as it has been in the Mundellian literature:

$$I_1 I + I_2 < 0 \tag{3.33}$$

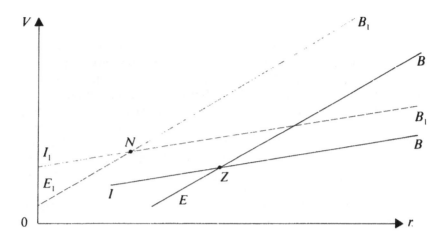

Figure 3.1

Hence, dV/dt is uniquely negative.

But, if the Ford–Sen effect is operative: (3.30) does not hold; neither does (3.31), with A_2 now being negative, rather than positive; and so, if it is then maintained that the left-hand side of equation (3.33) *is* to be regarded as the Slutsky condition, dV/dt *can* be positive. In equation (3.29) the term $I(1 - A_1) - A_2$ will now be positive, and the second term involving the Slutsky condition, will become positive. Hence, if the Marshall–Lerner effect is weak, then the chance of $dV/dt > 0$ is that much greater. In addition, if the *Niehans paradox* happens to prevail, so that the Marshall–Lerner condition is not satisfied ($I_2r - X_1 + I > 0$), then this, combined with the Ford–Sen effect, will guarantee that in a stable open-economy Mundellian model, a general tariff must be expansionary.

As far as the impact of the tariff on the exchange rate is concerned we discover that:

$$\frac{dr}{dt} = \left\{ (A_1 - 1)r^2[II_1 + I_2] - r^2I_1 \ [I(I - A_1) - A_2] \right\} |J|^{-1}$$

(3.34)

If the Ford–Sen effect is present, dr/dt is not uniquely signed.

The situation can be illustrated in Figure 3.1.

The after-tariff internal and external balance schedules are I_1B_1 and E_1B_1, respectively. We deduce from equation 3.26 that:

$$\left. \frac{dV}{dt} \right|_{r} = \frac{r^2[I_1I + I_2] + r[I(1 - A_1) - A_2]}{A_1 - rI_1 - I}$$

(3.35)

for the shift on the *IB* schedule. The shift in the *EB* schedule consequent upon the imposition of the tariff is:

$$\frac{\mathrm{d}V}{\mathrm{d}t}\bigg|\, r = \frac{-r^2[I_1 I + I_2]}{rI_1} \tag{3.36}$$

with the Slutsky condition holding, this expression is positive: hence the *EB* schedule shifts to the left in Figure 3.1. That this must happen is obvious enough: at given *r*, any increase in the tariff (from any level) must reduce imports via the price effect and since exports remain the same, output must rise to revive the demand for imports so that they re-attain their former level to preserve balance of payments equilibrium.

The *IB* schedule can shift in either direction or remain where it is even if the Ford–Sen effect, $A_2 < 0$, is satisfied and the Ford–Sen condition, $(I + rI_2 - X_1) - A_2 > 0$ is fulfilled. But, naturally, if the behavioural para-meters in the home economy are such that $\mathrm{d}V/\mathrm{d}t > 0$, expression (3.35) must be positive; and *IB* shifts to $I_1 B_1$ in Figure 3.1. The economy moves from *Z* to *N*. The exchange rate has appreciated (i.e. *r* has fallen): exports have fallen, reducing the demand for the domestic output, but the fall in the domestic economy's terms of trade must be such (i.e. *r* must have fallen proportionately more than *t* has risen) as to stimulate the domestic economy's absorption in terms of home goods via the Ford–Sen effect, to dominate the fall in export demand. If the Laursen–Metzler effect had existed then the fall in the domestic terms of trade would cause that absorption to fall, which would aggravate the impact on domestic output of the fall in export demand generated by the fall in the exchange rate.

3 Demand-side contractionary devaluation
Even if the Marshall–Lerner effect happens to be present, the Harberger expansionary effects of the devaluation of a country's otherwise fixed exchange rate will not emerge, so the recent literature has maintained, if there exist 'supply side' effects in the devaluing country's economy. Such effects could emerge through the need for imported intermediate goods in the production process, whose price could be raised by the devaluation (*ceteris paribus*). The consequence could be that the favourable impact of the devaluation of exports is counter-balanced by an increase in the domestic price of exports; and domestic demand for the domestic output could also fall because of a reduction in real income. The presence of 'real wage resistance' in the domestic economy could lead to a similar contrac-tionary outcome in the macro economy of the devaluing country (see, for example, Krugman and Taylor 1978).

The kind of absorption effect considered in this paper can result in contractionary devaluation because of 'demand side' influences. The devaluation, *ceteris paribus*, will improve the terms of trade and *reduce absorption in terms of home goods* by domestic residents and so can produce a fall in domestic output if the foreign price-elasticity of demand for the home country's goods is not 'sufficiently' high.

To demonstrate this important 'demand side' proposition, we use a model based on three market clearing equations. The first is for domestic output; the second is for money market; and the third is for the balance of payments. With fixed exchange rate, naturally, the balance of payments (B) becomes an endogenous variable. We also know that any balance of payments surplus or deficit will represent an increase or decrease in the country's foreign currency reserves: unless these changes are sterilized/ neutralized they will lead to changes in the domestic stock of money. With the domestic prices of 'the home good' and 'the foreign good' set at unity the three market clearing equations are written as:

$$A(V,r,i) + X(r) - rI(V,r,i) - V = 0 \qquad (3.37)$$

$$M^d(V,i) - M^s = 0 \qquad (3.38)$$

$$X(r) - rI(V,r,i) = B \qquad (3.39)$$

The notation not previously defined is: i is the rate of interest; $M^d(\cdot)$ is the demand for money; and M^s is the supply of money; with r now the fixed exchange rate.

Ex definitione:

$$dM^s = dD + dR \qquad (3.40)$$

where: D is the domestic component of high-powered money and R is the value (again in domestic currency units) of foreign currency reserves. Again, *ex definitione:*

$$dR = B \qquad (3.41)$$

Let us assume, for the sake of argument, that the Central Bank does not engage in active stabilization policy so that any change in D can only materialize through a change in reserves and the Central Bank's sterilization/neutralization of that change. Hence:

$$dD = -(1 - w)dR \qquad (3.42)$$

where w indicates the extent to which any increase in reserves is sterilized:

if $w = 0$, the Central Bank sterilizes the whole of any increase in foreign reserves. Thus:

$$dM^s = wdR = wB \qquad (3.43)$$

We discover from equations (3.37) − (3.39) and (3.43) that:

$$
\begin{bmatrix}
(A_1 - rI_1 - 1) & (A_3 - rI_3) & 0 \\
M_1 & M_2 & -w \\
-rI_1 & -rI_3 & -1
\end{bmatrix}
\begin{bmatrix}
dV \\
di \\
dB
\end{bmatrix}
=
\begin{bmatrix}
rI_2 - X_1 + I - A_2 \\
0 \\
rI_2 - X_1 + 1
\end{bmatrix}
dr \qquad (3.44)
$$

Thus:

$$\frac{dv}{dr} = \frac{(A_2 + X_1 - rI_2 - I)(M_2) - A_3(rI_2 - X_1 + I) + A_2 wI_3 r}{|J|} \qquad (3.45)$$

The trace of the Jacobian in (3.44) must be negative for stability and its determinant must also be negative. The trace condition is satisfied immediately. The determinantal condition will definitely be met if w is zero. Suppose for the sake of illustration that that is the case. Then if the Ford-Sen condition does obtain, the numerator in equation (3.45) can be positive, and hence dV/dr be negative: the Niehans paradox *per se*, of course, would produce that outcome. However, if $w > 0$, the Niehans paradox will not guarantee that result: the Ford-Sen effect ($A_2 < 0$) would now help to strengthen the negative impact on output of a devaluation.

The impact of the devaluation on the balance of payments is uncertain:

$$\frac{dB}{dr} = \left\{ (rI_2 - X_1 + I)[(A_1 - 1)M_2 - M_1 A_3] + [M_1 I_3 - I_1 M_2] rA_2 \right\} |J|^{-1} \qquad (3.46)$$

although a casual inspection of equation (3.46) would lead us to expect that the devaluation would improve the balance of payments. We can, indeed, state categorically that such an outcome will emerge if the Ford-Sen effect holds and the interest sensitivity of imports is small.

The reduction in domestic output brought about by the devaluation, and assisted by the Ford-Sen absorption effect, will serve to reduce imports, so supporting the devaluation's direct impact on the volume of imports. The reduction in macroeconomic activity will cause a fall in the rate of interest (as equation 3.44 can confirm), which will have little effect on increasing imports if the interest sensitivity of imports is indeed small.

The increase in r, meanwhile, has increased exports: and if the Marshall–Lerner condition is satisfied the pure price effect of the devaluation must be to raise the value of exports by more than the value of imports (which in regard to pure price effects, of course, can rise only because their valuation, via r, has increased). So combining price, interest rate and income effects, the balance of payments must improve.

4   Monetary and fiscal policy under flexible exchange rates

The conventional wisdom in open economy macro models, generated by the pioneering Mundell–Fleming models, is that: monetary policy is the only effective stabilization policy to adopt in a situation where exchange rates float freely; fiscal policy will be otiose, its initial impact on output being ultimately crowded out by exchange rate changes. This proposition is regarded as a 'strong result' in the literature. It is possible to demonstrate that the presence of the Ford–Sen effect is necessary to overturn it, and, indeed, that the effect can be sufficiently powerful to do so.

The model is in the Mundell–Fleming tradition. It assumes that there is perfect capital mobility between the two economies in the world (though we could relax this supposition) and so interest-rate parity holds:

$$i = i^* + \frac{\dot{r}}{r} \tag{3.47}$$

where i is the domestic (nominal) rate of interest; i^* is the 'rest of the world' interest rate; and $\dot{r}/r$ is the (expected) rate of depreciation of the exchange rate. At equilibrium, naturally, $i = i^*$. We assume that expected inflation is zero: so that we are concerned only with nominal interest rates; again, a standard, simplifying, hypothesis. Given that we have both flexible exchange rates and perfect capital mobility, the balance of payments equation is replaced by equation (3.47), with $\dot{r}/r = 0$, for equilibrium. The other two equations in the model for the domestic economy are for internal balance, the usual 'IS' schedule and for the money market.

In effect:

$$A(V,r,i) + X(r) - rI(V,r,i) + G - V = 0 \tag{3.48}$$

$$M_d\left(\frac{V}{P}, i\right) - \frac{M^s}{P} = 0 \tag{3.49}$$

The full model is equations (3.48) and (3.49) with i replaced by i^* from equation (3.47), and $\dot{r}/r = 0$, uncovered interest parity. Again, as can be gathered by implication from equation (3.48), we have normalized the domestic price of the domestic output and the foreign output at unity in the respective currencies. Hence, r denotes the terms of trade. We note one important point about the demand for money equation; it is written in real terms, but the price deflator is the price of the 'basket of goods' (P), i.e. it is the consumer price-index, which in effect, should be the deflator in open economy models.

Then:

$$P = \Phi(P_h, P_f, r, \delta) \tag{3.50}$$

where: P_h is the domestic price of the home good; P_f is the foreign price of the foreign good; and δ is the share in absorption of the foreign good.

Let us assume that:

$$P = r\delta^{\frac{-1}{\Omega}} \tag{3.50(a)}$$

So that we could imagine that all expenditure were for consumption purposes, based on a 'social utility function' for the home economy of the CES kind, (3.50a) would be a Samuelson–Swamy (1974) 'ideal consumer price index' in the Fisher sense (see the Appendix; where δ is defined). So when r alters, so too does δ.

Differentiation of equation (3.48) and (3.49) yields:

$$\begin{bmatrix} (A_1 - rI_1 - 1) & (A_2 + X_1 - rI_2 - I) \\ M_1 P & m(M^s - M_1 V) \end{bmatrix} \begin{bmatrix} dV \\ dr \end{bmatrix} = \begin{bmatrix} -dG + (rI_3 - A_3)di^* \\ PdM^s - P^2 M_2 di^* \end{bmatrix} \tag{3.51}$$

where:

$$m = [1 - r^\Omega \partial^{-1}] \partial^{1+\Omega/\Omega} > 0 \tag{3.51a}$$

Hence:

$$\frac{\partial V}{\partial G} = m(M_1 V - M^s) |J|^{-1} \tag{3.52}$$

where

$$|J| = m(M^s - M_1 V)(A_1 - rI_1 - 1) - M_1 P[A_2 + X_1 - rI_2 - I] \tag{3.53}$$

$$\frac{\partial V}{\partial M^s} = \left\{ -P[A_2 + X_1 - rI_2 - 1] \right\} |J|^{-1} \tag{3.54}$$

How do these two multipliers compare with those in the Mundell–Fleming literature? In that literature P is ignored in the money demand equation, even though if r if fully floating, P will be flexible and to assume the one varies whilst the other is constant is a contradiction in terms in a flex-price model. We find that:

$$\frac{\partial V}{\partial G} = \frac{0}{-M_1[A_2 + X_1 - rI_2 - I]} = 0 \tag{3.55}$$

$$\frac{\partial V}{\partial M^s} = \frac{-[A_2 + X_1 - rI_2 - I]}{-M_1[A_2 + X_1 - rI_2 - I]} > 0 \tag{3.56}$$

But, we note that the conventional assumption is that the Laursen–Metzler condition holds, this means that the determinant of the system, which is the denominator in (3.55) and (3.56) is negative, given that $M_1 > 0$. Indeed, the sign requirement on $|J|$ *is* negative: although the economic model is essentially third-order and the determinant of the full system should be negative, since the domestic rate of interest must alter as the economy adjusts to the world rate of interest consequent upon a random disturbance to the economy (even if i^* itself does not alter), we have essentially three dynamic equations. Output will increase when there is excess demand for output; the interest rate will increase when there is excess demand for money; and the exchange rate will increase when the world interest rate lies above the domestic interest rate. Essentially, the resultant determinantal equation is derived from the Jacobian in equation (3.51) bordered by the column vector: $[(A_3 - rI_3)M_2K_1]$ and the row vector: $[0 \ 0 \ K_1]$; where K_1 is the adjustment of the exchange rate to an excess of i^* over i. The condition that that Jacobian has a negative determinant is precisely the condition that is required to render the Jacobian in (3.51) negative.

So, what does the Ford–Sen condition imply for the Mundell–Fleming result? If we consider equation (3.56) we see, in the light of the above comments, that monetary policy is not a feasible policy to adopt to expand output in the Mundell–Fleming version of their own model because it creates instability.

In regard to equations (3.53) and (3.54) which embody the introduction of the consumer price index into the money market equilibrium, we observe that $m(M^s - M_1V)$ should, initially, be positive to enable stability to occur. We can assume that this is the case, with $m(M^s - M_1V)$ not large enough to violate the condition that the trace of the Jacobian also be negative. *In that case, $\partial V/\partial G > 0$; fiscal policy is expansionary and stable.* Furthermore, we deduce that *monetary policy is contractionary*; but also stable.

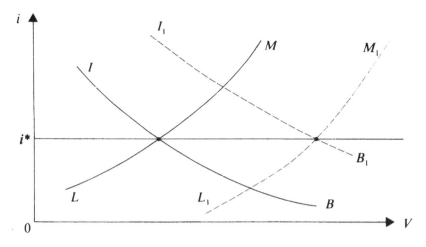

Figure 3.2

The outcome in the case of fiscal policy can be depicted in Figure 3.2. The increase in G shifts the IB schedule to the right in (i, V) space. The fiscal expansion lowers the exchange rate and so shifts the $L - M$ schedule $(M^d M^s)$ to the right also, even though there has been no direct accommodatory monetary policy. The fiscal expansion has lowered the exchange rate, and increased domestic absorption in terms of domestic goods (via the Ford–Sen effect). The reduction in the exchange rate has reduced the *general price level (P)*, and so has prevented the domestic rate of interest rising above the world rate and causing r to rise. Hence, the increase in the real supply of money has prevented a crowding-out of the increase in government expenditure, due to a rise in the exchange rate. That the value of r does fall when an increase in G leads to an increase in V can be confirmed from equation (3.51).

The situation for an increase in high-powered money is portrayed in Figure 3.3.

The case where monetary expansion leads to a contraction of output will be one where r is increased so that, in terms of (i, V) space, the 'LM' (i.e. $M^d M^s$) schedule shifts to the left; and with increased r so too must the IB (internal balance) schedule.

5 Assignment of stabilization policies under flexible exchange rates

It is now a standard proposition in the open economy macro literature that: under flexible exchange rates and perfect capital mobility, monetary policy should be directed to the internal objective of policy, whilst fiscal policy should be directed to the external objective. The internal objective

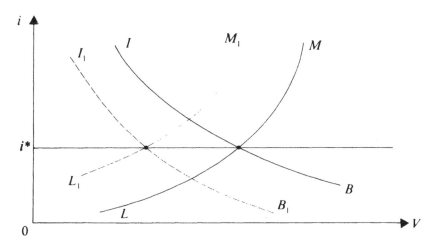

Figure 3.3

is usually taken to be to maintain output at one target level, $\bar{V}$; and the external objective is taken (under flexible exchange rate, that is) to be the maintenance of one exchange rate level, $\bar{r}$ (see Turnovsky 1977, Chapter 9, whose expository model we have followed).

The results obtained in the preceding section would lead us to expect that we could overturn that proposition, and this turns out to be the case. We assume the orthodox policy adjustment rules for the money stock and government expenditure:

$$\dot{G} = \alpha_{11}(V - \bar{V}) + \alpha_{12}(r - \bar{r}) \qquad (3.57)$$

$$\dot{M}^s = \alpha_{21}(V - \bar{V}) + \alpha_{22}(r - \bar{r}) \qquad (3.58)$$

where the dot over G and M^s indicates a time derivative. A *policy assignment* in the Mundell sense (1962, 1964) would require the government to set either α_{11} and α_{22} at zero or to set α_{12} and α_{21} at zero.

V and r will have reduced form equations which we can write in general form, as:

$$V = F(G, M^s) \qquad (3.59)$$

$$r = K(G, M^s) \qquad (3.60)$$

These equations will imply values of $\bar{G}$, $\bar{M}^s$ to meet $\bar{V}$ and $\bar{r}$. Linearizing (3.57) and (3.58) about the equilibrium that is defined by (3.59) and (3.60):

$$\dot{G} = \alpha_{11} [F_1(G-\bar{G}) + F_2(M^s-\bar{M}^s)] + \alpha_{12}[K_1(G-\bar{G}) + K_2(M^s-\bar{M}^s)]$$
$$(3.61)$$

$$\dot{M}^s = \alpha_{21}[F_1(G-\bar{G}) + F_2(M^s-\bar{M}^s)] + \alpha_{22}[K_1(G-\bar{G}) + K_2(M^s-\bar{M}^s)]$$
$$(3.62)$$

Let: $x_1 = G - \bar{G}$ and $x_2 = M^s - \bar{M}^s$. We can write (3.61) and (3.62) as:

$$\begin{bmatrix} \dot{x}_1 \\ \dot{x}_2 \end{bmatrix} = \begin{bmatrix} \alpha_{11}F_1 + \alpha_{12}K_1 & \alpha_{11}F_2 + \alpha_{12}K_2 \\ \alpha_{21}F_1 + \alpha_{22}K_1 & \alpha_{21}F_2 + \alpha_{22}K_2 \end{bmatrix} \begin{bmatrix} x_1 \\ x_2 \end{bmatrix} \qquad (3.63)$$

This equation applies to the adjustment of the economic system when both policy variables are altered to meet both policy targets, in the neighbourhood of equilibrium. Of course, if (3.59) and (3.60) are always linear then (3.63) provides a description of global adjustment also.

Now let us take the model of section 4.

Then we have:

$$F_1 = \frac{\partial V}{\partial G} = \frac{m(M_1 V - M^s)}{|J|} \quad F_2 = \frac{\partial V}{\partial M^s} = \frac{-P[A_2 + X_1 - r'_2 - I]}{|J|} \qquad (3.64)$$

$$K_1 = \frac{\partial r}{\partial G} = \frac{M_1 P}{|J|}; \ K_2 = \frac{\partial r}{\partial M^s} = \frac{(1 + rI_1 - A_1)}{|J|}$$

where: $|J| = m(M_1 V - M^s)(A_1 - rI_1 - 1) - M_1 P[A_2 + X_1 - rI_2 - I]$.

For stability we require: the trace of the coefficients matrix in 3.63 to be negative and its determinant to be positive.

Under flexible exchange rates without the inclusion of the consumer price index (when m becomes zero) and of the Ford–Sen condition in the Mundell–Fleming model, we recall that:

$$\frac{\partial V}{\partial G} = 0; \quad \frac{\partial V}{\partial M^s} > 0 \qquad (3.65)$$

$$\frac{\partial r}{\partial G} < 0; \quad \frac{\partial r}{\partial M^s} > 0$$

These conditions, together with the stability conditions, require that the government set: $\alpha_{11} = \alpha_{22} = 0$; $\alpha_{12} > 0$ and $\alpha_{21} < 0$. Hence, fiscal policy should be employed to maintain the external target, whilst monetary

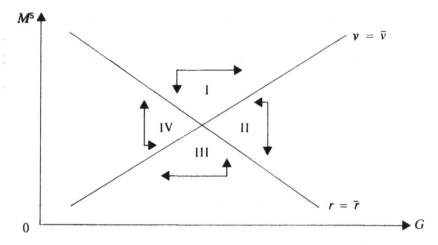

Figure 3.4

policy should be utilized to attain the internal target (see equations (3.57) and (3.58)).

In our model if:

$$F_1 = \frac{\partial V}{\partial G} > 0; \ F_2 = \frac{\partial V}{\partial M^s} < 0; \ K_1 = \frac{\partial r}{\partial G} < 0; \text{ and } K_2 = \frac{\partial r}{\partial M} < 0 \qquad (3.66)$$

it follows that the stability requirements are satisfied if: $\alpha_{12} = \alpha_{21} = 0$, $\alpha_{22} > 0$ and $\alpha_{11} < 0$. In that situation, the assignment of policies is the reverse of the standard rule, and is:

$$\dot{G} = \alpha_{11}(V - \bar{V}); \ a_{11} < 0 \qquad (3.67)$$

$$\dot{M^s} = \alpha_{22}(r - \bar{r}); \ a_{22} > 0 \qquad (3.68)$$

The situation is as illustrated in Figure 3.4. The schedule $V = \bar{V}$ is derived by setting equation (3.59) equal to V; and, similarly, the schedule $r = \bar{r}$, is obtained by setting equation (3.60) equal to $\bar{r}$. The slope of $V = \bar{V}$ is positive, from the signs of F_1 and F_2 in (3.66), whilst the slope of $r = \bar{r}$ is negative, since K_1 and K_2 have the same sign.

In the four phases we have:

I   Domestic recession.
    Excess supply of money causing $r > \bar{r}$.
II Domestic excess demand.
    Excess supply of money causing $r > \bar{r}$.
III Domestic excess demand.
    Excess demand for money causing $r < \bar{r}$.
IV Domestic recession.
    Excess demand for money causing $r < \bar{r}$.

6   The international transmission of demand shocks

We have mentioned earlier on that the main task which Laursen and Metzler (1950) set themselves was to determine whether or not flexible exchange rates would enable a country to insulate itself from output movements, economic fluctuations, in another country. Their general conclusion, based on a wider view in their text than the two-country mathematical model they employed in their Appendix was this:

> If capital movements can be effectively controlled, there is hardly any doubt that flexible exchange rates will cushion some countries to a considerable extent against the economic shocks of business cycles in other parts of the world . . . Nevertheless, the whole tenor of the preceding argument has been that the shock absorption performed by flexible exchange rates will by no means be perfect . . . We have seen, however, that output will not rise and fall simultaneously in all parts of the world, as under the gold standard. Instead, the rate of economic activity will probably fall moderately in some parts of the world while other parts of the world are enjoying a period of expansion . . . (Laursen and Metzler 1950, p 291).

In their formal mathematical appendix, however, they demonstrate that, given reasonable stability conditions, the comparative static findings indicate that a random shift in the one country's output will cause an opposite movement in the output of the other country. These findings rely heavily on the Laursen–Metzler effect.

If we label the countries 1 and 2, as they do, their model can be summarized in equilibrium (with no capital flows, balance of trade always zero and prices of domestic goods constant) as:

$$V_1 = A_1(V_1, r) + \alpha_1 \tag{3.69}$$

$$V_2 = A_2(V_2, 1/r) \tag{3.70}$$

$$I_1(V_1, r) = r I_2(V_2, 1/r) \tag{3.71}$$

The parameter α_1 represents a demand shock in country 1; V, I, and r are output, imports and the exchange rate. The latter is defined as we have defined it, with the home country taken to be country 1.

The two comparative statics results they obtain are:

$$\frac{dV_1}{d\alpha_1} = \frac{1}{\Delta}\left\{(1 - w_2)I_1(\eta_1 + \eta_2 - 1) - m_2 s_2\right\} \tag{3.72}$$

$$\frac{dV_2}{d\alpha_1} = \frac{1}{\Delta}(-m_1 s_2) \tag{3.73}$$

The term $(\eta + \eta_2 - 1)$ is just the Marshall–Lerner condition written in terms of elasticities at the point of equilibrium:

$$\eta_1 + \eta_2 - 1 = I_1 - \frac{\partial I_1}{\partial r} - \frac{\partial I_2}{\partial(1/r)} \tag{3.74}$$

Δ is the determinant of the Jacobian of the system and is:

$$\Delta = (1 - w_1)(1 - w_2)I_1(\eta_1 + \eta_2 - 1) - s_1 m_1(1 - w_2) - s_2 m_2(1 - w_1) \tag{3.75}$$

where:

$$w_1 = \frac{\partial A_1}{\partial V_1}; \ w_2 = \frac{\partial A_2}{\partial V_2}; \ m_1 = \frac{\partial I_1}{\partial V_1}; \ m_2 = \frac{\partial I_2}{\partial V_2};$$

$$s_1 = \frac{\partial A_1}{\partial r}; \text{ and } s_2 = \frac{\partial A_2}{\partial(1/r)}$$

Following Samuelson's Correspondence Principle, Laursen and Metzler demonstrate that the sign of Δ is crucial to the dynamic stability of the model; in what must have been one of the first formal, sophisticated, analyses of stability in open economy macro models. They argue that Δ must be positive for stability in their system: as a third-order system (in V_1, V_2 and r) the Routhian sufficient conditions for stability require Δ to be negative; since it is $-\Delta$ which is the constant term in the third-order characteristic equation of the system. It is that constant term *per se* which should be positive; and it is always equal to $(-1)^n$, when n is the order of the systems.

Now, suppose that we do take Δ as positive: it follows at once that the numerator of (3.72) must also be positive, and hence the home country's output expands consequent upon a positive demand shock. In the case of the foreign country, output must fall if the Laursen–Metzler effect holds.

Imagine that the Ford–Sen effect obtains instead. The Marshall–Lerner condition now only needs to hold weakly (or to be zero) and Δ will be positive: the strong Marshall–Lerner condition relied upon by Laursen and Metzler is no longer necessary. The overall outcome will be that both economies move in tandem: there is complete interdependence in the world economy.

If Δ is taken as negative, then the existence of the Ford–Sen effect requires the presence of the Niehans paradox (i.e. non-satisfaction of the Marshall–Lerner condition) to generate stability. In that event: $dV_1/d\alpha_1$ remains positive, but $dV_2/d\alpha_1$ becomes negative. The 'no capital flow' Laursen–Metzler model makes it impossible for $dV_2/d\alpha_1 = 0$.

The movement in the equilibrium exchange rate is given by:

$$\frac{dr}{d\alpha_1} = \frac{1}{\Delta} \, (m_1(1 - w_2)) \tag{3.76}$$

Should Δ be taken as negative, then under the Laursen-Metzler condition the home country's output might stay fixed, whilst that of the foreign country rises, and this would be consistent with an appreciation of the home currency. When Δ is negative and the Ford–Sen effect also obtains then the home country's output increases, that of the second country falls meanwhile; and the home currency appreciates. The reason for that is the fact that the Marshall–Lerner condition does not hold, which permits the model to be stable.

Appendix: The CES utility function and the corresponding 'ideal' price index

Let the utility function be

$$U = (ax_1^{-\beta} + bx_2^{-\beta})^{-1/\beta} \tag{A1}$$

and the budget restraint, y, be:

$$p_1x_1 + p_2x_2 = y \tag{A2}$$

Therefore, from utility maximization we deduce that:

$$\frac{x_1p_1}{y} = \frac{1}{1 + [\frac{b}{a}]^{\frac{1}{1+\beta}} [\frac{p_2}{p_1}]^{\frac{\beta}{1+\beta}}} \tag{A3}$$

The share of good 2 in expenditure is

$$\frac{x_2p_2}{y} = \frac{1}{1 + [\frac{b}{a}]^{\frac{1}{1+\beta}} [\frac{p_1}{p_2}]^{\frac{\beta}{1+\beta}}} \tag{A4}$$

Both shares depend upon relative prices.

Now consider the Samuelson–Swamy (1974) 'ideal' index number

$$P = \left[\frac{p_1^{\Omega}}{c} + \frac{p_2^{\Omega}}{d} \right]^{1/\Omega} \tag{A5}$$

Without loss of generality, we may set $c = d = 1$ in (A5) and $a = b = 1$ in (A1). It follows that:

$$\Omega = \frac{\beta}{1+\beta} \text{ or } \beta = \frac{\Omega}{1+\Omega} \tag{A6}$$

because the consumer price index is the price index derived from the *expenditure function* to (A1) with *utility* set at *unity*.

The expenditure function $E(\cdot)$ is, indeed:

$$E = (p_1^{\Omega} + p_2^{\Omega})^{1/\Omega} U \tag{A7}$$

This standard representation of the expenditure function, of course, follows by choosing x_1 and x_2 to minimize the expenditure that needs to be made to obtain a designated level of utility. That exercise produces, for a level of utility, U:

$$x_1 = p_1^{-z/\beta} (p_1^z + p_2^z)^{1/\beta} U \tag{A8}$$

$$x_2 = p_1^{-z/\beta} (p_1^z + p_2^z)^{1/\beta} U \tag{A9}$$

where: $z = \beta/1 + \beta$. Substitution of equations (A8) and (A9) into equation (A2) produces equation ($\bar{\text{A}}7$), with $y = E$.

References

Bhagwati, J. and Johnson, H. G. (1961) 'A generalised theory of the effects of tariffs on the terms of trade', *Oxford Economic Papers*, vol. 13, pp 225–253.

Dornbusch, R. (1982) 'Consumption opportunities, and the real value of external debt', *Journal of Development Economics*, vol. 9, pp 93–101.

Ford, J. L. and Sen, S. (1985) *Protectionism, Exchange Rates and the Macroeconomy*, Blackwell, Oxford.

Harberger, A. C. (1950) 'Currency depreciation, income and the balance of trade', *Journal of Political Economy*, vol. 58, pp 47–60.

Krugman, P. (1982) 'The macroeconomics of protection with a floating exchange rate', in: *Rochester Conference Series on Public Policy*, vol. 16, North-Holland, Amsterdam, pp 141–182.

Krugman, P. and Taylor, L. (1978) 'Contractionary effects of a devaluation', *Journal of International Economics*, vol. 8, pp 445–456.

Laursen, S. and Metzler, L. A. (1950) 'Flexible exchange rates and the theory of employment', *Review of Economics and Statistics*, vol. 32, November, pp 281–299.

Mundell, R. A. (1961) 'Flexible exchange rates and employment policy', *Canadian Journal of Economics*, vol. 27, pp 509–517.

Mundell, R. A. (1962) 'The appropriate use of monetary and fiscal policy for internal and external stability', *I.M.F. Staff Papers*, vol. 9, pp 70–79.

Mundell, R. A. (1964) 'A reply: capital mobility and size', *Canadian Journal of Economics*, vol. 30, pp 421–431.

Niehans, H. (1975) 'Some doubts about the efficacy of monetary policy under flexible exchange rates', *Journal of International Economics*, vol. 5, pp 275–281.

Obstfeld, M. (1982) 'Aggregate spending and the terms-of-trade: is there a Laursen–Metzler effect?', *Quarterly Journal of Economics*, vol. 97, pp 251–270.

Samuelson, P. A. and Swamy, S. (1974) 'Invariant economic index numbers and canonical duality: survey and synthesis', *American Economic Review*, vol. 64, pp 566–573.

Svensson, L. E. O. and Razin, A. (1983) 'The terms-of-trade and the current account: the Harberger–Laursen–Metzler effect', *Journal of Political Economy*, vol. 91, pp 97–125.

Tower, E. (1973) 'Commercial policy under fixed and flexible exchange rates', *Quarterly Journal of Economics*, vol. 87, pp 436–454.

Turnovsky, S. J. (1977) *Macroeconomic Analysis and Stabilisation Policies*, Cambridge University Press, Cambridge.

4. Macroeconomic policy effectiveness in the open economy: the Niehans paradox re-visited

Introduction

The so-called Niehans paradox is one of the most interesting examples of the whole class of Mundell–Fleming models which analyse the impact of macroeconomic policies under flexible exchange rates. It was formulated by Niehans (1975), though he himself did not call it a 'paradox'. The model showed that under certain conditions, which were fairly restrictive, expansionary monetary policy would actually *reduce* aggregate output, thus having a paradoxical and rather perverse effect on the macroeconomy.

The theoretical implications of this conclusion are rather unique. Almost all Mundell–Fleming type models tend to show that monetary policy is generally more potent under flexible exchange rates; the real controversy is about the efficacy of fiscal policy. Monetary expansion (contraction) not only increases (decreases) output, price level or inflation, but also tends to exacerbate the effects in the short run: hence the phenomenon of 'overshooting'. The Niehans effect, showing that the equilibrium value of output will fall (rise) as money supply increases (decreases), is therefore a radically different conclusion from the overall class of results in the field. It is also important to note, as we will demonstrate later, that fiscal policy is indeed expansionary in the Niehans formulation as in the traditional Keynesian models; hence there is an element of role reversal from the celebrated Mundellian conclusion regarding effective monetary/ineffective fiscal stance of the authorities.

As Niehans himself pointed out, his conclusion seemed to be supported by the stylized facts and therefore had a strong element of realism. The German case, where the Bundesbank has always pursued a conservative monetary policy, tending to keep money growth under strict control, seems to show that output (growth) can actually rise even when there is a monetary contraction. Clearly, the German miracle cannot be explained by macroeconomics alone. The point is that restrictive money, under flexible exchange rates, may not be recessionary. The example of the United States, under Reagan, is clearly another example of the reversal of the Mundellian paradigm and a vindication of the 'paradox'. Monetary growth has been strongly controlled by the Fed, leading to high interest rates and the overvaluation of the dollar. But the massive rise in government expenditure (led by military spending) and the high levels of the fiscal deficit have kept the economy buoyant at least within the short to medium term framework of macro analysis. This is what the Niehans model will predict. As regards the UK, both the fiscal and monetary stance were regressive in the early Thatcher years. But massive asset sales have allowed the government to increase its spending even though it is not reflected in the PSBR; this is clearly a special 'wealth effect'; the budget deficit is not a good indicator of demand creation. Government expenditure has been relatively high, in recent years, as well as being accompanied by a reduction in the direct tax burden; all these are evidence of expansionary fiscal policies. On the other hand, high interest rates show that effective monetary controls are crucial policy measures. Under these circumstances, the Niehans paradox would claim, unlike Mundell–Fleming, that aggregate output (growth) would rise, as has indeed been the case.

With flexible exchange rates and perfect capital mobility, the effect of money on output will work through the exchange rate (via interest rate changes). Thus the crucial link is the monetary effect of exchange depreciation (devaluation). In the Niehans model output falls, as money supply increases, because the Marshall–Lerner (*ML*) condition works in the opposite direction. A devaluation leads to a reduction in the trade balance and hence to a negative multiplier. The negation of the ML condition seems a very strong and restrictive assumption indeed, since all macro models accept it as an article of faith. However, there are numerous reasons to believe that it may be inoperative, at least within the lifetime of a macroeconomic model — the short-run. The simplest formulation of the ML condition is usually supported by the empirical fact that the relevant export elasticity is greater than one. But this is not necessarily true for mature industrial economies (such as the UK) nor for the developing countries (primary producers). In any case, the condition regarding export elasticity is derived from trade being always balanced; in a model with capital flows there is no reason to believe that trade balance is zero except in 'full equilibrium'. More complex formulations (say with exports requiring intermediate imported inputs) do not show the ML condition is automatically correct.

In spite of these comments, we shall show in our model that ML is neither necessary nor sufficient for the existence of the paradox. This removes one standard criticism of the case as originally proposed by Niehans, viz. the negation of Marshall–Lerner. Hence the claim, that the conclusion rests on odd or pathological assumptions fails to hold.

The second assumption made by Niehans, implicitly, was that of adaptive or static or neutral expectations. Therefore, the 'elasticity of expectations' is always less than unity (see Allen and Kenen (1980). Dornbusch (1976) makes the strong and forceful criticism that, at least in long-run equilibrium, expectations should be fulfilled. The elasticity assumption is too restrictive. But when the elasticity is made equal to unity (so that long term expectations are rational) then the model becomes *unstable*. Thus the negation of *ML* produces instability and invalidates any comparative statics experiments (by Samuelson's Correspondence Principle). This is a potentially more serious critique.

Our model, described below, will demonstrate that provided we use the notion of a saddle point equilibrium the difficulties associated with instability do not arise. We will also assume, right from the beginning, rational expectations. (Turnovsky (1981) has also stipulated rational expectations in his analysis which relates to the Niehans paradox.) The criticism that rapidly adjusting endogenous expectations will destabilize the Niehans model is not true either. Assuming rational expectations, flexible exchange rates, perfect capital mobility, with or without the Marshall–Lerner condition, the Niehans paradox will still hold. The taxonomy that we produce later makes it one out of several possibilities; nevertheless, *at a theoretical level* it is possible to have a situation wherein an increase in the money supply reduces output. The practical implications, in terms of stylized facts, have been briefly discussed earlier.

The basic model

Commodity market equilibrium is given by

$$E(Y, e, i) + T(Y, e) + G = Y \tag{4.1}$$

where E is total expenditure of the private sector (or absorption), T is the trade balance, G is government spending. Aggregate output is Y, while e is the nominal exchange rate and i the rate of interest. We note that

$$E_2 = (1 - \epsilon)I, \; 1 > E_1 > 0, \; E_3 < 0, \; T_1 < 0 \tag{4.2}$$

The first of these expressions is the Laursen–Metzler effect (*LM*) where ϵ is the elasticity of expenditure with respect to income and I the level of imports. For various reasons, discussed elsewhere as the Ford–Sen effect, E_2 can be positive or negative (Ford and Sen 1988). The domestic price level is unity.

The Marshall–Lerner condition (*ML*), which Niehans emphasized, is, of course, $T_2 = \partial T/\partial e$. We shall be agnostic, at this stage, about its sign; conventional logic asserts $T_2 > 0$ while the paradox requires $T_2 < 0$.

To emphasize the monetary effects of exchange rate depreciation, we equate 'real' money supply and demand. Thus

$$\frac{M}{Q} = L\left[\frac{PY}{Q}, i\right]$$ (4.3)

and Q the aggregate price index is

$$Q = (eP^*)^\delta P^{1-\delta}$$ (4.4)

Given P and P^* are set at unity we have

$$[M/e^\delta] = L(Y/e^\delta, i)$$ (4.5)

From (4.5), taking total differentials of logs, making appropriate transformations, we get

$$di = [\hat{M}/L_2] - [x\hat{Y}/L_2] - [\delta(1-x)\hat{e}/L_2]$$ (4.6)

A hat ^ implies proportional rate of change; $\hat{M} = dM/M$. x is the income elasticity of the demand for money. The conventional assumption is that $x<1$. Thus (4.6) gives implicitly a functional form for the interest rate

$$i = i(Y, e, M)$$ (4.7)

and

$$i_1>0, i_2>0, i_3<0$$ (4.8)

Under perfect mobility of capital, interest parity and *RE* we have

$$(\dot{e}/e)^{\exp} = \dot{e}/e = i(Y, e, M) - i^*$$ (4.9)

The problem with analysing stability for equations of the type (4.9) is well known. Essentially, $i_2>0$: hence $\partial\dot{e}/\partial e>0$, near the steady (stationary) state, giving unstable trajectories. Since the exceptional variable, e, is a jump or non-predetermined variable under *RE*, we need a stabilizing influence on the system. Rapid adjustment of expectations (under *RE*) tend to destabilize and need to be compensated by the dynamics of the backward-looking *non*-predetermined variables.

The obvious candidate, given the constancy of domestic price level, is for Y to be the non-predetermined variable. Its dynamics, predicated on the usual inventory mechanism, is postulated to be:

$$\dot{Y} = \alpha[E(Y, e, i) + G + T(Y, e) - Y] \quad (\alpha = 1) \tag{4.10}$$

We have kept to the basic IS/LM open economy representation, of the elemental macro-model, simply because the Niehans paradox was first analysed within this framework. However, since the major criticisms are focused on the *stability* issue, we have introduced dynamics right from the beginning. In a sense, the lead is given by the Samuelsonian Correspondence Principle; a proper knowledge of stability conditions is a prerequisite for comparative statics, which will be done later. A novel feature of this simple textbook model, however, is that we start thinking of unstable roots relatively early in the analysis simply because of the characterization of exchange dynamics (equation (4.9)).

To analyse stability we look at the relevant Jacobian of the system (4.10) and (4.9)

$$J = \begin{bmatrix} a_{11} & a_{12} \\ a_{21} & a_{22} \end{bmatrix} \tag{4.11}$$

where

$$\left. \begin{array}{l} a_{11} = E_1 + T_1 - 1 < 0 \\ a_{12} = E_2 + T_2 \quad ? \\ a_{21} = i_1 > 0 \\ a_{22} = i_2 > 0 \end{array} \right\} \tag{4.12}$$

Two comments are in order. First, the partials are evaluated in the close neighbourhood of equilibrium ($\dot{Y} = 0 = \dot{e}/e$). Hence, the evaluations of a_{ij} are done by putting $i = i^*$. For points away from general equilibrium this is not strictly true. But for comparative statics results it does not matter and (4.12) will suffice.

The second, more important, issue is the sign of $E_2 + T_2$. We choose to be agnostic and explore *all* the possibilities open to us simply because this sign is the key to the original Niehans paradox. Note that neither Niehans (the proposer) nor Dornbusch (the critic) analysed the implications of the E_2 term (*LM* effect). Their focus was only on T_2, i.e. Marshall–Lerner. What we get, however, is the *joint* effect whereby it is the sum of the two effects that matter. Thus, Niehans claimed that $T_2 < 0$; hence the paradox; Dornbusch refutes this in terms of stability. But it is quite possible for $T_2 < 0$ and $E_2 + T_2 > 0$; the outcome will be different. On the other hand, if Ford–Sen (1988) is valid and $E_2 < 0$, then we can still get the Niehans paradox with Marshall–Lerner operating and $T_2 > 0$. The nexus between the paradox and *ML* is therefore severed. In a sense, *ML* holding or not, is neither necessary nor sufficient for the 'paradox' or 'normal' results.

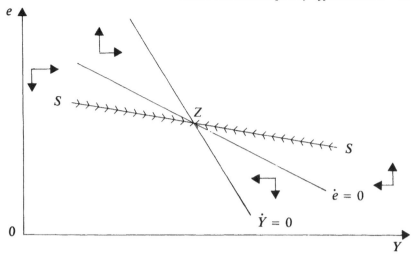

Figure 4.1   Case A

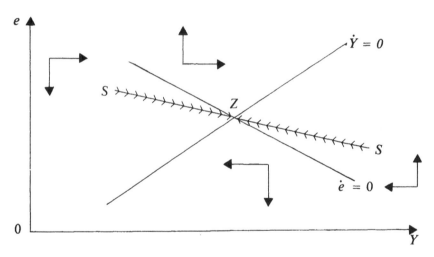

Figure 4.2   Case B

The validity of the debate, and its important implications for macro-policy, are now shifted to a much larger ground. Henceforth, we shall consider the total effect $E_2 + T_2$ and analyse the different cases on this basis rather than concentrating on the narrower range of issues regarding ML.

Stability requires the signing of $|J|$, which in turn depends on the assumptions made for $E_2 + T_2$. There are three possibilities, named Cases *A, B, C,* and depicted in the phase diagrams, Figures 4.1, 4.2, 4.3.

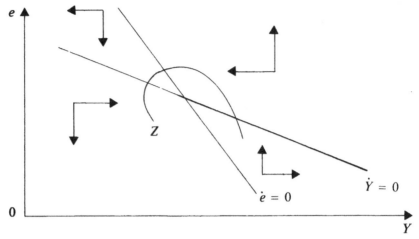

Figure 4.3   Case C

Case A.   Here $a_{12} = E_2 + T_2 < 0$. The Jacobian can be either sign. In this case, we have $|J| < 0$. Then the slope of $\dot{Y} = 0$ and $\dot{e} = 0$ are both negative in the (e, Y) plane. But $\dot{e} = 0$ is flatter. Since the product of the roots is negative we preclude complex roots. In addition, we must have one positive and one negative root. The equilibrium is a saddle-point and *SS* gives the (stable) saddle path. *SS* is downward sloping as expected for interest parity.

Case B.   Here $E_2 + T_2 > 0$. $|J|$ *must* be negative. Hence a saddle point equilibrium once again. The difference with the previous case is that $\dot{Y} = 0$ is now upward rising. In a sense, this is a conventional case where, for *IS* equilibrium, as output rises (increase in aggregate supply) demand is boosted by exchange depreciation (a rise in e). In the previous case $(E_2 + T_2 < 0)$ a devaluation would not increase demand either because *ML* was not working (as in Niehans) or that *LM* was perverse (as in Ford–Sen) or both.

Case C.   Here $a_{12} = E_2 + T_2 < 0$ and $|J| > 0$ — the counterpart of Case A. Cycles must occur since $(a_{11} - a_{22}) = E_1 + T_1 - 1 - i_2 < 0$.

The paradox and macroeconomic policy
General equilibrium is defined as

$$\dot{Y} = 0 = \dot{e}/e \qquad (4.13)$$

We first consider the effects, in equilibrium, of monetary and fiscal policy on the exchange rate, for the above mentioned cases, *A, B* and *C*. From (4.10), (4.9) and (4.13) we get

Table 4.1

	Effect of				
	G		M		Remarks
	$\dfrac{\partial Y^*}{\partial G}$	$\dfrac{\partial e^*}{\partial G}$	$\dfrac{\partial Y^*}{\partial M}$	$\dfrac{\partial e^*}{\partial M}$	
Case A: $E_2 + T_2 < 0,\ |J| < 0$	+	−	−	+	Niehans paradox
Case B: $E_2 + T_2 > 0,\ |J| < 0$	+	−	+	+	No paradox Mendell-Fleming result
Case C: $E_2 + T_2 < 0,\ |J| > 0$	−	+	+	−	No paradox Unrealistic

$$[\partial e^*/\partial M] = i_3[1 - E_1 - T_1]/|J| \tag{4.14}$$

$$[\partial e^*/\partial G] = i_1/|J| \tag{4.15}$$

The effects depend on the sign of $|J|$, since other partials are signed unambiguously. Given $i_3 < 0$, $[\partial e^* \partial M] >$ or < 0 depending on whether $|J| <$ or > 0. Similarly, since $i_1 > 0$, $\partial e^*/\partial G$ has the same sign as $|J|$.

We also have, from (4.10), (4.9) and (4.13),

$$[\partial Y^*/\partial M] = i_3[E_2 + T_2]/|J| \tag{4.16}$$

$$[\partial Y^*/\partial G] = -i_2/|J| \tag{4.17}$$

The effect of fiscal policy on output, from (4.17), depends clearly on the sign of $|J|$ with the derivative having the opposite sign.

Equation (4.16) delivers the Niehans paradox for Case A (remember $i_3 < 0$). In effect, if $|J|$ and $[E_2 + T_2]$ have the same signs, we will have the Niehans paradox in the sense that an increase in money supply will decrease output and lower unemployment. Note that Case A gives the conventional Keynesian effect for fiscal policy; it is expansionary.

The various alternatives are summarized in Table 4.1. The two parameters affecting two endogenous variables give rise to 12 possible alternatives for policy changes in the Mundell–Fleming framework.

Theory will take us no further than this taxonomy. To discuss plausibility we need some casual empirical observations. It seems that Case C is not generally observable. The fiscal policy result is particularly counter-intuitive. Exchange rate behaviour, following monetary change, is also odd: expansion causes an appreciation of exchange rate when interest parity would claim that the domestic currency should weaken. We concentrate on Cases A and B.

Case B is similar to the Mundell–Fleming–Dornbusch model, with both monetary and fiscal policy working in the right direction; exchange rate also behaves in 'plausible' fashion. Monetary policy works as expected. Fiscal policy is effective, since the monetary effects of devaluation are exploited in the money market equilibrium conditions. Additional G raises i which causes an incipient capital inflow, thus appreciating the currency. This dampens the multiplier. However, the fall in e causes aggregate price index to fall since imports are now cheaper. The supply of real balance rises and causes an excess supply of 'real' money. This warrants a fall in i. Aggregate demand is boosted directly as well as taking off the bullish pressure on the exchange rate. Thus crowding out is lower and output (and employment) can rise in the open economy. In the traditional Mundell–Fleming model, $i_2 = 0$; hence $[\partial Y^*/\partial G] = 0$. Here $i_2 > 0$. Exchange depreciation does affect the LM curve.

The most interesting case, from our point of view, is Case A. Fiscal policy effects are as before. Concentrate then on the Niehans paradox $(\partial Y^*/\partial M < 0)$ essentially dictated by the condition that $[E_2 + T_2]$ is negative. The previous literature ignored E_2 and concentrated on the ML condition T_2. Niehans's original claim turns out to be substantially correct, since if $E_2 = 0$ and $T_2 < 0$, then output will decline consequent to monetary expansion. This is, of course, a sub-case of Case A. Dornbusch's contention that the paradox cannot hold in the long run, with exchange rate expectations fully adapting, is not valid. The Niehans model does not lead to instability provided stability is defined in the sense of saddle paths (as in the *RE* literature). Without making any *ad hoc* assumptions about the nature of endogenous expectations, and its speed of adjustment, we can derive the (Niehans) paradoxical result in equilibrium. Rather, *RE* implies that the 'elasticity of expectations' is always equal to unity. This is the case where it has been claimed that the Niehans paradox will not hold except by violating stability. But this is precisely our Case A, where using *RE* and perfect adjustment of expectations both in the short and long run, we have demonstrated the possibility of the paradox. As the comparison with Case A and Figure 4.1 indicates, there are no problems with achieving equilibrium (after the monetary change) provided some fairly standard restrictions are accepted. Thus the Niehans paradox is consistent with *stable RE* paths.

Consider the situation of a monetary contraction. The rate of interest will rise, causing an incipient capital inflow. This will strengthen the domestic currency and cause an appreciation of the exchange rate. *ML* claims that the trade balance will worsen. *LM* claims that expenditure (measured in home goods) will fall and saving will rise. Both effects, under normal circumstances, will reduce aggregate demand and output will fall. But if either of the two conditions (or both) fails to hold then the opposite will occur. A fall in the exchange rate may improve the trade balance (as claimed in Niehans). Alternatively, exchange depreciation reduces saving and increases effective demand. If the joint effect is sufficiently strong in the postulated direction, so that $[E_2 + T_2] < 0$, then aggregate demand will rise consequent to contractionary monetary policy. Hence output rises as money stock is reduced – the Niehans paradox!

What about stability — the crucial criticism? We concentrate on Case *A* and observe the dynamics of the system consequent to a fall in money supply. The initial situation is depicted by the dotted lines in Figure 4.4 with equilibrium at Z_1 and the saddle path labelled S_1S_1. Figure 4.4 gives the behaviour of the economy *provided* we restrict ourselves to 'small' changes within a close neighbourhood of the original equilibrium. The $\dot{Y} = 0$ line does not shift, since it is not affected by M, and is given at general equilibrium by

$$Y = E(Y, e, i^*) + T(Y, e) + G = 0 \qquad (4.18)$$

The $\dot{e}/e = 0$ line shifts downwards. For a given Y, as M falls and i rises, the exchange rate must appreciate (e falls) to make $i = i^*$. The new equilibrium at Z_2 shows a currency appreciation (as expected) and an output increase (à la Niehans). S_2S_2 is the stable path for the (new) equilibrium Z_2.

Since Y is a predetermined variable and e is non-predetermined, e 'jumps' and falls rapidly from Z_1 to F to catch the saddle path. The initial exogenous shock, the decline in M, is assumed to be *unanticipated*. After the economy reaches F quickly ('instantaneously') it coasts asymptotically towards Z_2 along the unique stable trajectory S_2S_2. There is no overshooting and the Niehans paradox is fully justified. The attainment of the new equilibrium at Z_2 also allays the alleged fears about the stability of the system.

Similar analysis can be conducted for *anticipated* and *temporary* changes. Four possibilities can be examined: (i) unanticipated and permanent change in M (as in Figure 4.4); (ii) anticipated and permanent; (iii) unanticipated and temporary; (iv) anticipated and temporary.

Up until now the formal analysis was conducted on the basis of 'infinitesimal' changes in the neighbourhood of equilibrium $i = i^*$. Thus

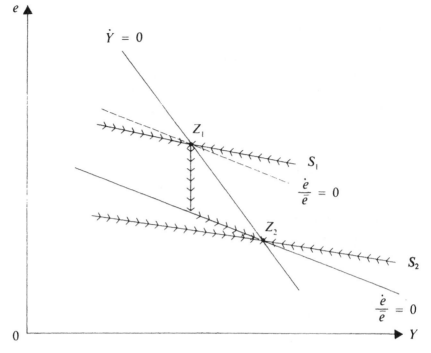

Figure 4.4

the $\dot{Y} = 0$ curve did not shift when money supply changed since i was kept equal to i^* in equation (4.18). But if i is made a function of M and inserted into the IS equation, we can still derive similar results. Then

$$\dot{Y} = E(Y, e, i(Y, e, M)) + G + T(Y, e) - Y \qquad (4.19)$$

$$\dot{e}/e = i(Y, e, M) - i^* \qquad (4.20)$$

At equilibrium $\dot{Y} = \dot{e}/e = 0$, hence Y^* and e^* are the same. The Jacobian is now

$$J' = \begin{bmatrix} E_1 + E_3 i_1 + T_1 - 1 & E_2 + T_2 + E_3 i_2 \\ i_1 & i_2 \end{bmatrix}$$

The determinant $|J'|$ is the same as $|J|$ earlier. So also are the sign configurations of Table 4.1. The only difference is in the dynamic paths as depicted in Figure 4.4. Note also that the signs of the *individual* elements of the Jacobian remain unchanged as do the signs of the slopes of $\dot{Y} = 0$ and $\dot{e}/e = 0$. All this is for Case A.

Consider now the impact of a fall in M. The $\dot{Y} = 0$ line shifts rightwards (upwards). The effects shown in Figure 4.4 are heightened. There is an even greater rise in Y due to the initial fall in M. The Niehans effect is indicated even more strongly.

References
Allen, P. R. and P. B. Kenen (1980) *Asset Markets and Exchange Rates*, Cambridge University Press, Cambridge, pp242–250.
Dornbusch, R. (1976) 'Exchange rate expectations and monetary policy', *Journal of International Economics*, vol.6, pp231–244.
Ford, J. L. and S. Sen (1988) 'The Ford-Sen (non Laursen-Metzler) effect and the negation of standard propositions in open economy macroeconomics', Essay 3 in this Collection.
Niehans, J. (1975) 'Some doubts about the efficacy of monetary policy under flexible exchange rates', *Journal of International Economics*, vol.5, pp275–281.
Turnovsky, S. J. (1981) 'Monetary policy and foreign price disturbances under flexible exchange rates: a stochastic approach', *Journal of Money, Credit and Banking*, vol.13, no.2, pp156–176.

5. Co-ordination, commercial and stabilization policies under alternative wage-setting regimes in a two-country model with a flexible exchange rate

1 Introduction

The recent (end-1987) turmoil on international financial markets once more brought to the forefront of economic debate the issue of policy co-ordination amongst the Western European countries, the US and Japan. It was argued that only a framework of co-operation would enable the gains of the 1982–85 economic boom to be retained and not to be dissipated by yet another recession. Western governments, however, did not appear to be over-enthusiastic towards such a viewpoint. At the centre of the ensuing policy debate was the different emphasis placed on fiscal policy by the Western and Japanese economies on the one hand, and by the US government, on the other. It has been suggested, in effect, that the stance of fiscal policy is too tight in the European and Japanese economies, whilst it is too lax in the US. The US government has, as a consequence, persistently requested West Germany and Japan, in particular, to adopt a more expansionary fiscal policy, and so assist the US in its locomotive role in the world's economy: these requests have also fallen on stony ground. The main reason for this appears to be the nature of the labour markets in the different economies. Branson and Rotenberg (1980), amongst others, have demonstrated that the econometric evidence indicates that the seven Western industrialized countries, Europe and Japan face *real wage resistance*, while the US and Canadian economies exhibit *nominal wage rigidity*. This suggests that whilst fiscal expansion might be successful in stimulating the macroeconomy in North America, it might only lead to inflation and thence to recession in Western Europe and Japan.

In this paper we develop a two-country model to examine the role of fiscal policy within and across countries against a background of different assumptions about the wage-setting regimes experienced in each country. The model is not a two-country model of the 'small open economy, rest of the world' paradigm: it is a fully-interdependent model. Naturally, we hypothesize that the two countries encapsulate the main macro-economic characteristics of two *broad blocs* of economies, Western/Japanese and

North American, including their labour markets (for a *real sector* model along these lines see Corden and Turnovsky 1983).

We shall also evaluate the effects of monetary policy and, a new feature of this model, of *commercial policy*. We shall see later that in regard to fiscal macro-stabilization policies, we merely re-inforce the conclusions already reached by Argy and Salop (1983) and Van der Ploeg (1987): namely, that the most successful 'co-operative' policy to adopt will be one wherein the country with nominal wage rigidity pursues an expansionary fiscal policy while the country which has real wage resistance does likewise: yet, to make the paper complete pedagogically, we also consider situations where both countries, alternately, have real wage resistance and nominal wage rigidity. It has not proved feasible, however, to solve these two country models analytically for the *levels* of the endogenous variables even by judicious linearization of key behavioural functions; as a consequence we cannot solve the co-ordination/conflict issues over stabilization strategies by first of all unscrambling the optimal levels of the one country's policy instruments on a *ceteris paribus* basis, which will permit its government's objective functions (e.g., the level of economic welfare) to be maximized. In effect, this means that we cannot deduce, analytically, the different countries' policy reaction curves. The implications of this are two-fold: on the one hand, we cannot deduce what is the optimal mix of the 'levels of policies' for either country to adopt, having to content ourselves with investigation of the multiplier effects of policy on the main determinants of economic welfare, output and the consumer price index; and, on the other hand, we have to evaluate the desirability of policy co-operation by reference to own-country and cross-country multiplier effects.

Our starting point will be the traditional Mundell model of a Keynesian type with fixed wages and prices, and perfect capital mobility. In such a framework monetary policy is alleged to expand output at home and abroad. The standard rationalization of this outcome is as follows. A monetary expansion at home will cause excess supply of real money at the initial level of the interest rate. That will stimulate home output, whilst the exchange rate will depreciate due to capital outflows. Since the model is of a two-country world, we know that the overall balance of payments must be in equilibrium and, therefore, capital that leaves the home country must end up in the foreign country. Moreover, the home country will have a trade balance surplus, while the foreign country will have a trade balance deficit, so that the currency of the foreign country will necessarily appreciate. That will lead to a decline in foreign output. Lower output abroad is consistent with foreign money market equilibrium (and the assumption that Mundell made was that domestic money demand is deflated by the *domestic* price level). Since money supply in the world has increased, and, as a result, the interest rate has fallen, a constant money supply and (domestic) price level abroad will require a drop in foreign output to bring the foreign money market into equilibrium once again. When we examine the case of nominal wage rigidity at home and abroad we will show that apart from anything else, if we deflate the money balances by the *consumer price index* then foreign output will rise, even in a Mundellian framework (Ford and Sen (1988b) have already drawn attention to the crucial nature of the price deflator).

As far as expansionary fiscal policy is concerned, using the Mundellian framework, the analysis goes as follows. If domestic government expenditure increases, home output rises, with the interest rate being forced up because of the excess demand for money. Consequently, the exchange rate will appreciate, causing capital inflow, which has to be matched by a trade balance deficit. Now, that will imply that the foreign currency depreciates, there is a trade balance surplus and capital flows abroad, while output also rises. As we will demonstrate those results are independent of the price deflator for money balances.

As we have already mentioned, the divergence in the labour market that is observed between the producer's real wage (own-product real wage) and the consumer's real wage for the home and the foreign country is a major element in recent research on open-economy macroeconomics; and we will develop our models along similar lines. The introduction of the supply side of the economy will provide new results for the effectiveness of the alternative policies, and in many cases we will observe a reversal in the role of monetary and fiscal policy. But all previous studies which have incorporated different wage-setting regimes have analysed only monetary and fiscal policy. They have not been concerned with commercial policy, except for Ford–Sen (1985) in the context of a small economy–rest of the world model. We will consider commercial policy, demonstrating that it can be beneficial to both countries, depending on whether the Laursen–Metzler effect, Metzler paradox, or the Marshall-Lerner condition hold or not.

We will distinguish and analyse four alternative cases depending on the assumptions we make about the wage indexation in either country. At the one extreme real wage resistance prevails in both countries, while at the other extreme we have the case of nominal wage rigidity throughout the world. In between these two extremes, we analyse the two intermediate cases, with the home country facing RWR or NWR and the foreign country NWR or RWR, respectively.

Monetary policy provides unambiguous results in all cases (for both multiplier effects of policies and in terms of implications for co-ordination of strategy). The effects of fiscal policy, and especially of commercial policy, are hard to unscramble, even for basic multipliers. Furthermore, as we proceed from a world of real wage resistance towards a world of nominal wage rigidity the effects of all three policies become increasingly difficult to derive. Consequently, we will limit the presentation of the underlying algebraic manipulations, and for each case we will discuss the economics of the alternative economic policies with the use of a summary table, typical *IS, LM* schedules, and, where appropriate, aggregate demand and supply schedules.

In the next section we begin with the case of real wage resistance at home and abroad. Section 3 will cover the case of real wage resistance at home and nominal wage rigidity abroad. Section 4 analyses the case of nominal wage rigidity at home and real wage resistance abroad. Finally, Section 5 analyses the case of nominal wage rigidity at home and abroad. In each section we consider both domestic multipliers and inter-dependencies of policies between the two countries.

2 The two-country model with real wage resistance at home and abroad

a. The model
We consider now a two-country world with floating exchange rates, and with real wage resistance at home and abroad. There is perfect capital mobility between highly integrated financial markets. Furthermore, economic agents form their expectations (exp.) about future movements of the exchange rate (e) in a rather simplistic way, since they assume static expectations, implying that $(\dot{e}/e)^{\text{exp}} = 0$. This will enable us to equilibrate domestic (r) and foreign (r^*) interest rates:

$$r = r^* \tag{5.1}$$

Therefore, as in the one-country model, the interest rate will be fixed at the world rate, but in contrast to the case of the small open economy the expanding country is assumed to be able to affect the interest rate, producing, therefore, a new monetary equilibrium at home and abroad.

With *perfect* capital mobility, the balance of payments equilibrium condition, now over both trade and capital accounts, must be explained by the equilibrium condition given by (5.1). With flexible exchange rates and perfect capital mobility, the balance of payments must balance in full equilibrium.

Firms produce goods at home and can sell either at home or abroad. We further assume that there is imperfect substitution between home and foreign goods. Then the domestic and foreign goods markets equilibria are given by:

$$Y = E(Y + t\sigma M, \sigma(1 + t), r) + X(Y^*, \sigma, r^*) -$$
$$(1 + t)\sigma M(Y + t\sigma M, \sigma(1 + t), r) + G \tag{5.2}$$

$$Y^* = E^*(Y^*, \sigma, r^*) + M(Y + t\sigma M, \sigma(1 + t), r) -$$
$$\left[\frac{1}{\sigma}\right] X(Y^*, \sigma, r^*) + G^* \tag{5.3}$$

Here, the left-hand side of equation (5.2), for example, depicts the level of output in the home country; whilst the right-hand side represents total (real) expenditure on home output, written in absorption or expenditure format. Similar considerations apply to equation (5.3) which relates to the foreign country; the asterisk is used to denote foreign values or magnitudes. The notation we have adopted is standard, but we provide a legend using the home country as the reference point:

- Y is real income in domestic units or output

  M is the quantity of imports

  X is the quantity of exports

  t is the *ad valorem* tariff (which is levied in this model solely by the home country)

  σ is eP^*/P

  e is the units of domestic currency required for the purchase of a unit of foreign currency

  P is the domestic price level

  r is the rate of interest

  G is real government expenditure

  $t\sigma M$ is the tariff revenue raised from the general tariff, t, imposed on imports.

Expenditures at home and abroad are alleged to depend on domestic income, the terms of trade, and the interest rate; with the only difference being in the presence of commercial policy, where income at home is increased by the tariff revenue, and the domestic and world terms of trade differ. Moreover, exports are taken to be a function not only of the terms of trade, σ, but also of the income of the other country and the interest rate. Since this is a two-country model, naturally, the exports and imports of the home country are the imports and exports of the foreign country.

The supply of output will be determined by means of an explicit supply schedule, which we shall consider presently. We note now that the goods markets are hypothesized to clear instantaneously: equations (5.2) and (5.3) are always satisfied.

In regard to the financial sectors of the two economies, we posit the existence of only a limited asset menu. It is simply confined to home currency and home government bonds for each country separately. These financial markets are also assumed, following convention, to clear instantaneously. The home and foreign money markets are described by the following equilibrium conditions:

$$\frac{H}{P} = (1 + t)^{1 - \beta\sigma 1 - \beta L} \left[\frac{Y + t\sigma M}{(1 + t)^{1-\beta} \sigma^{1-\beta} - \beta}, r \right]$$ (5.4)

and

$$\frac{H^*}{P^*} = \sigma^{\beta^* - 1} L^*(\sigma^{1 - \beta^*} Y^*, r^*)$$ (5.5)

The home and foreign money supply (high-powered money supply) have each been deflated by the corresponding consumer price index: after elementary manipulation we deduce equations (5.4) and (5.5). The home and foreign country consumer price indices are *defined* to be, respectively:

$$Q = P^\beta [eP^*]^{(1 - \beta)}$$ (5.6)

$$Q^* = (P^*)^{\beta^*} \left[\frac{P}{e} \right]^{1 - \beta^*}$$ (5.7)

The respective money supplies are controlled by the respective governments or their Central Bank. The bond markets are excluded from the model via Walras's Law.

Finally, we turn to consider the supply side of the model for the composite outputs produced by the two economies, namely, Y and Y^*. We assume that these outputs are generated by Cobb–Douglas production functions which, under the assumption of profit maximization, lead to these aggregate supply schedules:

$$Y = a \left[\frac{P}{W} \right]^\delta; \qquad\qquad \delta > 0$$ (5.8)

and,

$$Y^* = a^* \left[\frac{P^*}{W^*} \right]^{\delta^*}; \qquad\qquad \delta^* > 0$$ (5.9)

where W and W^* are, respectively, the money wages in the home and the foreign country.

We assume these two wage-formation processes:

$$\frac{W}{Q} = (1 - \kappa)\frac{\bar{W}}{Q} + \kappa\bar{w} \tag{5.10}$$

and

$$\frac{W^*}{Q^*} = \frac{(1 - \kappa^*)\bar{W}^*}{Q^*} + \kappa\bar{w}^* \tag{5.11}$$

Here, $\bar{w}$ is the fixed real wage and $\bar{W}$ is the fixed nominal wage. Hence, workers are potentially concerned with the standard of living, not just with their own product wage (w/P) as are producers. Should K, the adjustment coefficient, equal unity, we have the situation where there is full real wage resistance, essentially; as the consumer price index alters, workers push for, and receive, a fully compensating change in their money wage. In the cases where the adjustment coefficients K and K^* are zero we have the case of money wage rigidity, when nominal wages are constant.

Thus, under real wage resistance, the variant of labour supply behaviour assumed for this form of our two-country model: $W = \bar{w}Q$ and $W^* = \bar{w}^*Q^*$. Upon substituting these two relationships into the aggregate supply schedules, these become:

$$Y = a[(1 + t)^{\beta - 1}\sigma^{\beta - 1}(\bar{w})^{-1}]_\delta \tag{5.12}$$

and

$$Y^* = a^*[\sigma^{1 - \beta^*}(\bar{w}^*)^{-1}]^{\delta^*} \tag{5.13}$$

Hence, we see the now well-established outcome, that, in the case of real wage resistance aggregate supply of output is determined completely by the terms of trade.

We close the model with the definition of the world terms of trade, defined previously:

$$\sigma = \frac{eP^*}{P} \tag{5.14}$$

We employ this equation, rather than incorporate it into our basic equations (such as the expenditure equation), since it does simplify the mathematical analysis of the model and the interpretation of its results, despite preventing us from reducing the dimensions of the model. For the same reason, we utilize the goods market equilibrium equations (5.2) and (5.3) together with the two countries' supply schedules, rather than substituting the latter into the left hand side of (5.2) and (5.3), respectively. Hence, we have seven equations to solve for seven unknowns. The equations are (in the order in which we have used them): (5.2), (5.4), (5.12), (5.3), (5.5), (5.13) and (5.14). The endogenous variables are: Y, Y^*, P, P^*, $r(\equiv r^*)$, e and σ. The exogenous variables are; H, H^*, G, G^* and t.

b. Policy Exercises

When we differentiate totally the seven equations, and assume that the *initial* values of e, P, P^* and σ are unity, with the *initial* tariff set at zero, we deduce that:

$$A \, dy = dx \tag{5.15}$$

where A, the Jacobian of the system, is:

$$
\begin{bmatrix}
(E_1 - M_1 - 1) & X_1 & 0 & 0 & (E_3 - M_3 + X_3) & 0 & (X_2 - \epsilon M - M_2) \\
L_1 & 0 & H & 0 & L_2 & 0 & (1 - \beta)L(1 - \eta) \\
1 & 0 & 0 & 0 & 0 & 0 & a\delta(1 - \beta)(\bar{w}^{-1})^\delta \\
M_1 & (E^*_1 - X_1 - 1) & 0 & 0 & (E^*_3 + M_3 - X_3) & 0 & (M_2 - \epsilon^* X - X_2) \\
0 & L_1^* & 0 & H^* & L_2^* & 0 & (1 - \beta^*)L^*(\eta^* - 1) \\
0 & 1 & 0 & 0 & 0 & 0 & a^*\delta^*(\beta^* - 1)(\bar{w}^{*-1})^{\delta^*} \\
0 & 0 & 1 & -1 & 0 & -1 & 1
\end{bmatrix} \tag{5.16}
$$

and:

$$dy = [dY \ dY^* \ dP \ dP^* \ dr \ de \ d\sigma]' \tag{5.17}$$

$$
dx =
\begin{bmatrix}
-dG + [(MM_1 + M_2) + (\epsilon - E_1)]dt \\
dH + [(1 - \beta)L(\eta - 1) - L_1 M]dt \\
a\delta(\beta - 1)(\bar{w}^{-1})^\delta \, dt \\
-dG^* - (MM_1 + M_2) \, dt \\
dH^* \\
0 \\
0
\end{bmatrix} \tag{5.18}
$$

In simplifying the Jacobian to produce the matrix given by (5.16) we have invoked the *Laursen-Metzler effect*, in the way it has been formulated in the traditional literature, so that: $E_2 = (1 - E_1)M$ and $E^*_2 = (1 - E^*_1)X$, for the home and the foreign country, respectively. *Ceteris paribus*, we are entitled to do so because of our assumptions about the construction of the consumer price indices (see again Ford and Sen (1988b). Additionally, we have been able to effect simplifcations to the Jacobian by using the own-real income elasticity of real expenditures in the two countries (denoted by ϵ and ϵ^*) and the real income elasticities of money demand (η and η^*). We have, of course, also followed convention by denoting a partial derivative of a function with respect to one of its arguments by the order of the argument in the function; thus, $\partial E/\partial Y = E_1$.

The neatest formulation we can deduce for the determinant of the Jacobian, despite the above simplifications, is this, the sign of which is indeterminate *a priori*:

$$
\begin{aligned}
|J| = HH^*\{a\delta(1 - \beta)(\bar{w}^{-1})^\delta[(E^*_3 + M_3 - X_3)(1 - E_1) + M_1(E_3 + E^*_3)] + \\
(X_2 - M_2)(E_3 + E^*_3) + \epsilon^*X(E_3 - M_3 + X_3) - \epsilon M(E^*_3 + M_3 - X_3) + \\
a^*\delta^*(\beta^* - 1)(\bar{w}^{*-1})^{\delta^*}[(M_3 - X_3 - E_3)(1 - E^*_1) - \\
X_1(E_3 + E^*_3)]\}
\end{aligned} \tag{5.19}
$$

However, on the basis of dynamic analysis, the Samuelsonian correspondence principle requires us to sign $|J|$ as negative for stability. We assume that that is the case and accordingly utilize restrictions on the various elements of J which it implies, when we evaluate the policy multipliers.

As can be appreciated from equations (5.15) – (5.18), the effects of monetary policy (operating via increases in either H or H^* or both) are easy to deduce. The repercussions on either economy of alterations, for example, in its own fiscal policy or in that of the country admit of only extreme, complex expressions. These are not reproduced here: instead we present the qualitative outcomes that can be deduced from the relative partial derivatives. These are catalogued in Table 5.1 for the home country.

We shall consider the consequence of monetary and fiscal policy in the foreign country, for both its output and that of the home country, shortly, when we comment more specifically on co-ordination. For the moment, we consider Table 5.1.

The only unambiguous results, as we would expect, are provided by monetary policy. Measures by the Central Bank in the home country to raise output and (real) economic welfare will be unsuccessful: monetary

Table 5.1.   *Qualitative effects of commercial and stabilization policies by the home country*[1]

	Y	Y^*	P	P^*	r	e	σ
Expansionary Monetary policy	0	0	+	0	0	+	0
Expansionary Fiscal policy	+	−	$+^{\epsilon}$	$+^{\epsilon}$	+	$-^{\epsilon}$	−
Imposition of a general tariff	$+^{\epsilon}$	−	$+^{\epsilon}$	$+^{\epsilon}$	$+^{\epsilon}$	$-^{\epsilon}$	−

[1] ϵ denotes most likely outcome.

policy is 'classically neutral'. This must be the outcome under the classical production conditions of the model and the control operated on supply by the real wage mechanism.

The ultimate result of the increase in the domestic money stock is to raise both the domestic price level (P) and the rate of exchange (so there is a depreciation) both in the same proportion, leaving the focal *real* variable, the world terms of trade (σ), unaltered. Since there has been no change in money market conditions in the foreign country, the new equilibrium rate of interest, subsequent upon the increase in the domestic money stock, is the same as hitherto, and there is no movement in the foreign price level. The immediate impact of the change in the domestic money stock is on the domestic rate of interest, which will fall and, via the subsequent capital outflow, upon the exchange rate, e will rise. The latter then generates an increase in the demand for domestic output (via import substitution and an expansion of export demand). This brings about an increase in the rate of interest. At the same time we have to imagine a process whereby the increase in the exchange rate (e) leads to an increase in the money wage, via the (successful) attempts of workers to maintain their real wage. Consequently, profit maximizing producers reduce the level of domestic output to its previous (pre-money supply expansion) magnitude. When the new equilibrium is attained all real variables return to their previous values. Only e and P have altered, but their ratio stays constant.

The case of monetary expansion in one of the countries, in a situation of real wage rigidity, is readily seen in sum by a diagrammatical analysis based on aggregate demand and aggregate supply. Figure 5.1 illustrates these two schedules for the home country. The aggregate (AS) supply schedule (equation 5.12) when there is no tariff, provides us with a unique supply schedule, which relates output solely to the terms of trade.

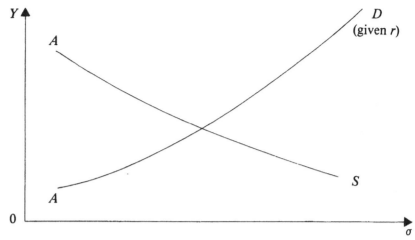

Figure 5.1

In view of the fact that output does only depend upon the terms of trade, for the case of no tariff and no government expenditure (or, obviously, for the case where these policy parameters are constant), we can transform the aggregate demand (*AD*) schedule, given by the right-hand side of equation (5.2), so that *Y* depends upon σ, for given r (because Y^* which influences X is dependent upon σ also). Clearly, only the *AD* schedule for the home country can potentially be affected (indirectly) by a change in the money stock (*H*), should it alter the domestic rate of interest. Since at the final equilibrium the latter has to remain at its previous equilibrium level, in this model, an increase in H cannot affect either Y or σ; and, therefore, with σ fixed, Y^* cannot alter. Monetary policy here has the classical neutrality effect both at home and abroad.

We turn now to the situation when government expenditure (*G*) increases in the home country. Output must expand at home, whilst it declines abroad. The 'world' interest rates increase; initially, the domestic rate of interest is pushed up by the demand expansion, and this drags along with it the foreign interest rate. When the new equilibrium is finally attained, interest rates are still, initially, above their pre-expansion values. The interest rate changes affect the exchange rate, via capital flows initially, and thereafter through trade flows: *e* probably falls, so that there is an exchange rate appreciation for the expanding country. Indeed, if $\eta^* > 1$, *e* falls, and the foreign price level increases; and if simultaneously, $\eta > 1$, the domestic price level also increases. As such, as far as a purely domestic expansion engendered by fiscal policy is concerned, these findings are the opposite of the Mundellian results: fiscal policy is not a locomotive, but a beggar-thy-neighbour policy.

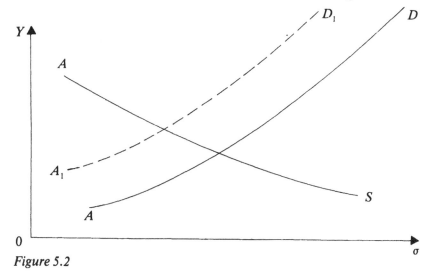

Figure 5.2

The position for fiscal policy can be summarized graphically by means of the *AD* and *AS* schedules. In Figure 5.2 we have the home country's aggregate supply schedule, which is identical to that drawn in Figure 5.1, of course, since aggregate supply is fiscally neutral. The aggregate demand schedule shifts to the north-west with any increase in government expenditure (G): with the schedule being dependent upon the rate of interest, we recall. Any increase in r will shift the aggregate demand schedule to the south-east: however, the increase in r (which will reduce home and foreign demand for domestic goods) brought about when G increases is not sufficient to crowd out the fiscal expansion. Therefore, though aggregate demand shifts back from A_1D_1 partially towards AD, it never re-attains the schedule *AD*.

Finally, for the real wage resistance version of this two-country model, we come to the employment of commercial policy, operating through an *ad valorem* tariff on imports, by the domestic government. Some of the multiplier effects are uniquely signed, and the remainder are only just short of being so, as complex as the particular multipliers happen to be. Their likely signs are indicated in Table 5.1. These will be the *exact* signs if the income elasticities of money demand in the two countries are: $\eta < 1$ and $\eta^* > 1$.

In those circumstances, both domestic and foreign output respond positively and negatively, respectively, to the imposition of the tariff. This suggests that the negative influence which the tariff will have on the terms of trade and the positive effect it will have on the interest rate, both having a negative effect on domestic expenditure, must be more than offset by the income effect of the tariffs. That is, in the home country the increase in income by the amount of the tariff revenue will cause output at home to rise in the final equilibrium. Output declines abroad as a result of this strong income effect at home; although the terms of trade have been deteriorating there, the rise in the level of interest rate can cause demand to fall in the foreign country.

The value of the Metzler paradox $(X_2 - M + eM_1M) < 0$, plays some role in determining the signs of $\partial e/\partial t$ and $\partial \sigma/\partial t$, but its role is minimized in a two-country model. The final sign of the change in the domestic terms of trade $\sigma(1 + t)$ is unknown *a priori*. It is not true that it is always negative. Mundell (1961), Krugman (1982) and Eichengreen (1981, 1983) mistakenly assume that this is always the case. Their arguments possibly hold for very specific cases. As Ford and Sen (1985) have shown, if we work through the mathematics then the final outcome on the domestic terms of trade depends on the initial value of σ or of e (if we have normalized for the price levels) which is positive, and on the value of $\partial \sigma/\partial t$ or $\partial e/\partial t$. The latter can be positive or negative. If it is positive, then $\sigma(1 + t)$ will rise, which implies an increase in aggregate demand and thus of output. If it is negative, output can still rise if $\partial \sigma/\partial t$ is less than σ; while it must fall otherwise. In essence, naturally, the value of $\sigma(1 + t)$, of σ in effect, is determined by the simultaneous adjustment of demand and supply.

In sum, at home we will have home currency appreciation, a trade balance surplus, while the domestic price level rises. The terms of trade improve. Abroad we will observe currency depreciation, a trade balance deficit, and the price level rising. The interest rate rises as well.

In respect of commercial policy, a two-dimensional diagrammatic treatment cannot provide any results or insights. The aggregate demand/supply picture can merely inform us that with a full general equilibrium analysis of the system, any qualitative change to both Y and σ is possible. Thus, the introduction of a tariff must shift the aggregate schedule in a south-westerly direction (in Figure 5.2) and alters its shape. The aggregate demand schedule could shift to the north-west to an extent whereby output is increased and the (world) terms of trade decreased: the tariff revenue will increase income for any value of the terms of trade, but the rate of interest and the level of exports will not stay constant. If r does increase at the final equilibrium and Y^* fall, then these factors will move aggregate demand to the south-east. The net effect of the shifts (dependent as they are, *ceteris paribus*, on the revenue produced from the tariff) is problematical and reflects the elasticity, expenditure, money demand effects, noted previously. Even if we insert the fact that at the equilibrium, Y^* must simply depend upon σ, we can still make no progress with the AS/AD diagram, because we cannot determine the tariff revenue and the rate of interest without solving the full model. Hitherto, for example, for the case of a monetary expansion, we had a zero tariff revenue, and at equilibrium a fixed rate of interest. It was then possible to use the home country's *AD/AS* diagram to solve for the *equilibrium* value of Y and of σ; and hence of Y^*.

In the consideration of the three types of economic policy that the home country might adopt we have drawn attention to their implications for the foreign country. Monetary policy has no effect on the foreign economy; fiscal expansion harms it by reducing its output and its real economic welfare (absorption in terms of the basket of goods); and commercial policy does likewise.

But what are the consequences for the home country if monetary and fiscal expansion are pursued by the foreign government? Take first of all the position in respect of monetary policy. As expected, *ex hypothesi*, we do confirm that $\partial Y^*/\partial H^* = 0$ and $\partial Y/\partial H^* = 0$.

For fiscal policy the outcome is as follows:

$$\frac{\partial Y}{\partial G^*} = |J|^{-1}[HH^* a\delta(\beta - 1)(\bar{w})^{-\delta}(E_3 - M_3 + X_3)] < 0 \qquad (5.20)$$

$$\frac{\partial Y^*}{\partial G^*} = |J|^{-1}[HH^* a^*\delta^*(1 - \beta^*)(\bar{w}^*)^{\delta^*}(E_3 - M_3 + X_3)] > 0 \qquad (5.21)$$

These results, and they must be, are identical qualitatively with those for a fiscal expansion in the home country. However, as they must under this country-symmetric model, not only do they mirror each other qualitatively, but multiplier-by-multiplier they are the same quantitatively except for differences in the behavioural parameters of their respective demand and supply functions. The full results for domestic fiscal expansion are:

$$\frac{\partial Y}{\partial G} = |J|^{-1}[HH^* a\delta(\beta - 1)(\bar{w})^{-\delta}(X_3 - M_3 + E_3^*)] > 0 \qquad (5.22)$$

$$\frac{\partial Y^*}{\partial G} = |J|^{-1}[HH^* a^*\delta^*(1 - \beta^*)(\bar{w}^*)^{-\delta^*}(X_3 - M_3 + E_3^*)] < 0 \qquad (5.23)$$

Equations (5.20) – (5.23) inform us that no form of co-operation over fiscal policy will be feasible under real wage resistance in both countries. The beggar-thy-neighbour nature of fiscal policy where it is invoked in either country separately to improve its own economic situation, cannot be countervailed by the two governments desiring to co-ordinate their attempted expansion. The symmetry of the fiscal policy multipliers given in equations (5.20) – (5.23) determine that outcome. In effect, we can

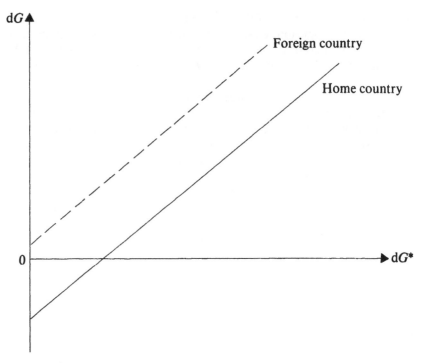

Figure 5.3

envisage an attempt at co-operation emanating from the desire of each government to raise its level of output (and employment) by some designated amount, so that each country has a target, dY^T and dY^{*T}. Then, the two countries working together should ideally select the change in government expenditure that each will institute according to this system:

$$\begin{bmatrix} \dfrac{\partial Y}{\partial G} & \dfrac{\partial Y}{\partial G^*} \\[2ex] \dfrac{\partial Y^*}{\partial G} & \dfrac{\partial Y^*}{\partial G^*} \end{bmatrix} \begin{bmatrix} dG \\[2ex] dG^* \end{bmatrix} = \begin{bmatrix} dY^T \\[2ex] dY^{*T} \end{bmatrix} \qquad (5.24)$$

The matrix in (5.24) is singular. This is because the 'reaction curves' of the two countries can never intersect here: in fact, they are parallel to each other.

The general situation is portrayed in Figure 5.3.

It would not bring any lasting benefit to, say, the home country to expand government expenditure if it saw dG^* at zero: the gain it managed to lever would be only short lived. The foreign country would retaliate by choosing a value for dG appropriate to the dG it observed for the home country. In essence, if we imagine that policy design is based on moving the economy in this or that direction, a kind of differential game would be induced (see, for example, Miller and Salmon (1984); and Henderson (1984), for a clear statement of co-ordination issues).

The only form of lasting policy, which will evolve from co-ordination is one which involves commercial policy in the home country and fiscal policy in the foreign country. We have not formally analysed the situation where a general tariff is also imposed by the foreign country, but in a situation where there is the same wage-determination process in both countries, the qualitative effect of general tariffs, imposed on a *ceteris paribus* basis, by either country separately are identical. Accordingly, an attempt by either country to steal a march on the other by imposing a tariff (or by increasing any existing tariff) would ultimately be self-defeating; and there can be no basis for co-operation, since the situation mirrors that for fiscal policy. However, when only the home country imposes a general tariff, the impacts on Y and Y^* are not necessarily linearly related, as are $\partial Y/\partial G$ and $\partial Y^*/\partial G$, so that the equivalent matrix to that in equation (5.24) is not necessarily singular:

$$\begin{vmatrix} \dfrac{\partial Y}{\partial t} & \dfrac{\partial Y}{\partial G^*} \\[2mm] \dfrac{\partial Y^*}{\partial t} & \dfrac{\partial Y^*}{\partial G^*} \end{vmatrix} \geq 0 \tag{5.25}$$

In fact, the two tariff multipliers referred to qualitatively in Table 5.1 and the text are as follows:

$$\frac{\partial Y}{\partial t} = |J|^{-1}HH^*[a\delta(\beta-1)(\bar{w}^{-1})^{\delta}a^*\delta^*(\beta^*-1)(\bar{w}^{*-1})^{\delta^*}\{(1-E_1^*)$$
$$(E_3 - M_3 + X_3) + X_1(E_3 + E_3^*)\}] > 0 \tag{5.26}$$

$$\frac{\partial Y}{\partial t} = |J|^{-1}HH^*[a^*\delta^*(\beta^*-1)(\bar{w}^{-1})^{\delta^*}[a\delta(\beta-1)(\bar{w}^{-1})^{\delta}\{(E_1 - 1)$$
$$(E^*_3 + M_3 - X_3) - M_1(E_3 + E_3^*)\} - (MM_1 + M_2)(E_3 + E^*_3) - $$
$$(E_3^* + M_3 - X_3)(\epsilon - E_1)] < 0 \tag{5.27}$$

The situation might be as depicted in Figure 5.4.

The optimum values of dt and dG^* being, naturally, the values that satisfy:

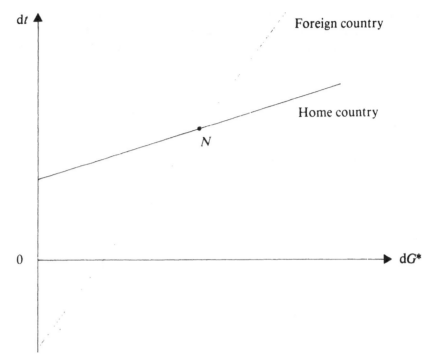

Figure 5.4

$$\begin{bmatrix} \dfrac{\partial Y}{\partial t} & \dfrac{\partial Y}{\partial G^*} \\[2ex] \dfrac{\partial Y^*}{\partial t} & \dfrac{\partial Y^*}{\partial G^*} \end{bmatrix} \begin{bmatrix} \mathrm{d}t \\[2ex] \mathrm{d}G^* \end{bmatrix} = \begin{bmatrix} \mathrm{d}Y^{\mathrm{T}} \\[2ex] \mathrm{d}Y^{*\mathrm{T}} \end{bmatrix} \tag{5.28}$$

3   Two-country model with real wage resistance at home and nominal wage rigidity abroad

a.   The model

In the introduction we mentioned the policy debate between Europe and Japan, on the one side, and the US, on the other. It was argued that the former faces real wage resistance (RWR) while the latter faces nominal wage rigidity (NWR). Therefore, the economics and policy implications of 'European' (home) and US (abroad) interdependence can be described and analysed by an assymetric world where at home we have RWR and abroad NWR. This analysis will give us the opportunity to evaluate the effects of conventional stabilization policies and compare them with previous conclusions. Moreover, we will highlight the consequences of the imposition of a general tariff imposed by the European economies on imports from the US; which is not such a fanciful possibility given impending European Union in 1992.

The framework of the two economies is identical to the one we already used in the case of RWR at home and abroad, except that the aggregate supply side will be altered to permit the presence of nominal wage rigidity abroad. It is assumed that there, the nominal wage always remains at its initial level, independently of any change in domestic and foreign prices. Therefore, changes in the exchange rate will have no direct effect on employment in the foreign economy, since movements in the customers' price index are not taken into consideration by the workers in the formation of wage demands. Equation (5.11) is replaced by:

$$W^* = \bar{W}^* \equiv l^* \tag{5.29}$$

When the level of employment in the foreign economy has been determined at the appropriate wage rate, it will be transformed into a supply of foreign real output through the aggregate production function given by (5.9). Substitution of (5.29) into (5.9) gives the relevant aggregate supply for the foreign economy:

$$Y^* = a^* \left[\frac{P^*}{l^*} \right]^{\delta^*} \tag{5.30}$$

Hence, we conclude that in the case of nominal wage rigidity, the supply of output is determined by the foreign price level. Therefore, while the terms of trade determine the supply of output at home, in the foreign country it is its own price level which determines the supply of output there. This difference in output determination is central to understanding the different policy effects in the two countries; and hence the current policy debate.

The two-country model for this case can be summarized by the following seven equilibrium equations:

$$Y = E(Y + t\sigma M, \sigma(1 + t), r) + X(Y^*, \sigma, r^*) - (1 + t)\sigma M \\ (Y + t\sigma M, \sigma(1 + t), r) + G \tag{5.31}$$

$$Y^* = E^*(Y^*, \sigma, r^*) + M(Y + t\sigma M, \sigma(1 + t), r) - \\ \left[\frac{1}{\sigma} \right] X(Y^*, \sigma, r^*) + G^* \tag{5.32}$$

$$\frac{H}{P} = (1 + t)^{1 - \beta} \sigma^{1 - \beta} L \left[\frac{Y + t\sigma M}{(1 + t)^{1 - \beta} \sigma^{1 - \beta}}, r \right] \tag{5.33}$$

$$\frac{H^*}{P^*} = \sigma^{\beta^*-1} L^* \left[\sigma^{1-\beta^*} Y^*, r^* \right] \tag{5.34}$$

$$Y = a \left[(1+t)^{\beta-1} \sigma^{\beta-1} \bar{W}^{-1} \right]^{\delta} \tag{5.35}$$

$$Y^* = a^* [P^* l^{*-1}]^{\delta^*} \tag{5.36}$$

$$\sigma = \frac{eP^*}{P} \tag{5.37}$$

The model solves for the values of the seven endogenous variables Y, Y^*, P, P^*, r, e and σ given the values of the exogenous variables G, G^*, H, H^* and t.

b. Policy exercises

We totally differentiate equations (5.31) – (5.37) and assuming that initial values of e, P, P^* and σ are equal to unity, and $t = 0$ initially, we obtain the following Jacobian matrix of the complete system:

$$
\begin{bmatrix}
(E_1 - M_1 - 1) & X_1 & 0 & 0 & (E_3 - M_3 + X_3) & 0 & (X_2 - \epsilon M - M_2) \\
L_1 & 0 & H & 0 & L_2 & 0 & (1 - \beta)L(1 - \eta) \\
1 & 0 & 0 & 0 & 0 & 0 & a\delta(1 - \beta)(\bar{w}^{-1})^{\delta} \\
M_1 & (E^*_1 - X_1 - 1) & 0 & 0 & (E^*_3 + M_3 - X_3) & 0 & (M_2 - \epsilon^* X - X_2) \\
0 & L_1^* & 0 & H^* & L_2^* & 0 & (1 - \beta^*)L^*(\eta^* - 1) \\
0 & 1 & 0 & -a^*\delta^*(l^* - 1)^{\delta^*} & 0 & 0 & 0 \\
0 & 0 & 1 & -1 & 0 & -1 & 1
\end{bmatrix}
\tag{5.38}
$$

The vector of endogenous (dy) variables is:

$$dy = [dY \; dY^* \; dP \; dP^* \; dr \; de \; d\sigma]' \tag{5.39}$$

and the vector of policy changes (dx) is:

$$
dx = \begin{bmatrix}
-dG + [(MM_1 + M_2) - (\epsilon - E_1)]dt \\
dH + [(1 - \beta)L(\eta - 1) - L_1 M] \, dt \\
a\delta(\beta - 1)(\bar{w})^{-\delta} dt \\
-dG^* - (MM_1 + M_2) \, dt \\
dH^* \\
0 \\
0
\end{bmatrix}
\tag{5.40}
$$

Table 5.2. Qualitative effects of commercial and stabilization policies by the home country[1]

	Y	Y^*	P	P^*	r	e	σ
Expansionary Monetary policy	0	0	+	0	0	+	0
Expansionary Fiscal policy	+	$+^\epsilon$	$+^\epsilon$	$+^\epsilon$	$+^\epsilon$	$-^\epsilon$	$-$
Imposition of a general tariff	$+^\epsilon$	$+^\epsilon$	+	$+^\epsilon$	+	$-$	$-^\epsilon$

[1] ϵ denotes most likely outcome.

The determinant of (5.38) is:

$$
\begin{aligned}
|J| = &\ -H\,[H^*\{a\delta(1-\beta)(\bar{w}^{-1})^\delta[M_1(E_3+E^*_3)-(E^*_3+M_3-X_3)(E_1-1)]\} + \\
&+ E^*_3(X_2-\epsilon M-M_2)-E_3(M_2-\epsilon^* X-X_2)+(X_3-E_3)(\epsilon M+\epsilon^* X)] - \\
&- a^*\delta^*(l^{*-1})^{\delta^*}\{(1-\beta)L^*(\eta^*-1)[(E_3+E^*_3) - (E^*_1-1)(E_3-M_3+X_3)] + \\
&+ E_3(M_2-\epsilon^* X-X_2)L^*_1 - L^*_1 E^*_3(X_2-\epsilon M-M_2) + (E^*_1-1)(X_2-\epsilon M-M_2)L^*_2 + \\
&+ (M_3-X_3)(\epsilon^* X+\epsilon M)L^*_1 + X_1 L^*_2(\epsilon M+\epsilon^* X) + \\
&+ a\delta(1-\beta)(\bar{w}^{-1})^\delta[L^*_2\{(E_1-1)(E^*_1-X_1-1)-M_1(E^*-1)\} + \\
&+ L^*_1[E_3 M_1 + E_1 X_3 - X_3 + M_3 - E^*_3(E_1-M_1-1)-L_1 E_1 M_3]\}]
\end{aligned}
\tag{5.41}
$$

It is clear that the sign of $|J|$ is indeterminate *a priori*, but dynamic analysis once again requires us to sign it negatively. It is worth noticing that the value of the Jacobian is not independent of the value of the foreign income elasticity of demand for money, and that ties together the price level movements and the foreign aggregate supply side. As always, we have been concerned with the sign of the Laursen–Metzler effect in both countries which has to be positive in this particular model, we recall. The Marshall–Lerner condition is assumed positive while the role of the Metzler paradox is once again important to an evaluation of the effects of commercial policy in the two economies. Table 5.2 summarizes the qualitative results of the three policies, when invoked by the domestic economy. These results first of all show us that as soon as the foreign country experiences nominal wage rigidity the output and price effects of fiscal expansion and tariff imposition are more difficult to trace than in the case of RWR at home and abroad. In the case of monetary expansion the effects on output and prices are identical to the previous situation. Once again, the domestic price level rises in the same proportion as the money supply, causing the interest rate to return to its initial level, and forcing an equivalent exchange rate depreciation and thus the trade balance of the home country remains unchanged. Since there is no effect of the monetary expansion at home on the foreign price level, we observe no change in output there, and the foreign economy is still insulated from any effects of the monetary expansion at home. Therefore, the home economy again will bear the cost of expansion, in the form of inflation and exchange rate depreciation.

In the case of a fiscal expansion at home we observe an increase of output at home and abroad. While output rises at home unequivocally, in the foreign economy that will only be the case if the foreign income elasticity of money is less than one (or equal to one). But if $\eta^* > 1$ then the outcome on foreign output will be ambiguous; and it is possible that it declines. The importance of the value of η^* becomes clear and this is missed by Argy and Salop (1983), as well as by Van der Ploeg (1987). Should $\eta > 1$ and $\eta^* < 1$ then the price level at home and abroad will increase and that will certainly raise world output. Thus, with fiscal expansion at home, there will be a rise in aggregate demand for domestic output creating excess demand for real money and raising the interest rate, there will be capital inflows and a trade balance deficit such that the exchange rate falls and the terms of trade improve. This will lead to an increase in the supply of home output. But an increase in the domestic and foreign price, given that the world money supply is fixed, is therefore necessary to produce money market equilibrium at home and abroad. That rise in the foreign price level, given nominal wage rigidity, will cause foreign producers' real wage to fall; so firms will hire more workers and output increases abroad.

As far as commercial policy is concerned, the imposition of a tariff on imports by the home country will cause similar results to those of fiscal policy but the initial impact and the adjustment process are very different. Domestic output will rise because of a strong income effect (which raises the demand for it), and because of a fall in the domestic terms of trade (which raises its supply). We expect that the income effect will offset the negative effect of the improvement of the domestic terms of trade and the rise in the interest rate. In the foreign country, output rises as well, because of the existence of nominal wage rigidity. The inflationary pressures that the imposition of a tariff will cause in the foreign country, via foreign money market equilibrium, will force the real wage to decline there. Accordingly, producers will hire more labour, and the supply of output will increase subsequently.

The values of the income elasticity at home and abroad are important again and they must be such that $\eta \leqslant 1$ and $\eta^* \geqslant 1$, to generate the results summarized in Table 5.2 for the case of commercial policy. Should the

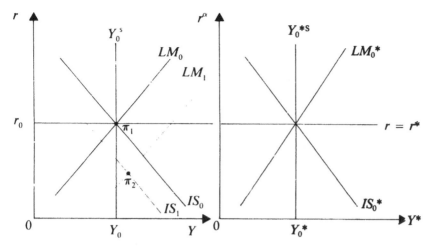

Figure 5.5 Monetary expansion in a RWR–NWR world

values of η, η^* be reversed it is feasible for foreign output to decline, though it could still rise.

Figure 5.5 analyses the case of a *monetary expansion* at home. The initial increase in money supply will create an excess supply of real balances and that will shift LM_0 rightwards, increasing aggregate demand for domestic output. As a consequence, the interest rate falls in order to bring equilibrium in the money market, given that the supply of output is fixed at the moment. The domestic price level will begin to rise, causing the terms of trade to improve, and resulting in capital outflows which will put pressure on the exchange rate to depreciate. The improvement in the terms of trade stimulate output at home. In addition, the fall in the interest rate will cause private expenditure to rise, while the fall in the terms of trade through the Laursen–Metzler effect will have the opposite effect. The IS_0 schedule shifts leftwards but not by much, and temporary equilibrium is, say, at point π_2.

In the foreign country, no changes are observed. Since the supply of output there depends on the foreign price level and not on the terms of trade, changes in the terms of trade and the exchange rate will not affect the supply of foreign output. In the home country, we will move back to the original position when the domestic price level increases proportionately as much as the money supply. That will produce money market equilibrium at home and therefore the interest rate returns to its original level, and with the exchange rate depreciation just matching the rise of the domestic price level; the terms of trade returns to its initial level. Home aggregate demand and supply will return to their initial equilibrium levels.

In contrast, the *home* economy's *fiscal policy* will most probably become a locomotive policy. The final outcome of an increase in government spending in the home country will depend on the value of the domestic and foreign income elasticity of demand for money. Although home output rises uniquely, foreign output rises if and only if $\eta^* \leqslant 1$, while it is possible for it to decline if $\eta^* > 1$. The domestic and foreign price levels will rise if $\eta \geqslant 1$ and $\eta^* \leqslant 1$. However, if $\eta < 1$ and $\eta^* > 1$ then it is possible that there will be a deflationary effect generated by home fiscal expansion. Finally, the interest rate falls and the exchange rate appreciates as long as $\eta^* < 1$. The inflationary effect of the fiscal expansion is very important for the output expansion in the foreign country, since with nominal wage rigidity there, a change in the domestic price level is the only channel by which output abroad can change. Thus, if with fiscal expansion at home, *P** falls, then the real wage abroad will rise and consequently output declines there. We provide some heuristic comments on what might be happening when domestic fiscal expansion produces world output expansion, and later we will refer to the case when output abroad declines.

The immediate consequence of fiscal expansion at home is an excess demand for domestically-produced goods. This leads to an excess demand for real money balances; the interest rate rises for any given level of output (since the nominal money supply is fixed). The rise in the interest rate will reduce the home and (foreign) demand for goods; moreover, it will stimulate capital inflows into the home country, causing the home currency to appreciate, whilst the terms of trade will improve. That will serve to give a new boost to domestic output.

Therefore, the home country will find itself in the new equilibrium at point π_2 on Figure 5.6. In the foreign country we also have an increase in the demand for foreign output, and so IS^*_0 shifts rightwards. Money market equilibrium at home and abroad suggests that with $\eta > 1$ and $\eta^* < 1$, there will be excess supply of real money in the world and the domestic and foreign price levels must rise to produce equilibrium in the money market at home and abroad. These new money market equilibria are reflected by the shift of the LM_0, LM^*_0 schedules leftwards. The rise in the foreign price level will cause foreign producers' real wage to fall and as a result they will hire more workers, expanding the supply of output abroad. The new equilibrium abroad will be at point π^*_2

If $\eta < 1$ and $\eta^* > 1$, then we could find that output abroad is falling rather than rising. This could occur because there will be an excess demand for real money balances world wide and the domestic and foreign price levels must fall to produce money market equilibrium. While wages are indexed to the overall price index at home, and since the exchange rate has appreciated, output still expands at home, because a lower consumer price

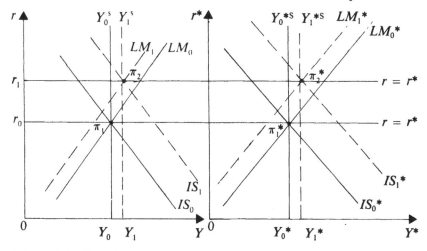

Figure 5.6 Fiscal expansion at home in a RWR–NWR world

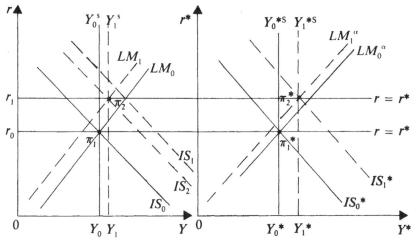

Figure 5.7 Tariff imposition in a RWR–NWR world

index leads to lower nominal wage demand, (initially) to a decline of the home wage rate, and thus to higher output. But the fall in the foreign price level will have an immediate effect on the rise in the foreign wage rate and that will result in a fall in output and employment abroad. Thus, in contrast to earlier studies such as Argy and Salop (1983) and Van der Ploeg (1987) it cannot be demonstrated uniquely that fiscal expansion in Europe will cause an increase in output and employment in the US.

We now turn to offer some analysis of the effects of the imposition of a tariff, by the home country. As before, in Figure 5.7 we are given the initial equilibrium conditions in the goods and money markets as well as aggregate supply in both countries.

When the home country imposes a tariff on imports from abroad, the immediate consequence, of course, is that these goods become more expensive, persuading domestic residents to shift expenditures towards domestic goods. We recall that the absorption function describes private expenditure on both domestic and foreign goods and, therefore, it is not a simple matter to identify exactly the size of the shift of the private expenditure towards domestically produced goods: but the effect will be to move IS_0, the initial IS curve, rightwards to IS_1. The fall in imports will cause the trade balance to improve, exerting a downward pressure on the exchange rate, leading to an improvement in the terms of trade, σ. Assuming once again that the domestic terms of trade fall in the final equilibrium, this will have a negative effect on home expenditure, but one that is not sufficient to nullify the expansionary income effect of the tariff. So IS_1 will shift back towards the initial position π_1. But higher real income at home, accompanied by a fixed real money supply, will provoke an excess demand for real money balances. For any given level of income, the interest rate must rise; and this will also cause some reduction in home expenditure. To maintain money market equilibrium, though, we require that the domestic price level rises, because with the assumption of $\eta \leqslant 1$ there will be excess supply of real money balances, even with a moderate rise in the interest rate. Domestic output also rises but not by much and the home economy finds its new equilibrium position at point π_2.

In the foreign economy we will also observe a moderate rise in output. In contrast to the first case where we have RWR abroad, and therefore adjustments in the foreign consumers' price index prevent there being any effect on foreign supply, NWR permits some expansion abroad. The deterioration of the terms of trade abroad stimulates foreign aggregate demand, which offsets the negative effect of a higher interest rate, and demand rises there. IS^*_0 shifts rightwards. But exchange rate changes are not taken into consideration by foreign workers who care only about a particular level of the nominal wage. Given $\eta^* \geqslant 1$ money market adjustments abroad require that the foreign price must rise to clear the market. But a higher level of the foreign price enables the foreign real wage to fall and employers are induced to hire more labour, increasing foreign output. The new equilibrium for the foreign economy is π^*_2. The final outcome, therefore, is that although the home economy faces real wage resistance, nominal wage rigidity abroad permits world output and employment to rise, consequent upon the levying of the tariff. Therefore, in the case where the foreign country faces NWR the home country can expand output by the use of a tariff without causing retaliation from the foreign country, since output rises there as well. Tariffs need not be a beggar-thy-neighbour instrument. With full information by both governments about the world model, there is no need for co-operation nor for the foreign country (the USA) to indulge itself in conventional stabilization policies as antidotes to the repercussions of the home country's (Europe's) tariff.

In the preceding evaluation of the three forms of economic policy, we have considered the adoption of policies by the home country only. This provides some insights into the likely need for co-ordination of policies, or for retaliation. But to comment on those matters in a little more detail, we need to consider the multiplier effects on both countries of monetary and fiscal policy followed by the foreign country also. Since the qualitative results in such situations are identical with home country policies pursued in a NWR (Home), RWR (Abroad) regime, we return to the question of co-ordination at the end of the next section, which concentrates on that regime.

4   Two-country model with nominal wage rigidity at home and real wage resistance abroad

a.   The model

Let us now consider commercial and stabilization policies in a model where the home economy faces nominal wage rigidity while the foreign economy faces real wage resistance. The imposition of a general tariff on European products by the US would have important policy pointers, since in the last couple of years we have observed increasing protectionism in the US against a number of European goods: this trend might well be enhanced from 1992, even if Europe imposes only minimal tariffs against the US.

The framework used in this section is essentially the same as that of Section 3. The difference is that the wage process in the home economy is represented by the following, rather than by equation (5.8):

$$W = \overline{W} = l \tag{5.42}$$

The home country's supply schedule will be:

$$Y = a \left[\frac{P}{l} \right]^{\delta} \tag{5.43}$$

Home output is now determined by the domestic price level, whilst foreign output depends upon the terms of trade.

The two-country model can be summarized by the four equilibrium conditions together with the equations for supply and the terms of trade:

$$Y = E(Y + t\sigma M, \sigma(1 + t), r) + X(Y^*, \sigma, r^*) - $$
$$(1 + t)\sigma M(Y + t\sigma M, \sigma(1 + t), r) + G \tag{5.44}$$

$$Y^* = E^*(Y^*, \sigma, r^*) + M((Y + t\sigma M, \sigma(1 + t), r) - \left[\frac{1}{\sigma}\right] X(Y^*, \sigma, r^*) \tag{5.45}$$

$$\frac{H}{P} = (1 + t)^{1 - \beta} \sigma^{1 - \beta L} \left[\frac{Y + t\sigma M}{(1 + t)^{1 - \beta} \sigma^{1 - \beta}}, r \right] \tag{5.46}$$

$$\frac{H^*}{P^*} = \sigma^{\beta^* - 1} L^*(\sigma^{1\,\beta^*} Y^*, r^*) \tag{5.47}$$

$$Y = a[Pl^{-1}]^{\delta} \tag{5.48}$$

$$Y^* = a^* [\sigma^{1 - \beta^*} \overline{w}^{* - 1}]^{\delta^*} \tag{5.49}$$

$$\sigma = \frac{eP^*}{P} \tag{5.50}$$

The model will once again solve for the values of the endogenous variables Y, Y^*, P, P^*, r, e and σ given the values of the exogenous variables G, G^*, H, H^* and t.

b. Policy exercises

We totally differentiate equations (5.44) – (5.50) and assuming again that the initial value of e, P, P^* and σ are equal to unity and that of t is zero, we have:

$$J = \begin{bmatrix} (E_1 - M_1 - 1) & X_1 & 0 & 0 & (E_3 - M_3 + X_3) & 0 & (X_2 - \epsilon M - M_2) \\ L_1 & 0 & H & 0 & L_2 & 0 & (1 - \beta)L(1 - \eta) \\ 1 & 0 & a\delta(l^{-1})^{\delta} & 0 & 0 & 0 & 0 \\ M_1 & (E^*_1 - X_1 - 1) & 0 & C & (E^*_3 + M_3 - X_3) & 0 & (M_2 - \epsilon^* X - X_2) \\ 0 & L_1^* & 0 & H^* & L_2^* & 0 & (1 - \beta^*)L^*(\eta^* - 1) \\ 0 & 1 & 0 & 0 & 0 & 0 & a^*\delta^*(\beta^* - 1)(\overline{w}^{* - 1})^{\delta} \\ 0 & 0 & 1 & -1 & 0 & -1 & 1 \end{bmatrix} \tag{5.51}$$

$$dy = [dY \; dY^* \; dP \; dP^* \; dr \; de \; d\sigma]' \tag{5.52}$$

and

Table 5.3. *Qualitative effects of commercial and stabilization policies by the home country*[†]

	Y	Y^*	P	P^*	r	e	σ
Expansionary Monetary policy	+	+	+	$-^\epsilon$	−	+	+
Expansionary Fiscal policy	$+^\epsilon$	?	$+^\epsilon$	$+^\epsilon$	+	$-^\epsilon$	?
Imposition of a general tariff	+	$-^\epsilon$	+	$+^\epsilon$	+	−	−

[†]ϵ denotes most likely outcome when $\eta<1$ and $\eta^*\geqslant 1$; ? indicates an ambiguous result.

$$dx = \begin{bmatrix} -dG + [(MM_1+M_2) - (\epsilon-E_1)]dt \\ dH + [(1-\beta)L(1-\eta) - L_1M]\,dt \\ 0 \\ -dG^* - (MM_1+M_2)\,dt \\ dH \\ 0 \\ 0 \end{bmatrix} \qquad (5.53)$$

$|J|$ is an unwieldy expression and it is relegated to a note.[1] We sign it as a negative by stability requirements. To assist us to sign the numerator of the policy multipliers we again assume that the Marshall–Lerner condition holds; the Laursen–Metzler condition effect is always present, we remember; and alternative assumptions are made about the Metzler paradox.

Table 5.3 summarizes the qualitative results of the alternative policies under consideration: we have assumed that $\eta<1$ and $\eta^*\geqslant 1$. As we can readily observe as soon as we move towards a less indexed economy that pursues active economic policy the qualitative results are altered quite dramatically, especially for the case of monetary expansion.

With the home country facing nominal wage rigidity any *monetary expansion* it undertakes will cause world output to rise and now both countries experience an increase in output. Monetary policy is not a beggar-thy-neighbour policy. For this to be so the domestic price level must rise while the terms of trade improve from the point of the foreign country (that is, σ must deteriorate). Furthermore, the interest rate falls and together with the deterioration in the terms of trade this will prompt an increase in the domestic demand for domestic output. This is strengthened by the rise in exports consequent upon the rise in foreign income.

But the change in the terms of trade has a negative impact (via the Laursen–Metzler effect) on the expenditure on foreign output abroad. To be consistent with higher output supply there the fall in the interest rate must have been sufficient to offset the negative own-demand effect of the terms of trade. From the foreign money market we discover that the fall in the interest rate and the increase of real income, (given that we have assumed that the income elasticity of demand for money, η^*, is greater than or equal to unity) will create an excess demand for real balances; necessitating a fall in the domestic price level and, eventually, in the consumer price index there.[2]

Fiscal expansion at home when there is nominal wage rigidity will cause domestic output to rise, which will require an increase in the domestic price level. But the effect of the fiscal expansion on the terms of trade and, consequently, on foreign output is ambiguous. It is possible that foreign output expands but it is more likely that the terms of trade will improve for the foreign country and that means foreign output falls.[3] Therefore, in contrast to the previous model, fiscal policy can expand the home economy at the foreign country's expense. The interest rate rises and the resultant capital inflows will cause the exchange rate to appreciate and the trade balance goes into deficit. That will lead to deflationary effects due to the improvement of the terms of trade, the rise in interest and the fall in foreign output, but they do not offset the beneficial effect on aggregate demand caused by the initial increase in domestic government expenditures. With the interest rate rising, and terms of trade falling (assuming, remember, that $\eta \leqslant 1$) there will be an excess supply of real money balances; so P must rise to re-establish equilibrium. The foreign country will experience capital outflows, exchange rate depreciation and a trade surplus. Aggregate demand falls there because of the rise in the interest rate which more than offsets the inflationary effect that the terms of trade will have on foreign aggregate demand for foreign output. In the foreign money market the fall in output and the increase in the interest rate (given $\eta^* \geqslant 1$), will produce an excess supply of real money and, therefore, the foreign price level must rise so that money market equilibrium can be re-attained.

An *imposition of tariffs* on the imports from the foreign country, when the home country faces nominal wage rigidity at home, will cause domestic output to rise, and with it a rise in the domestic price level. It is probable that foreign output will fall, because the terms of trade, σ, have improved in the final equilibrium. This implies that the domestic price increases by more than the foreign price level when it is adjusted for the exchange rate. Given that $\eta \leqslant 1$ and $\eta^* \geqslant 1$, money market equilibrium at home and abroad requires that prices rise, while the world interest rate must also rise to compensate for the rise in domestic income, partly attributable to the tariff revenue. It must be true then that in the home country the stimulative effects of a rise in income (and in real income, since the terms of trade improve) more than offset the negative effect of the improvement of the domestic terms of trade, $\sigma(1 + t)$, and the rise of the world interest rate on domestic aggregate demand on home and foreign goods. By contrast, the combined expansionary effects on foreign aggregate demand of expansion in the home country and the deterioration of the terms of trade need to be more than offset by the rise in the interest rate in order for foreign output to fall. On the basis of the assumptions made about η and η^* we expect that the home currency appreciates. We see then that although the expanding country faces nominal wage rigidity and the foreign country real wage resistance, commercial policy is once again a beggar-thy-neighbour policy.

What about the scope for *co-ordination* of economic policies? To supplement the comments we have already made on this question in this section and Section 4 we can consider Tables 5.2 and 5.3 initially for monetary and fiscal policy.

Table 5.2 informs us that monetary expansion by the home country in a RWR (Home), NWR (Abroad), world is of no benefit to either country; but at least it does not have harmful transmission effects on the foreign country. Now, suppose that simultaneously with the expansion of the domestic money supply, the foreign Central Bank engineers an expansion of high-powered money. The consequences, as Table 5.3 confirms, will be expansion of output and employment in both countries.

Definite improvements in both countries' output will ensue if in a RWR, NWR world, the country with RWR conducts fiscal policy, whilst the NWR country forsakes such a policy. Naturally, the empirical values of the relevant parameters will determine whether fiscal expansion is beneficial to both countries under NWR(H), RWR(A).

The 'certain success' strategy is for the NWR country to pursue monetary policy while the RWR country utilizes fiscal policy. Suppose then, that we have the wage-determining mechanisms assumed in this section, for target changes in Y and Y^*, the optimal monetary and fiscal policies are provided by the solution to:

$$
\begin{bmatrix} \dfrac{\partial Y}{\partial H} & \dfrac{\partial Y}{\partial G^*} \\[2ex] \dfrac{\partial Y^*}{\partial H} & \dfrac{\partial Y^*}{\partial G^*} \end{bmatrix} \begin{bmatrix} \mathrm{d}H \\[2ex] \mathrm{d}G^* \end{bmatrix} = \begin{bmatrix} \mathrm{d}Y^{\mathrm{T}} \\[2ex] \mathrm{d}Y^{*\mathrm{T}} \end{bmatrix} \tag{5.54}
$$

where the elements of the multiplier matrix are given in a note.[4] Even if

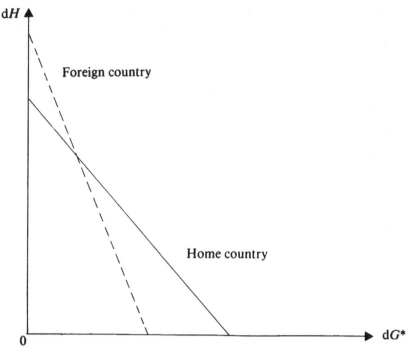

Figure 5.8

$dY^T = dY^{*T}$, the relative multipliers are such as to lead to the type of reaction curves depicted in Figure 5.8.

Consider now the policy implications raised by the introduction of a general tariff by the home country. The tariff will be unambiguously advantageous to both economies if the tariff-levying country faces real wage resistance (on our assumptions that for the two income elasticities of money demand ($\eta > 1$ and $\eta^* < 1$). A commercial policy conducted by the RWR country could be a substitute for fiscal policy and it could be operated in conjunction with monetary policy in the NWR country. In view of the fact that we have limited the policy objectives of the governments in the two economies to attainment of only one target each, a combination of commercial policy/monetary policy, cannot dominate a combination of fiscal policy/monetary policy. If we were to broaden the policy-makers' horizon to encompass, say, movements in their respective consumer price indices (*ceteris paribus*, inflation) then even in this world of 'certainty' a mix of policies involving the imposition of a general tariff by one of the countries could become optimal. But the widening the scope of the authorities' objectives is a task for another paper. The limited consideration we have given to 'target for output changes' is sufficient to indicate the complex, and complicated, nature of such an exercise; which is intractable without recourse to numerical analysis.

5 Two-country model with nominal wage rigidity at home and abroad
a. The model
In this final section we endeavour to provide some useful results from a model in the Mundellian tradition, in the sense that money wages are rigid in both countries. However, the respective price levels are not assumed to be fixed. As in all previous cases, money balances at home and abroad are deflated by the respective consumer price indices, and price levels must change in order to re-establish money market equilibrium. More than that, changes in the domestic prices will cause the production of home and foreign output to rise or fall. The terms of trade play no role in output determination. Recalling Mundell's results we have that while fiscal policy will expand world output, monetary policy is a beggar-thy-neighbour policy. We will show that we confirm the Mundellian results with respect to fiscal policy, but monetary policy *can* produce an increase in world output under certain circumstances. Commercial policy in this framework will also have expansionary effects in both countries. A model of extensive worldwide 'money illusion' could describe policy repercussions for the blocs such as EFTA, on the one hand, and the US, on the other.

The two money wages, we recall from our previous discussion, will be:

$$W = l \tag{5.55}$$

and

$$W^* = l^* \tag{5.56}$$

The complete model will now be described by:

$$Y = E(Y + t\sigma M, \sigma(1 + t), r) + X(Y^*, \sigma, r^*) - \\ (1 + t)\sigma M(Y + t\sigma M, \sigma(1 + t), r) + G \tag{5.57}$$

$$Y^* = E^*(Y^*, \sigma, r^*) + M(Y + t\sigma M, \sigma(1+t), r) - \left[\frac{1}{\sigma}\right] X(Y^*, \sigma, r^*) \tag{5.58}$$

$$\frac{H}{P} = (1+t)^{1-\beta} \sigma^{1-\beta} L\left[\frac{Y + t\sigma M}{(1+t)^{1-\beta} \sigma^{1-\beta}}, r\right] \tag{5.59}$$

$$\frac{H^*}{P^*} = \sigma^{\beta^* - 1} L^*(\sigma^{1-\beta^*} Y^*, r^*) \tag{5.60}$$

$$Y = a[P.l^{-1}]^{\delta} \tag{5.61}$$

$$Y^* = a^* [P^*.l^{*-1}]^{\delta^*} \tag{5.62}$$

$$\sigma = \frac{eP^*}{P} \tag{5.63}$$

b. Policy exercises

When we differentiate (5.58) – (5.64) totally, choosing units so that initially, as before: $e = P = P^* = \sigma = 1$ at $t = 0$ (hence $dt \equiv t$), we have this Jacobian:

$$
\begin{bmatrix}
(E_1 - M_1 - 1)\,X_1 & 0 & 0 & (E_3 - M_3 + X_3) & 0 & (X_2 - \epsilon M - M_2) \\
L_1 & 0 & H & 0 & L_2 & 0 & (1 - \beta)L(1 - \eta) \\
1 & 0 & -a\delta(l^{-1})^{\delta} & 0 & 0 & 0 & 0 \\
M_1 & (E^*_1 - X_1 - 1) & 0 & 0 & (E^*_3 + M_3 - X_3) & 0 & (M_2 - \epsilon^* X - X_2) \\
0 & L_1^* & 0 & H^* & L_2^* & 0 & (1 - \beta^*)L^*(\eta^* - 1) \\
0 & 1 & 0 & -^*\delta^*(l^{*-1})^{\delta^*} & 0 & 0 & 0 \\
0 & 0 & 1 & -1 & 0 & -1 & 1
\end{bmatrix}
\tag{5.64}
$$

The vector of endogenous variables is the same as previously (see equation (5.53)). The exogenous variable (dx) vector is:

$$
dx = \begin{bmatrix}
-dG + [(MM_1 + M_2) - (\epsilon - E_1)]dt \\
dH + [(1 - \beta)L(\eta - 1) - L_1 M]\,dt \\
0 \\
-dG^* - (MM_1 + M_2)\,dt \\
dH^* \\
0 \\
0
\end{bmatrix}
\tag{5.65}
$$

We sign $|J|$ as negative: but it is impossible to simplify $|J|$ to impose the extra condition on parameter values which will guarantee that sign: the expression for $|J|$ is again relegated to a note.[5]

Table 5.4 summarizes the qualitative results of the alternative policies in a NWR world, when $\eta \leqslant 1$ and $\eta^* \geqslant 1$. The final outcomes in this model are extremely difficult to untangle, even when the two income elasticities of money demand assume those ranges.

Table 5.4. Qualitative effects of commercial and stabilization policies by
the home country[†]

	Y	Y^*	P	P^*	r	e	σ
Expansionary Monetary policy	+	$-^\epsilon$	+	$-^\epsilon$	−	+	+
Expansionary Fiscal policy	+	+	+	+	+	−	−
Imposition of a general tariff	+	$+^\epsilon$	+	$+^\epsilon$	+	−	−

[†]ϵ denotes most likely outcome: occurs when $\eta \leqslant 1$ and $\eta^* \geqslant 1$.

With the home and foreign country facing nominal wage rigidity a
monetary expansion at home will increase domestic output while decreasing output abroad. This is the familiar Mundell result. Monetary policy in
this framework is a beggar-thy-neighbour policy. (But this is not a unique
outcome, since altering the values of η and η^* can alter it). Nevertheless,
the domestic and foreign price levels will change in the new final equilibrium, because of money market adjustments in the two countries, which
by affecting the respective producers' wage, influence supply at home and
abroad, via the aggregate production functions. Thus, the inclusion of an
explicit supply side in the two economies provides a clear link between
output supply and price changes. But, in part, the effects of price changes
are due to our deflating the money balances at home and abroad by the
respective consumer price index. This allows exchange rate adjustments to
affect the supply of money, and given the values of η and η^* to force
adjustments in P and P^*; this is excluded from the Mundellian framework. If it were the case that $\eta^* < 1$ it would be likely that foreign output
and the foreign price level would also rise. As $\eta^* \to 0$ the possibility of that
occurrence increases. So, a monetary expansion at home will raise the
domestic price level and, hence, home output rises while the foreign price
level and foreign output fall. Moreover, the increase in real money supply
will cause the interest rate to fall, causing capital outflows and exchange
rate depreciation, leading to a trade balance surplus (or to a decline in the
trade deficit). The exchange rate depreciation will finally cause a fall in the
terms of trade which will be strengthened by the rise in the domestic price
level as well. The fall in the interest rate along with the deterioration of the
terms of trade must offset the deflationary effect which the drop in foreign
output causes. In the foreign country we will observe that there will be

capital inflows, currency appreciation and a trade deficit, as it approaches equilibrium.[6]

In the case of a domestic fiscal expansion, output increases both at home and abroad. The price levels should rise in both countries, reducing producers' real wage and, therefore, increasing employment and output worldwide. At home, the interest rate rises causing capital inflows, exchange rate appreciation and a trade balance deficit. In the domestic economy we must have that the positive effect of the increase in government expenditures and the rise in foreign output will offset the deflationary effect of the fall in the terms of trade. In the foreign country the deterioration of the terms of trade and the increase in the domestic output should offset the deflationary effect of the rise in the interest rate and aggregate demand must rise at home and abroad. Money market adjustments, given the values of the respective income elasticities of demand for money, will clear when the respective price levels rise. Certainly, the foreign economy will face capital outflows, currency depreciation and trade surplus, as it approaches equilibrium.[7]

Finally, in the case of commercial policy we will have that the imposition by the domestic economy of a tariff will cause world output to rise. Under our assumptions that both economies face nominal wage rigidity and that $\eta \leqslant 1$, $\eta^* \geqslant 1$, the stimulative effects of a higher income due to the tariff revenue, and the rise in foreign output should more than offset the negative effect of the rise in interest rate and the possible fall in the domestic terms of trade. The trade balance goes into surplus and the exchange rate appreciates. In the foreign country, the deterioration of the terms of trade and the increase in home output will more than offset the negative effect of the rise in the interest rate. Given the values of η and η^* money market adjustments will clear provided the respective price levels rise. It is this inflationary effect of the tariff which will cause the respective real wages to fall and, therefore, output and employment to rise worldwide.

We can deduce the following heuristic arguments again to attempt to explain in more detail how those results summarized above might have been generated by the three different economic policies. We begin with a monetary expansion.

A monetary expansion at home will cause the real money supply to rise and that will cause an excess supply of money at the initial level of the interest rate and so the interest rate falls to preserve money market equilibrium; and aggregate demand for domestic output rises. The fall in the interest rate will cause capital outflows, exchange rate depreciation and a further increase in the demand for domestic output, while the trade balance goes into surplus. The depreciation of the exchange rate will cause the terms of trade to deteriorate, further increasing the aggregate demand for domestic output, via the Laursen–Metzler effect. So in the home country the expansionary effects of a lower interest rate, depreciation of the exchange rate and the deterioration of the terms of trade will more than offset the deflationary effect of a possible fall in foreign income. In the money market we have that given the interest rate and income, a rise in the terms of trade (and assuming that $\eta \leqslant 1$ will cause the demand for real money to be less than the supply of money) will be accompanied by a rise in the domestic price level. But a rise in the domestic price level will cause domestic firms' real wage to fall and output supply rises.

In the foreign country opposite effects are observed. The improvement of the terms of trade dampens the aggregate demand for foreign output. This must offset the positive effect of a lower interest rate and the increase in the domestic economy's output. The resulting trade deficit and currency appreciation will further cause demand for output to decline. Supply of foreign output falls, with foreign producers' wage rising, given that the foreign price level falls to re-instate money market equilibrium abroad $(\eta^* \geqslant 1)$.

Consider fiscal expansion. This will increase directly the aggregate demand for domestic output. This, in turn, will cause excess demand for real money balances and the interest rate will rise, partially offsetting the expansionary effect of the initial fiscal expansion. At the same time, the rise in the interest rate will cause capital inflows and currency appreciation, with the trade balance going into deficit. The terms of trade will improve, producing a strengthening of domestic demand for domestic output. Furthermore, with fixed money supply the fall in the terms of trade, given also the rise in the interest rate and that $\eta \leqslant 1$, will create an excess supply of money, forcing an increase in the domestic price level. The rise in the domestic price level will once again decrease domestic producers' real wage and output supply rises.

In the foreign country, the deterioration of the terms of trade along with the exchange rate depreciation and rising output at home will offset the negative effect of a higher interest rate and aggregate demand for foreign output also rises. Additionally, given that the money supply is fixed there, and the value of $\eta^* \geqslant 1$, there will be an excess supply of real money balances, causing the foreign price level to rise as well. Finally, with a lower real wage abroad, foreign output supply increases, too.

We turn to consider commercial policy. The immediate impact of the imposition of a tariff will be a fall in imports, and a rise in the domestic demand for domestic output. This will produce, given the fixed money supply, excess demand for real money balances, and the interest rate must rise to maintain money market equilibrium at home. This will partially offset the initial increase in the aggregate demand. The improvement of the current account (trade balance) will certainly put a downward pressure on the exchange rate and the *world* terms of trade improve. This appreciation will be strengthened by the capital flows, resulting in a higher interest rate. But, the improvement of the *world* terms of trade, and here we assume that the domestic terms of trade improve as well, will cause adjustments in the home goods and money market equations. Specifically, the domestic supply of, and demand for, real money balances both rise with the fall in the domestic terms of trade. But since $\eta \leqslant 1$, it must be the case that the supply rises more than the demand and the resultant excess supply of real money balances will mean that the domestic price level must rise to maintain money market equilibrium. But the rise in P will also have effects in the supply side of the economy. Since workers are concerned with a fixed nominal wage, W, an increase in P has no effect on the workers' employment decision, but changes the producers' real wage. Their real wages fall and as a consequence employment rises, leading to higher production of domestic output.

The combined stimulative effect of higher income at home and the deterioration of the terms of trade will cause aggregate demand abroad to rise and, in view of a fixed foreign real money supply a higher interest rate is required to re-establish equilibrium. The foreign economy will then be faced with capital outflows as well as a current account deficit which leads to an exchange rate depreciation and a deterioration of its terms of trade which, as noted above, has a positive effect on foreign demand. Moreover, the exchange rate depreciation and the terms of trade deterioration will cause a fall in both the supply and demand for foreign real balances for any level of interest rate. But assuming that $\eta^* \geqslant 1$, demand falls by more than supply and as a result we have an excess supply of real money balances, requiring that the foreign price must also rise to maintain equilibrium. Since the foreign economy faces nominal wage rigidity as well, changes in prices will not affect the foreign workers' decision about employment, but the real wage of producers' declines, provoking an increase in foreign output and employment.

What about the possibility of policy conflict and the scope for policy co-ordination in an inter-dependent world of two major blocs faced by nominal wage rigidity in their respective labour markets? The qualitative multiplier effects for *ceteris paribus* expansionary stabilization policy in the foreign country are deducible from Table 5.4, since the results of expansion by either country are (must be) symmetric, when they both have the same labour market and other conditions in general (even though the relevant behavioural parameters, a, a^*, . . . might differ, of course).

Hence, a policy conflict can only materialize if one of the countries decides to improve its own economic position by expanding its money stock. The other country will wish to retaliate. But both can be in a superior position by co-operating and in the process deciding that they will both pursue an expansionary fiscal policy. Alternatively, the home country could impose a general tariff whilst the foreign country adopts an expansionary fiscal stance.

6 Some conclusions

Mundell (1964) analyses a two-country model with a flexible exchange rate and perfect capital mobility under static expectations. The framework of the analysis was similar to the one-country model analysed by him (1961, 1963) and Fleming (1962). Implicit within this framework is the assumption that the *nominal* wage, in both countries, is fixed. The model does not explicitly take into account output supply considerations; this is unnecessary *ex hypothesi*. As in the case of the Mundellian one-country model, output is completely demand determined. It was in such a framework that the now classic results were derived that while monetary policy is a beggarthy-neighbour policy, fiscal policy is a locomotive policy. Mundell did not consider commercial policy in this two-country model.

Later works, namely, Argy and Salop (1983), Bruno and Sachs (1979), Branson and Rotenberg (1980) and Van der Ploeg (1987), took into consideration the supply side of the economies and the impact that flexibility of wages and prices will have on the effectiveness of monetary and fiscal policy; though we note that Argy and Salop excluded the terms of trade (Laursen–Metzler effect) from their expenditure function. It then emerged that there is an asymmetry in the supply side that can produce different policy outcomes. The authors showed that where workers are concerned with the real wage Mundell's results are only one possible outcome.

In this essay we have utilized a similar setting for a two-country model. However, the money market is also of a conventional type, with the exception that the nominal money supply is deflated by the consumer price index. Moreover, demands for real money balances are no longer homogeneous of degree one in prices, which make the final outcome sensitive to the respective value of the income elasticity of demand for money. In addition, we consider the four possible types of wage regimes, the existence of commercial policy, and the execution of stabilization policies in both countries simultaneously.

The general finding is that monetary policy is ineffective in stimulating domestic and foreign output, as long as the expanding country faces real wage resistance. In such a case the initial increase in the home money supply will only serve to raise the domestic price level by the same proportion. That will leave the world interest rate unchanged, while the exchange rate depreciates to offset the rise in prices. In other words, there is a one-to-one increase in the price level and the exchange rate, leaving the current account unaffected. In the foreign country, output, interest rates, the current account and prices will remain unchanged, and the increase in import prices is exactly offset by the foreign currency appreciation. These results diverge from those Mundell obtained. Monetary policy is now neutral, while Mundell (1964) shows that while it increases domestic output it decreases output abroad. Thus, we saw that the costs of monetary expansion in the form of inflation are borne solely by the expanding economy with the foreign economy completely insulated from any side-effects. However, when the expanding country faces nominal wage rigidity and the foreign country faces real wage resistance, world output rises, while if the foreign country also faces nominal wage rigidity then the home economy is likely to expand at the expense of the foreign economy (the Mundellian result). In the former case, the money supply expansion at home has an effect on the interest rate, with the price level rising by less than the money supply. Thus there will be expansion at home since real wages fall, while the improvement in the terms of trade abroad will also increase foreign output. In the latter case, the domestic output rises for the same reasons, but the foreign output will decline as long as foreign prices fall. However, it will rise if the foreign price level rises as well. In either case, the exchange rate depreciates at home, hence, it appreciates in the foreign country; certainly, in the former case the output of the home country rises by less than in the latter.

When we consider fiscal expansion at home, the final outcomes become more complex, and they depend on the respective income elasticities of demand for money. If the expanding country faces real wage resistance then while the home output will rise, foreign output falls if the foreign country also faces real wage resistance, while it rises if it faces nominal wage rigidity. In the home country we expect that the interest rate will rise, the exchange rate will appreciate and the domestic price level rises so that the terms of trade improve and output rises. But that means that the terms of trade deteriorate in the foreign country and that should imply, with RWR abroad, a drop in its output. By contrast, in the case of NWR abroad, a rise in foreign prices is consistent with a higher interest rate and deteriorating terms of trade; accordingly, there will be a fall in the real wage with a concomitant rise in output and employment there.

When the expanding country faces nominal wage rigidity, once again home output rises, with more or less the same effects for the home economy as before. However, the outcome for the foreign economy is not clear for the case of RWR. Since we are not sure what the final effect on the terms of trade will be, it is unclear if foreign output will rise or fall. The answer will depend on the specific value of several parameters in the foreign economy. Again, the home currency appreciates because of the capital inflows, while the price level rises at home. Consequently, the foreign currency will depreciate, and given the higher interest rate, the foreign price level rises. Should the foreign country also face nominal wage rigidity, the world output rises, because the real wage of foreign producers falls.

With respect to fiscal policy, the direction of change in the key variables depends crucially on the nature of fiscal finance. Frenkel and Razin (1987) analyse alternative means of budgetary finance in a two-country model under flexible exchange rates. Two alternatives are considered: a debt-financed or a tax-financed rise in government spending. Assuming that the initial debt is zero, they show that in the case of a debt-financed fiscal expansion the conventional Mundellian results are obtained. However, when a tax-financed fiscal expansion is undertaken (as in the case implicitly in our model, since we have assumed that any change in *G* is financed by a lump-sum tax; including such a tax explicitly in our model will only reduce the size of some of our coefficients, never alter their signs, and so leave our conclusions unaffected), then while domestic output is raised and the exchange rate depreciates, foreign output remains unchanged. This complete insulation of the foreign country is shown to result from the complete offsetting of the demand effects of the rise in government spending by the reduction in the domestic private sector demand for foreign output, induced by the depreciation of the currency. In addition, the interest rate remains unchanged.

As noted previously, the case of commercial policy in the context of a two-country model has not been discussed in the literature. We recall that in previous works that analyse the one country (Rest of the World) case, conventional theory argues that a tariff imposition will cause domestic output to fall (except for Ford and Sen (1985)). Guided by this notion, the apparent incontrovertibility of that view in a two-country model prevailed. All of the results based on Mundell's work (1961) and on subsequent works by Krugman (1982) and others assume that the domestic terms of trade always fall in the final equilibrium. If that were to be so, in demand determined models, it is quite obvious that, via the (positive) Laursen–Metzler effect, output must fall. Even given that effect, we have demonstrated that the terms of trade may or may not fall in the final equilibrium. Furthermore, when we consider also the supply side of the economy, it was shown that even if there is a fall in the domestic terms of trade this will cause *a rise* in domestic output (Eichengreen (1981, 1983) has supply side effects: he argues that only if the terms of trade fall in the long run can output increase and that this will not occur). Therefore, when we consider tariffs within the framework of the two-country model which we have developed, we find that they can increase the world output in some cases. Specifically, in the case where the foreign country faces RWR then independently of the wage-setting regime which prevails at home, foreign output falls. In this case the home country expands at the expense of the foreign economy. In such a case, the tariff will increase domestic income, the interest rate and the exchange rate appreciate, causing the *world* terms of trade to improve and therefore supply of domestic output rises. Demand for domestic output rises mainly because of the strong income effect of the tariff. The domestic price level will also rise. But the terms of trade abroad will deteriorate and that will cause the supply of output there to fall, while foreign demand also falls since the interest rate has risen and imports of the home country decline. In the case when the home country faces nominal wage rigidity, it is expected that with the inflationary effect of tariffs on the home economy, producers' real wages will fall so that domestic output and employment will rise.

When the foreign country faces nominal wage rigidity, then independently of the wage-setting regime that prevails in the home country, tariffs will increase home and foreign output. As before, the home output will rise either because the terms of trade have improved or because the domestic price level has risen. In the foreign country the price level rises and, therefore, since there exists NWR there, producers' real wages fall and foreign supply of output increases. In sum, the final outcome depends on whether tariffs are inflationary at home and abroad.

As we stated in our introduction, a difference in the labour markets of the Western economies is at the heart of the policy debate problem between the US and the Western European and Japanese economies. It has been argued that the fiscal stance is very tight in the Western European and Japanese economies while it is too loose in the US, and more should be done, therefore, by the respective governments to bring policies closer together to sustain the economic recovery.

Our findings indicate that as far as stabilization policies are concerned, the best outcome would be achieved when the country that faces NWR pursues expansionary monetary policy, with the RWR country pursuing expansionary fiscal policy. Furthermore, if the country with RWR (Europe) were to pursue commercial policy, then in order to avoid retaliation and recession, the country with NWR (US or Canada) should pursue expansionary monetary policy. Given the three types of economic policy, should the countries have several objectives in mind in their setting of policy (e.g. raising output subject to a change in the consumer price index), a combination of all three could be chosen by the harmonization of the governments' policy strategies.

Notes

1. $|J| = [(E^*_3 + M_3 - X_3)\{HH^*[X_1 a^* \delta^*(1 - \beta^*)(\bar{w}^{*-1})^\delta + (X_2 - \epsilon M - M_2)]\} +$

$$+ H^* a \delta(l^{-1}) \{(1 - \beta)L(1 - \eta)(E_1 - M_1 - 1) - (X_2 - \epsilon M - M_2)L_1 -$$

$$- a^* \delta^*(1 - \beta^*)(\bar{w}^{-1})^{\delta^*} L_1 X_1\} -$$

$$- (E_3 + X_3 - M_3)\{[(M_2 - \epsilon^* X - X_2) + a^* \delta^*(1 - \beta^*)(\bar{w}^{*-1})^{\delta^*}(E^*_1 - X_1 - 1)] \times$$

$$[HH^* - H^* a \delta(l^{-1})^\delta L_1 + H^* a \delta(l^{-1})^{\delta}(1 - \beta)L(1 - \eta)]\}$$

$$+ H^* a \delta(l^{-1})^\delta\{M_1 L_2(X_1 - EM - M_2) + a^* \delta^*(1 - \beta^*)(\bar{w}^{*-1})^{\delta^*}(1 - E^*_1) -$$

$$- (E_1 - M_1 - 1)L_2\}]$$

2. The complete discussion of the effects of monetary policy in a NWR-RWR world has been carried out under the assumption that the value of $\eta^* \geqslant 1$ which will produce a negative effect of a monetary expansion on the foreign price level. When $\eta^* < 1$ the final outcome is less obvious, but we believe that it will still be negative. The relevant multiplier is:

$$\frac{\partial P^*}{\partial H} = |J| \, a \delta(l^{-1})^\delta\{(1 - \beta^*)L^*(\eta^* - 1)[E_1 - 1)(E^*_3 + M_3 - X_3) - M_1(E_3 + E^*_3)]$$

$$+ L^*_2[(1 - E_1)(M_2 - \epsilon^* X - M_2) - M_1(\epsilon M + \epsilon^* X)]$$

$$+ a^* \delta^*(\beta^* - 1)(\bar{w}^{-1})^{\delta^*}[(E^*_1 - 1)(E^*_1 - X_1 - 1)L^*_2 + M_1(1 - E^*_1)L^*_2$$

$$+ L^*_1(1 - E_1)(E^*_3 + M_3 - X_3) + M_1 L^*_1(E_3 + E^*_3)]\}$$

3. The discussion of the effects of fiscal policy, as we explained in the text, is based on the values of η and η^*. We take $\eta \leqslant 1$ and $\eta^* \geqslant 1$. So the effects of fiscal expansion on domestic output, the domestic price level and the interest rate are given assuming that $\eta > 1$, while the effects on the foreign price level and the exchange rate are given assuming $\eta \leqslant 1$ and $\eta^* \geqslant 1$. If η and η^* take other values the outcomes are much more difficult to trace. The analysis in the text showed, with Table 5.3, the uncertain effect of fiscal expansion at home, on foreign output and the terms of trade. Since the foreign country faces RWR, we know that foreign output supply depends only on the terms of trade (positively). Thus the ambiguity in both results. The multipliers will help us to clarify this point:

$$\frac{\partial Y^*}{\partial G} = \frac{1}{|J|}\{H^* a^* \delta^*(\beta^* - 1)(\bar{w}^{-1})^{\delta^*}[a \delta(l^{-1})^\delta\{L_1(E^*_3 + M_3 - X_3) - M_1 L_2\} \quad (1)$$

$$+ H(E^*_3 + M_3 - X_3)]\}$$

$$\frac{\partial \sigma}{\partial G} = \frac{1}{|J|}\{-H^*[a \delta(l^{-1})^\delta\{L_1(E^*_3 + M_3 - X_3) - M_1 L_2\} + H(E^*_3 - M_3 - X_3)]\} \quad (2)$$

From expressions (1) and (2) it is clear that the ambiguity is caused by the sign of the term in the brackets which is the same for both:

$$L_1(E^*_3 + M_3 - X_3) - M_1 L_2 \quad (3)$$

If (3) is negative then foreign output falls and the terms of trade improve. If (3) is positive the final outcome on both variables is less clear, but it would be possible for foreign output to rise accompanied by a deterioration of the terms of trade.

4. $\dfrac{\partial Y}{\partial H} = -|J|^{-1}a\delta\, l^{-\delta}H^*[a^*\delta^*(1-\beta^*)(\bar{w}^*)^{-\delta^*}\{(E^*_1-X_1-1)(E_3+X_3-M_3)$

$$-X_2(E^*_3+M_3-X_3)\}$$

$$+ (E_3+X_3-M_3)(M_2-\epsilon^*X-X_2)-(E^*_3+M_3-X_3)(X_2-\epsilon M-M_2)]$$

$\dfrac{\partial Y^*}{\delta H} = |J|^{-1}H^*a\delta^*(\bar{w}^*)^{-\delta^*}a\delta l^{-\delta}[M_1(E_3+X_3-M_3)-(E_1-M_1-1)(E^*_3+M_3-X_3)]$

$\dfrac{\partial Y}{\partial G^*} = -|J|^{-1}H^*a\delta l^{-\delta}[L_2\{X_1a^*\delta^*(\beta^*-1)(\bar{w}^*)^{-\delta^*}-(X_2-\epsilon M-M_2)\}$

$$+ (1-\beta)L(1-\eta)(E_3-M_3+X_3)]$$

$\dfrac{\partial Y^*}{\partial G^*} = |J|^{-1}H^*a^*\delta^*(\beta^*-1)(\bar{w}^*)^{-\delta^*}[a_2\delta l^{-\delta}\{L_2(E_1-M_1-1)-L_1(E_3-M_3+X_3)\}$

$$- H(E_3-M_3+X_3)]$$

5. $|J| = -H\{H^*[E_3(M_2-\epsilon^*X-X_2)-E^*_3(X_2-\epsilon M-M_2)-(X_3-M_3)(E_3+E^*_3)]$

$$+ a^*\delta^*(l^{*-1})^{\delta^*}[(1-\beta^*)L^*(\eta^*-1)\{(1-E_1^*)(E_3+X_3-M_3)+X_1(E_3+E^*_3)\}$$

$$+ (X_2-\epsilon M-M_2)\{(E^*_1-X_1-1)L^*_2-L^*_1(E^*_3+M_3-X_3)\}$$

$$+ (M_2-\epsilon^*X-X_2)\{(E_3+X_3-M_3)L^*_1-L^*_2X_1\}]\}$$

$$+ a\delta(l^{-1})^{\delta}\{H^*[(1-\beta)L(1-\eta)\{(1-E_1)(E^*_3+M_3-X_3)+M_1(E_3+E^*_3)\}$$

$$+ L_2[(E_1-1)(M_2-\epsilon^*X-X_2)+M_1(\epsilon M+\epsilon^*X)\}$$

$$+ L_1\{E^*_3(X_2-\epsilon M-M_2)-E(M_2-\epsilon^*X-X_2)+(X_3-M_3)(\epsilon M+\epsilon^*X)\}]$$

$$+ a^*\delta^*(l^{*-1})^{\delta^*}[L^*_1\{L^*_2[(E_1-1)(M_2-\epsilon^*X-X_2)+(M_1(\epsilon M+\epsilon^*X)]$$

$$+ (1-\beta)L(1-\eta)[(1-E_1)(E^*_3+M_3-X_3)+M_1(E_3+E^*_3)]$$

$$+ L_1\{E^*_3(X_2-\epsilon M-M_2)-E_3(M_2-\epsilon^*X-X_2)+(X_3-M_3)(\epsilon M+\epsilon^*X)\}\}$$

$$- L^*_2[(1-\beta)L(1-\eta)[(1-E_1)(E^*_1-X_1-1)+M_1(E^*_1-1)]$$

$$+ L_1[(E^*_1-1)(X_2-\epsilon M-M_2)+X_1(\epsilon M+\epsilon^*X)]\}$$

$$+ (1-\beta^*)L^*(\eta^*-1)[L_2[(1-E_1)(E^*_1-X_1-1)+M_1(E^*_1-1)]$$

$$+ L_1[E_3(E^*_1-X_1-1)-E^*_3X_1-(X_3-M_3)(E^*_1-1)]\}]\}$$

6. The comparative statics results for monetary policy in NWR–NWR world are given as follows:

$\dfrac{\partial Y}{\partial H} = \dfrac{1}{|J|}[-a\delta(l^{-1})^{\delta}\{H^*[E_3(M_2-\epsilon^*X-X_2)-E^*_3(X_2-\epsilon M-M_2)+(X_3-M_3)(\epsilon M+\epsilon^*X)]$

$$+ a^*\delta^*(l^{*-1})^{\delta^*}[(1-\beta)L^*(\eta^*-1)\{(1-E^*_1)(E_3+X_3-M_3)+X_1(E_3+E^*_3)\}$$

$$+ (X_2-\epsilon M-M_2)\{(E_1-X_1-1)L^*_2-L^*_1(E^*_3+M_3-X_3)\}$$

$$+ (M_2-\epsilon^*X-X_2)\{(E_3+X_3-M_3)L^*_1-L^*_2X_1\}]\}] \tag{1}$$

$\dfrac{\partial Y^*}{\partial H} = \dfrac{1}{|J|}[a\delta(l^{-1})^{\delta}a^*\delta^*(l^{*-1})^{\delta^*}\{(1-\beta^*)L^*(\eta^*-1)[(E_1-1)(E^*_3+M^3-X_3)$

$$- M_1(E_3+E^*_3)]+(1-E_1)(M_2-\epsilon^*X-X_2)L^*_2-M_1L^*_2(\epsilon M+\epsilon^*X)\}] \tag{2}$$

$$\frac{\partial P}{\partial H} = \frac{1}{|J|} \left[-\{H^*[E_3(M_2 - \epsilon^*X - X_2) - E^*_3(X_2 - \epsilon M - X_2) + (X_3 - M_3)(\epsilon M + \epsilon^*X)] \right.$$

$$+ a^*\delta^*(l^{*-1})[(1 - \beta^*)(\eta^* - 1)\{(1 - E^*_1)(E_3 + X_3 - M_3) + X_1(E_3 + E^*_3)\}$$

$$+ (X_2 - \epsilon M - M_2)\{(E^*_1 - X_1 - 1)L^*_2 - L^*_1(E^*_3 + M_3 - X_3)\}$$

$$+ (M_2 - \epsilon^*X - X_2)\{(E_3 + X_3 - M_3)L^*_1 - L^*_2X_1\}\}]] \tag{3}$$

$$\frac{\partial P^*}{\partial H} = \frac{1}{|J|} \left[a\delta(l^{-1})^\delta\{(1 - \beta)L^*(\eta^* - 1)[(E_1 - 1)(E^*_3 + M_3 - X_3) - M_1(E_3 + E^*_3)] \right.$$

$$+ (1 - E_1)L^*_2(M_2 - \epsilon^*X - X_2) - M_1L^*_2(\epsilon M + \epsilon^*X)\}] \tag{4}$$

$$\frac{\partial r}{\partial H} = \frac{1}{|J|} \left[-a\delta(l^{-1})\{H^*[(1 - E_1)(M_2 - \epsilon^*X - X_2) - M_1(\epsilon M + \epsilon^*X)] \right.$$

$$+ a^*\delta^*(l^{*-1})^{\delta^*}\{(1 - \beta^*)L^*(\eta^* - 1)[(E_1 - 1)(E^*_1 - X_1 - 1) + M_1(1 - E^*_1)]$$

$$+ (1 - E_1)(M_2 - \epsilon^*X - X_2)L^*_1 - M_1L^*_1(\epsilon M + \epsilon^*X)\}] \tag{5}$$

$$\frac{\partial e}{\partial H} = \frac{1}{|J|} \left[-\{H^*[E_3(M_2 - \epsilon^*X - X_2) - E^*_3(X_2 - \epsilon M - M_2) + (X_3 - M_3)(\epsilon M + \epsilon^*X)] + \right.$$

$$+ a^*\delta^*(l^{*-1})[(1 - \beta^*)L^*(\eta^* - 1)\{X_1(E_3 + E^*_3) + (1 - E^*_1)(E_3 + X_3 - M_3)\}$$

$$+ (X_2 - \epsilon M - M_2)\{(E^*_1 - X_1 - 1)L^*_2 - L^*_1(E^*_3 + M_3 - X_3)\}$$

$$+ M_2 - \epsilon^*X - X_2)\{(E_3 + X_3 - M_3)L^*_1 - L^*_2X_1\}\}]$$

$$+ a\delta(l^{-1})^\delta[-\{(1 - \beta^*)L^*(\eta^* - 1)\{(E_1 - 1)(E^*_3 + M_3 - X_3) - M_1(E_3 + E^*_3)\}$$

$$+ L^*_2\{(1 - E_1)(M_2 - \epsilon^*X - X_2) - M_1(\epsilon M + \epsilon^*X)\}\}$$

$$+ H^*\{(E_3 + X_3 - M_3)M_1 - (E^*_3 + M_3 - X_3)(E_1 - M_1 - 1)\}$$

$$+ a^*\delta^*(l^{*-1})^{\delta^*}\{(E_1 - 1)(E^*_1 - X_1 - 1)L^*_2 + M_1(1 - E^*_1)L^*_2$$

$$+ (1 - E_1)(E^*_3 + M_3 - X_3)L^*_1 + M_1L^*_1(E_3 + E^*_3)\}]]] \tag{6}$$

Note that since $\partial\sigma/\partial H < 0$ then $\partial e/\partial H > \partial P/\partial H - \partial P^*/\partial H$.

7. The relevant comparative statics for the case of fiscal policy in a NWR-NWR world are:

$$\frac{\partial Y}{\partial G} = \frac{1}{|J|} \left[-a\delta(l^{-1})^\delta\{H^*[L_2(M_2 - \epsilon^*X - X_2) - (E^*_3 + M_3 - X_3)(1 - \beta)L(1 - \eta)] \right.$$

$$+ a^*\delta^*(l^{*-1})^{\delta^*}[(1 - \beta)L(1 - \eta)\{L^*_2(E^*_1 - X_1 - 1) - L^*_1(E^*_3 + M_3 - X_3)\}$$

$$+ L^*_2L^*_1(M_2 - \epsilon^*X - X_2) - L_2(E^*_1 - X_1 - 1)(1 - \beta^*)L(\eta^* - 1)]\}] \tag{1}$$

$$\frac{\partial Y^*}{\partial G} = \frac{1}{|J|} \left[a^*\delta^*(l^{*-1})^{\delta^*}\{(E^*_3 + M_3 - X_3)(1 - \beta^*)L^*(\eta^* - 1) - L_2(M_2 - \epsilon^*X - X_2)] \right.$$

$$+ a\delta(l^{-1})^\delta[(1 - \beta^*)L^*(\eta^* - 1)\{L_1(E^*_3 + M_3 - X_3) - M_1L_2\}$$

$$+ (1 - \beta)L(1 - \eta)M_1L^*_2L_1(M_2 - \epsilon^*X - X_2)]\}] \tag{2}$$

$$\frac{\partial P}{\partial G} = \frac{1}{|J|} \left[-\{H^*L_2(M_2 - \epsilon^*X - X_2) + a^*\delta^*[L^*_2L^*_1(M_2 - \epsilon^*X - X_2) \right.$$

$$+ (1 - \beta)L(1 - \eta)(E^*_1 - X_1 - 1)(E^*_3 + M_3 - X_3) - L^*_2(E^*_1 - X_1 - 1)$$
$$(1 - \beta^*)L^*(\eta^* - 1)]\}] \tag{3}$$

$$\frac{\partial P^*}{\partial G} = \frac{1}{|J|} \left[H\{(E^*_3 + M_3 - X_3)(1 - \beta^*)L^*(\eta^* - 1) - L^*_2(M_2 - \epsilon^*X - X_2)\} \right.$$

$$+ a\delta(l^{-1})^\delta\{(1 - \beta^*)L^*(\eta^* - 1)[L_1(E^*_3 + M_3 - X_3) - M_1L_2]$$

$$\left. + (1 - \beta)L(1 - \eta)M_1L^*_2 - L^*_2L_1(M_2 - \epsilon^*X - X_2)\} \right] \tag{4}$$

$$\frac{\partial r}{\partial G} = \frac{1}{|J|} \left[- \{H^*[a\delta(l^{-1})^\delta L_1\{M_1(1 - \beta)L(1 - \eta) - L_1(M_2 - \epsilon^*X - X_2) - H(M_2 - \epsilon^*X - X_2)\} \right.$$

$$+ a^*\delta^*(l^{*-1})^{\delta^*}[a\delta(l^{-1})\{L_1(E^*_1 - X_1 - 1)(1 - \beta^*)L(\eta^* - 1)$$

$$+ (1 - \beta)L(1 - \eta)M_1L^*_1 - L^*_1L_1(M_2 - \epsilon^*X - X_2)\}$$

$$\left. - H\{L^*_1(M_2 - \epsilon^*X - X_2) - (E^*_1 - X_1 - 1)(1 - \beta^*)L^*(\eta^* - 1)\}]\}\right] \tag{5}$$

References

Argy, V. and Salop, J. (1983) 'Price and output effects of monetary and fiscal policy in a two-country world under flexible exchange rates', *Oxford Economic Papers*, vol.35, pp228–246.

Branson, W. H. and Rotenberg, J. (1980) 'International adjustment with wage rigidity', *European Economic Review*, vol.13, pp309–332.

Bruno, M. and Sachs, J. (1979) 'Supply versus demand approaches to the problem of stagflation', in *Macroeconomic Policies for Growth and Stability: A European Perspective*, Symposium (ed. H. Giersch), Institüt fur Weltwirtschaft, Universität Kiel.

Corden, W. Max and Turnovsky, S. J. (1983) 'Negative international transmission of economic expansion', *European Economic Review*, vol.20, pp289–310

Eichengreen, B. J. (1981) 'A dynamic model of tariffs, output and employment and flexible exchange rates', *Journal of International Economics*, vol.11, pp341–359.

Eichengreen, B. J. (1983) 'Protection, real wage resistance and employment', *Weltwirtschaftliches Archiv*, vol.149, pp429–453.

Fleming, J. M. (1962) 'Domestic financial policies under fixed and under flexible exchange rates', *I.M.F. Staff Papers*, vol.9, pp369–379.

Ford, J. L. and Sen, S. (1985) *Protectionism, Exchange Rates and the Macroeconomy*, Basil Blackwell, Oxford.

Ford, J. L. and Sen, S. (1988b) 'Negation of the Laursen–Metzler effect and its implications for some standard propositions in open economy macromodels', Mimeographed, January; see this volume.

Frenkel, J. A. and Razin, A. (1987) 'The Mundell–Fleming model: a quarter century later', *I.M.F. Staff Papers*, vol.34, pp567–620.

Henderson, D. W. (1985) 'On transmission and co-ordination under flexible exchange rates: comment', in *International Economic Policy Co-ordination*, (eds W. H. Buiter and R. C. Marston), Cambridge University Press, Cambridge, pp24–31.

Krugman, P. (1982) 'The macroeconomics of protection with a floating exchange rate', *Carnegie-Rochester Conference Series on Public Policy*, vol.16, North-Holland, Amsterdam, pp141–182.

Laursen, S. and Metzler, L. (1950) 'Flexible exchange rates and the theory of employment', *Review of Economics and Statistics*, vol.32, pp281–299.

Miller, M. H. and Salmon, M. (1985) 'Policy co-ordination and dynamic growth', W. H. Buiter and R. C. Marston (eds), cited under D. W. Henderson, pp184–212.

Mundell, R. A. (1961) 'Flexible exchange rates and employment policy', *Canadian Journal of Economics*, vol.27, pp509–517.

Mundell, R. A. (1963) 'Capital mobility and stabilisation policies under fixed and flexible exchange rates', *Canadian Journal of Economics*, vol.29, pp475–485.

Mundell, R. A. (1964) 'A reply: capital mobility and size', *Canadian Journal of Economics*, vol.30, pp421–431.

Ploeg, F. van der (1987) 'International interdependence and policy co-ordination in economics with real and nominal wage rigidity', *Working Paper 986*, Centre for Labour Economics, London School of Economics.

6. Exchange rates, forward rates, domestic and Eurocurrency interest rates, Central Bank intervention and capital controls

1 Introduction

The advent of the Eurocurrency markets, at the beginning of the 1950s, and their subsequent expansion, have widened considerably the investment and borrowing opportunities which are available, to all market participants, in each national currency. Any investor, for example, may choose between investing in a national or in an international market; the latter may be subject to fewer regulations and to different risks than his own national market. Consequently, any attempt to model the determination of spot and forward exchange rates, together with domestic interest rates, even for a small open economy, must incorporate the Eurocurrency markets: *mutatis mutandis*, the analysis of the implications for financial markets of a change in government policy cannot be fully evaluated without the construction of a framework which integrates domestic and Eurocurrency markets.

As Johnston (1979) has argued poignantly:

> . . . this article . . . suggests that the Eurocurrency market is not independent of domestic banking systems and that, if capital flows are unrestricted, interest rates in the two markets are extremely closely related. Indeed, in such circumstances the Eurocurrency market appears very much as an integrated part of the domestic banking system, with even small changes in liquidity in one market generating compensating flows from the other . . . These considerations reinforce the main thesis of this article which is that the Euro-markets are not independent of domestic banking systems and that it is misleading to study them in isolation.
> (Johnson 1979, p46).

In this paper we construct such an integrated financial model for a small open economy. This will permit us to examine the determination of a variety of interest rates, besides the domestic interest rate, and to analyse the relationship between the forward premium (in the foreign currency market), domestic and foreign rates of interest. We shall be able to examine the impact on domestic interest rates, Eurocurrency interest rates and exchange rates (spot and forward rate) of exogenous disturbances emanating from intervention on the exchange markets by the domestic

Table 6.1.   Balance Sheet of UK non-bank residents

Assets[1,2]		Liabilities	
(1)	Base money B_d^a	(1)	To domestic banks in domestic currency L_d^a
(2)	Non-interest bearing demand deposits N_d^a	(2)	To domestic banks in foreign currency EL_f^a
(3)	Domestic deposits M_d^a		
(4)	Foreign currency deposits (in domestic banks) EM_f^a		
(5)	Domestic securities S_d^a		
(6)	Foreign currency securities ES_f^a		
(7)	Domestic equity K_d^a		

[1] Assets and Liabilities denominated in foreign currency are valued in domestic currency by multiplying by the exchange rate E, where E is defined as the domestic currency price of foreign currency.
[2] The superscript 'a' represents non-bank residents; the subscripts 'd' and 'f' domestic and foreign currency, respectively.

monetary authorities and the threat that they will impose controls on international capital movements.

2.   An outline of the integrated financial model

We can assume that the small open economy, the domestic economy, is the UK: the Rest of the World is represented by the US. The economic agents, or market participants, are as follows. In the UK we have: Non-bank residents; Domestic Banks; Eurobanks; and the Central Bank. As far as economic agents in the US are concerned, we need only to consider them at 'the economy level of aggregation'.

The balance sheets of UK market participants are provided in Tables 6.1 and 6.2. Table 6.1 sets out the portfolio composition of UK non-bank residents: their net worth (NW) being, of course, the difference between Assets and Liabilities. Domestic equities are included in their balance sheet, but for our purposes, as we shall see, are taken to be non-traded assets.

The domestic banks borrow by issuing domestic and foreign currency deposits to non-bank residents, as well as issuing non-interest-bearing demand deposits to non-bank residents. Banks can also borrow from non-residents. They lend to residents by holding domestic currency loans and

Table 6.2. *Balance Sheet of Domestic Banks*

Assets[1,2]		Liabilities	
(1) Bank reserves in domestic currency	$R_d{}^b$	(1) N.i.b. deposits	$N_d{}^b$
(2) Domestic currency loan to non-bank residents	$L_d{}^b$	(2) Domestic deposits of non-bank residents	$M_d{}^{b1}$
(3) Domestic currency securities	$S_d{}^b$	(3) Domestic deposits of non-residents	$M_d{}^{b2}$
(4) Foreign currency loaned to non-bank residents	$EL_f{}^b$	(4) Foreign currency deposits of non-bank residents	$EM_f{}^b$

[1]Assets and Liabilities denominated in foreign currency are valued in domestic currency by multiplying by the exchange rate E, where E is defined as the domestic currency price of foreign currency.
[2]The superscript 'b' represents non-bank residents; the subscripts 'd' and 'f' domestic and foreign currency, respectively.

Table 6.3. *Balance Sheet of Eurobanks*

Assets[1]		Liabilities	
Loans in sterling	eS^L	Deposits in sterling	eS^D
Loans in dollars	eD^L	NESP	$eS^L - eS^D$
		Deposits in dollars	eD^D
		NEDP	$eD^L - eD^D$

[1]Assets and Liabilities denominated in foreign currency are valued in domestic currency by multiplying by the exchange rate E, where E is defined as the domestic currency price of foreign currency.

foreign currency loans. They also lend to the domestic government, by holding domestic currency securities, and hold reserves of banks as shown in Table 6.3.

So, banks in the Eurocurrency markets are assumed to possess a simple balance sheet. They offer both Eurosterling and Eurodollar deposits/loans.

The Central Bank's balance sheet is presented in Table 6.4

The Central Bank issues domestic currency and domestic reserves as its

Table 6.4.   Balance Sheet of Central Bank

Assets[1,2]		Liabilities	
(1) Domestic currency securities	S_d^c	(1) Domestic currency by non-bank residents	B_d^c
(2) Foreign currency securities	ES_f^c	(2) Reserves held by banks	R_d^c

[1] Assets and Liabilities denominated in foreign currency are valued in domestic currency by multiplying by the exchange rate E, where E is defined as the domestic currency price of foreign currency.
[2] The superscript 'c' represents non-bank residents; the subscripts 'd' and 'f' domestic and foreign currency, respectively.

Table 6.5.   Balance Sheet of non-residents

Assets[1,2]		Liabilities	
Domestic (UK) deposits	M_d^f	Eurosterling loans	eS^L
Domestic (UK) securities	S_d^f	Eurodollar loans	eD^L
Eurosterling deposits	eS^D		
Eurodollar deposits	eD^D		

[1] Assets and Liabilities denominated in foreign currency are valued in domestic currency by multiplying by the exchange rate E, where E is defined as the domestic currency price of foreign currency.
[2] The superscript 'f' represents non-bank residents; the subscripts 'd' and 'f' domestic and foreign currency, respectively.

liabilities. It holds both domestic and foreign currency securities. The monetary base (B) of the UK economy is $Bd^c + Rd^c$.

Finally, we turn to the relevant aspects of the balance sheet of non-residents (i.e. of the US economy) which are depicted in Table 6.5.

A comparison of Tables 6.3 and 6.5 reveals one of the main, simplifying, assumptions: only foreigners deal in the Eurocurrency markets.

In sum, in terms of financial claims the model contains: money; domestic bank deposits; domestic bank loans; domestic securities; foreign securities; Eurosterling bank deposits; Eurosterling bank loans; Eurodollar bank loans; equities; spot foreign exchange; and forward foreign exchange. The latter figures in the model as agents endeavour to cover themselves against foreign exchange risk: and as yet, it has strictly not appeared.

These interest and exchange rates will be reduced to just four: the domestic interest rate (i_d); the Eurosterling rate (i_x); the spot exchange rate (E); and the forward exchange rate (fr). The last two will imply a value for the forward premium, fp. This simplification is accomplished by the following means: (1) the rate of interest on pure money is assumed to be zero; (2) the equity rate is assumed to be exogenous (as in Frantianni 1976); (3) the domestic bank deposit and loan rates are assumed to be determined perfectly competitively, so that the loan rate is a mark-up over the deposit rate, *and* domestic loans and domestic securities (bonds) are taken to be perfect substitutes by market participants (except from the Central Bank, of course), which means that the loan rate and the security rate are synonymous. This amalgamation of the loan and securities markets into a single market, normally referred to as the *credit market*, is now a conventional (but non-rationalized) procedure, following the seminal work of Brunner (1973). However, to be valid economically, it does require that securities are issued by non-bank residents as well as by the Central Bank: therefore, at best, loans and securities would be perfect substitutes for domestic (UK) banks, but be perfect complements for non-bank domestic (UK) residents. To make the combining of the two markets into one fully satisfactory, we should then assume that either non-bank residents have a supply of securities on the liabilities side of their balance sheet; or that there is an industrial sector which holds physical capital as assets, and which issues, as liabilities, equities and securities. This last will be the assumption we shall wish to carry forth implicitly in what follows; (4) by invoking a perfectly competitive assumption again, for Eurobanks there will be only one Eurosterling rate determined at equilibrium; (5) the foreign (US) security rate (i_s) is assumed to be exogenous; and (6) by the nature of the activities of Eurobanks there will be only one Eurodollar rate (i_f), and it will be assumed that the interest rate in the Eurodollar and US markets are tightly linked through flows of funds between them, to the extent that the two rates are equal $(i_f = i_s)$. [We recall that Johnston (1979) expects this; see also note (12)].

Essentially, then, we have markets to determine: the spot exchange rate (E); the forward exchange rate (fr); the domestic credit rate (i_d); and the Eurosterling rate (i_x). The forward premium (f_p) being deducible from the identity:

$$f_p \equiv (fr - E)/E \qquad\qquad (6.1)$$

We assume, in effect, that wealth (or net worth) and income, which will influence asset demand/liability supplies in a general portfolio analysis of market behaviour, are exogenous; in line with much of the literature on the modelling of international financial markets.

We shall see (in Section 3) that this set of variables can be further reduced because Eurobanks will maintain the Eurosterling rate at the interest parity level;

$$i_x = i_f + fp \tag{6.2}$$

Furthermore, if there is no capital control and domestic and Eurosterling assets have a high degree of substitutability, arbitrage activity between domestic banks and Eurobanks could be expected to produce this outcome:

$$i_d = i_f + fp \tag{6.3}$$

which, given (6.2), implies that $i_d = i_x$: the domestic credit rate equals the Eurosterling rate of interest (see note 12).

At this juncture we shall not set out the relevant market clearing equations for the model, together with the behavioural functions of the various market participants. These items, especially the specification of the portfolio behaviour of economic agents, are best presented as we proceed.

It is more appropriate for us now to consider the effect that the presence of Eurobanks has on the foreign exchange market and to consider Eurocurrency interest parity. This is the subject of the next section.

3.   Eurocurrency markets and foreign exchange markets

Over the years, the Eurocurrency markets have become highly integrated, while, by contrast, national credit markets have frequently appeared to follow independent courses. As a consequence, we observe that empirically, the forward premium has diverged quite markedly from interest parity with respect to national interest rates; but despite enormous shocks to the international monetary system over the recent decade, the forward premium has remained at interest rate parity with respect to Eurocurrency interest rates, as it did under fixed exchange rates.[1] The reasons why interest parity holds in Eurocurrency markets (in contrast to most national markets) are twofold: (a) Eurocurrency markets are largely free of capital controls and other restrictions which inhibit arbitrage between national markets, and (b) all Eurocurrency markets share an equal vulnerability to future capital controls, and thus expectations of future controls do not seem to inhibit arbitrage between Eurocurrencies.[2]

Knowing that interest parity holds for Eurocurrency interest rates, however, does not explain how transactions in the Eurocurrency markets and exchange markets influence Eurocurrency interest rates and the forward premium. It is to these matters that we now turn, for a regime of flexible exchange rates.

Recall that we shall refer to the US as the foreign market and to the dollar as the foreign currency, with sterling defined to be the home currency. Remember also that we have assumed that the US's own interest rate (i_s) is exogenous to our small open economy model; and by the same token, the Eurodollar rate (i_f) is taken to be equal to the US's domestic interest rate.

The balance sheet of Eurobanks (Table 6.3, in the previous section) informs us that they offer both Eurodollar deposits (loans) and Eurosterling deposits (loans). The respective interest rates are i_f and i_x: the deposit rate and the loan rate in a given Eurocurrency being assumed to be linked together by a competitive margin, which we can assume is zero. Only non-residents (see Table 6.5, in the previous section) are assumed to deal with Eurobanks.

All the assets and liabilities, separately, in the Eurobank portfolio are taken to be gross substitutes. So, for its customers, namely, US residents, at given net worth and income, their demand for Eurosterling deposits (eS^D) is assumed to be:

$$eS^D = es^D(i_x \overset{+}{-} fp; \, i_x \overset{+}{-} sp; \, \overset{-}{i_f}) \tag{6.4}$$

Here: $i_x - fp$ is the covered return on Eurosterling deposits; $i_x - sp$ is the uncovered return; the signs over the arguments in $eS^D(\cdot)$ indicate the signs of its respective partial derivatives; and the definition of sp, a speculative premium, is:

$$sp = \frac{E^e - E}{E} \tag{6.5}$$

where e denotes an expectation, so that sp is the expected proportionate change in the exchange rate.

If Eurobanks were to act merely as brokers, matching deposits and loans in each Eurocurrency, then the Eurosterling rate, i_x, would be determined solely by the interaction between the demand for Eurosterling deposits by non-bank investors and the supply of Eurosterling Loans by non-bank borrowers. Under this simplifying assumption, the Eurosterling interest rate would be i_x^* in Figure 6.1, where the non-bank excess supply of Eurosterling loans, $eS^L - eS^D$, is zero.

Eurobanks, however, typically assume a more active role in the Eurocurrency market since they often take a net loan position in one currency by converting funds obtained in another Eurocurrency market.[3] For

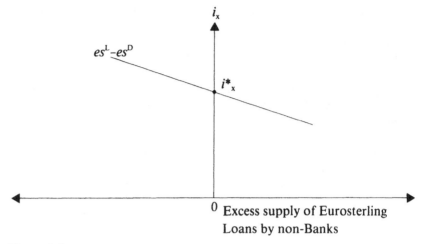

Figure 6.1

example, given a sufficient incentive, Eurobanks may convert Eurodollar deposits into sterling in order to increase Eurosterling loans, thereby increasing their net sterling loan position, NESP (see Table 6.3, above). Thus Eurosterling loans emanate from two sources: (1) Eurosterling deposits, and (2) sterling converted from dollars by Eurobanks. Equilibrium in the Eurosterling market must reflect the behaviour of Eurobanks as well as that of non-bank borrowers and lenders. Eurosterling loans must now equal the sum of Eurosterling deposits and the net Eurosterling position of the Eurobanks:

$$eS^L = eS^D + NESP \qquad (6.6)$$

Under the simplifying assumption that Eurobanks fully cover their net Eurocurrency positions, the excess demand for forward dollars by Eurobanks denoted by $N\hat{E}SP$ is simply their net Eurosterling loan position, NESP, which, as we have seen, must equal the excess supply of Eurosterling loans by non-banks, $eS^L - eS^D$. That is, since the Eurobanks are willing to accept whatever Eurosterling deposits or loans are offered at the prevailing interest rate, the excess demand for forward dollars by the Eurobanks must reflect the underlying excess supply of Eurosterling Loans ($eS^L - eS^D$) by non-bank borrowers and investors.[4] In effect, Eurobanks set the Eurosterling rate and non-banks determine the size of the net Eurosterling position which the Eurobanks assume.

As a result of the currency conversions by Eurobanks, the interest rate on Eurosterling (i_x) is closely tied to the interest rate on Eurodollars (i_f). To

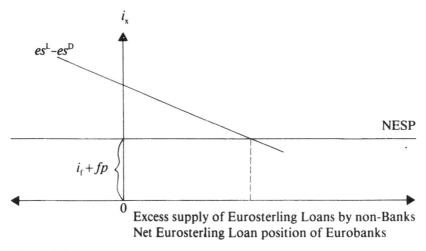

Figure 6.2

appreciate this, consider the case where Eurobanks are induced to convert dollar funds into sterling. To avoid the exchange risk associated with a net sterling loan position, the Eurobanks will normally cover that position with an equivalent purchase of forward dollars. The whole transaction will be profitable provided the interest rate on Eurosterling loans adjusted for the forward premium exceeds the interest rate paid on Eurodollar deposits. Then, ignoring transaction costs, the transaction will be profitable as long as $i_x - fp \geq i_f$.[5]

Competition between Eurobanks, in fact, keeps the interest rate charged on Eurosterling loans at a constant mark-up over the Eurodollar rate, the mark-up reflecting only the cost of the forward cover. That is, Eurobanks maintain the Eurosterling rate at the interest parity level:[6]

$$i_x = i_f + fp \qquad\qquad (6.7)$$

If the Eurodollar rate and the forward premium are taken as given, then the Eurosterling rate offered by the Eurobanks is determined as well. Eurobanks stand ready to offer Eurosterling loans and deposits at an interest rate of $i_x = i_f + fp$, so the NESP schedule of the Eurobanks in Figure 6.2 is perfectly elastic at this rate. Equilibrium in the market for Eurosterling, therefore, is achieved when the non-bank excess supply schedule intersects the NESP schedule at the interest parity rate.

The 'market equilibrium' shown in Figure 6.2, however, is, strictly, only a partial equilibrium, since the *forward premium* remains to be determined; for example, if Eurobanks seek to cover their net Eurosterling position in the forward market, the forward premium will have to adjust, leading to further changes in the Eurosterling rate. Furthermore, the demand for Eurosterling deposits eS^D, supply of Eurosterling loan eS^L, by non-bank investors or borrowers, and Eurobanks' net Eurosterling position are all involved in spot exchange market; thus these terms also influence the forward premium, and their function is similar to those of foreign-held domestic currency (sterling) deposits in domestic banks.

Indeed, the equation for eS^L is identical to that for eS^D given in equation (6.4), with the signs of all partial derivatives reversed. Accordingly, we can write the equation for *NESP*, in the more general manner, in which we can write equation (6.4), in the following, which is the equation used (in linear form) to derive Figure 6.2:

$$NESP = NESP \; (\overset{+}{i_x}, \; \overset{-}{i_f}, \; \overset{-}{fp}, \; \overset{+}{E}, \; \overset{-}{E^e}, \; \overset{-}{fr}, \; \overset{-}{sp}) \tag{6.8}$$

Hence:

$$N\hat{E}SP = N\hat{E}SP \; (\overset{+}{i_x}, \; \overset{-}{i_f}, \; \overset{-}{fp}, \; \overset{+}{E}, \; \overset{-}{E^e}, \; \overset{-}{fr}, \; \overset{-}{sp}) \tag{6.9}$$

4.   Equilibrium in the spot and forward foreign exchange markets
We can consider equilibrium in the two foreign exchange markets now that we have deduced the properties of the equilibrium in the Eurocurrency Markets, and have drawn-out their link with foreign exchange markets.

a.   The spot exchange market
Excess demand (X_E) for spot dollars will be:

$$X_E = S_f^a - \left[\frac{M_d^f + S_d^f}{E} + \frac{(eS^D + NESP - eS^L)}{E} \right] \tag{6.10}$$

where: S_f^a is the demand for dollars by non-bank UK residents in order to cover their demand for foreign (US) securities (see their balance sheet above, Table 6.1); M_d^f and S_d^f reflect the demand by non-residents (US residents) for domestic assets (see Table 6.5 above); and the term in round brackets represents the sale of dollars by foreigners and Eurobanks to cover their purchases of Eurosterling denominated assets (see Tables 6.3 and 6.5).

b. The forward exchange rate market

Excess demand in this market (X_{fr}) is given by:

$$X_{fr} = \frac{N\hat{E}SP}{e} + (\hat{M}^f_d + \hat{S}^f_d) - \hat{F}^a - ST \tag{6.11}$$

where:

$$\hat{F}^a = \hat{S}^a_f \tag{6.12}$$

and ST, which we have not used previously, is the excess supply of forward dollars of 'speculators and commodity traders'; we assume that:

$$ST = ST(\overset{+}{Q}, \overset{-}{M}, \overset{+}{fr}, \overset{-}{E}, \overset{-}{E^e}, \overset{+}{fp}) \tag{6.13}$$

Here, Q is the foreign economy's *orders* for domestic exports; and M is the home economy's *orders* for imports.

We have already specified the behavioural function for $N\hat{E}SP(\cdot)$; those for $\hat{M}^f_d$, $\hat{S}^f_d$ and $\hat{S}^a_f$ are assumed to be as follows:

$$\hat{M}^f_d = \hat{M}^f_d(\overset{+}{i_d}, \overset{-}{i_s}, \overset{+}{E}, \overset{-}{E^e}, fr, fp) \tag{6.14}$$

$$\hat{S}^f_d = \hat{S}^f_d(\overset{+}{i_d}, \overset{-}{i_s}, \overset{+}{E}, \overset{-}{E^e}, fr, fp) \tag{6.15}$$

$$\hat{S}^a_d = \hat{S}^a_f(\overset{-}{i_d}, \overset{+}{i_s}, \overset{-}{E}, \overset{+}{E^e}, fr, fp) \tag{6.16}$$

c. The excess demand functions for spot and forward exchange

These then can now be written as:

$$X_E = X_E(\overset{-}{i_d}, \overset{-}{i_x}, \overset{+}{i_f}(i_s), \overset{-}{E}, \overset{-}{E^e}, \overset{+}{fr}, \overset{+}{fp}) \tag{6.17}$$

$$X_{fr} = X_E(\overset{+}{i_d}, \overset{+}{i_x}, \overset{-}{i_f}(i_s), \overset{+}{E}, \overset{+}{E^e}, \overset{-}{fr}, \overset{-}{fp}) \tag{6.18}$$

d. Equilibrium in the spot and forward exchange markets

Now, let us assume that the domestic (UK) interest rate is a function of the Eurosterling rate (i_x). In fact, the particular interdependence between

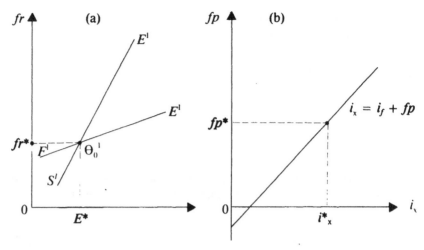

Figure 6.3

markets that we have assumed will produce such a relationship when the
model is solved completely as a general equilibrium model; and, in certain
conditions we can show that if we widen our model somewhat to include a
connection between Domestic Deposit Banks and the Eurobanks (see
note 12), i_d, in general equilibrium, will be similar to i_x. Making the
weaker assumption that $i_d = i_d(i_x)$, and for given expected future
exchange rate (E^e), together with i_f, equations (17) and (18) can be solved
for E and fr; hence for fp and for i_x.

When X_E is zero, equation (6.17), taken for simplicity to be linear,
provides us with the *ceteris paribus* relationship between fr and E portrayed in Figure 6.3(a) by $S'E'$. Likewise, equation (18) permits us to
describe the relationship between fr and E to maintain equilibrium in the
forward market, by $F'E'$. Figure 6.3(b) contains the schedules for
equilibrium in the domestic credit market and for simultaneous equilibrium conditions in the Eurocurrency markets, given the exogenous
$i_f(\equiv i_d)$. The slope of $S'E'$ will exceed that of $F'E'$ by the conditions that
guarantee stability of the complete (i.e. 3 equation) system.[7]

5. An integrated analysis of the domestic, foreign and Eurocurrency
markets

In the preceding sections we have analysed the equilibrium in the Eurocurrency and foreign exchange markets on a partial basis; a basis, however,
which was almost a complete general equilibrium basis. This is because of
the fact that the domestic (UK) economy is a small open economy, and the
simplifying assumption has been made that the Eurocurrency markets are

predominantly integrated with the US (foreign) money market. The interdependency between the UK private sector and other financial markets is taken largely to be with the US domestic market; whilst the US economic agents deal directly with both the UK market and the Euromarket, but, predominantly, do not regard Eurocurrencies as a substitute for UK domestic financial assets.

UK domestic financial behaviour does help determine the two exchange rates and so our model should, naturally, be solved as an integrated one of the two foreign exchange markets solved in conjunction with the domestic financial, or credit, market as we have transformed it into, following the literature in this field. So, we must now summarize the situation in the credit (c) market.

This market is a combination of the UK loan and securities markets we recall and excess demand there (X_c) is:

$$X_c = S_d^a + S_d^f + B - L_d^a - S_d \tag{6.19}$$

where, to complete our notation: S_d is the total supply of securities in the domestic economy; and B is the demand for both loans and domestic securities by Domestic Banks. Hence, X_c becomes the excess demand for securities; since the demand and supply of bank loans are netted-out in equation (6.19), with there being no domestic bank loans granted to foreigners, *per se* (though loans can be granted, we recall from Table 6.2, by domestic banks to domestic residents in foreign currency). Equation (6.19) does represent the securities/loans market equilibrium; but, by the behavioural assumption made, it also represents equilibrium in the loan market.

Those behavioural assumptions permit us to write:

$$X_c = X_c(\overset{+}{i_d}, \overset{+}{E}, \overset{-}{fr}, \overset{-}{fp}, \overset{-}{i_f}(= i_s), \overset{+}{E^e}) \tag{6.20}$$

The signs of the partial derivatives have an immediate economic rationale.

The schedules drawn in Figure 6.3(a) are, we recall, for a given value of the domestic interest rate. Now, it is not possible to construct schedules in (fp, i_d) space from the domestic credit market and the exchange markets, which permit us to close the model by simply adding one more diagram to Figure 6.3. We can, of course, construct such schedules for equilibrium in the domestic credit market and for simultaneous equilibrium in the spot and forward exchange markets. Such schedules depend upon fr and E. Likewise, though we can construct two schedules for both the domestic credit market and the exchange markets taken jointly, in (fr, i_d) space, those schedules depend upon E; with Figure 6.3(a) dependent upon it there is no way that a 'causal' diagrammatic analysis can be conducted. Even if i_d *is* uniquely tied to i_x (as it could possibly be if we permit Domestic Banks to engage in arbitrage activities in the Euromarket) a general equilibrium solution to solve for all three key endogenous variables requires a formal analysis, by using the excess demand functions in the three markets, the credit market; the spot exchange market; and the forward exchange market. Once the comparative statics properties of that three market system have been established the model can be changed into a two-dimensional diagrammatic representation, of course, by simple substitution of, say, the solution of fr from the $fr(\cdot)$, in terms of i_d and E, into the other two excess demand equations.

6. Comparative statics results

We now turn to the formal analysis of the comparative statics of the model, knowing that i_x can be determined as a forward premium mark-up on the (given) Eurodollar rate. Of course, such an analysis, under stable conditions, and for normalized values of the original values of the endogenous variables, represents a solution to the model. The policy disturbances which we shall investigate are: open market operations in the domestic securities market by the Central Bank; intervention by the Central Bank in the spot exchange market; intervention by the Central Bank in the forward market. The 'exogenous' disturbances we consider are: a change in the foreign (US) *orders* for domestic goods (which affects the forward market) and an alteration in the foreign (US) domestic interest rate (i_s) which is identical with the Eurodollar rate (i_f).

a.   An open market purchase of domestic securities by the Central Bank
The three excess demand equations, written in general form, are:

$$-X_c = -X_c(\overset{+}{i_d}, \overset{+}{E}, \overset{-}{fr}, \overset{-}{fp}, \overset{-}{i_f}(= i_s), \overset{+}{E^e}, \alpha) \qquad (6.21)$$

$$X_t = X_t(\overset{-}{i_d}, \overset{-}{E}, \overset{+}{fr}, \overset{+}{fp}, \overset{+}{i_f}, \overset{-}{E^e}, \theta) \qquad (6.22)$$

$$X_{fr} = X_{fr}(\overset{+}{i_d}, \overset{+}{E}, \overset{-}{fr}, \overset{-}{fp}, \overset{-}{i_f}, \overset{+}{E^e}, \beta) \qquad (6.23)$$

The securities (credit) market excess demand function, we notice, has in fact been written in excess supply format by multiplying it by minus one. This is because the pseudo-dynamics of the model (see note 7) are assumed to be of the neo-classical kind, so that E and fr respond positively to an excess demand in the spot and forward markets, respectively, whilst i_d responds positively to an excess supply of credit.

The parameters α, θ and β are the shift parameters which capture the policy interventions or the exogenous disturbances emanating from the US. The parameter α depicts the open market purchase of securities when (it) or its change is positive; when it is negative, the implication is that there has been an open market increase in the supply of securities. In all excess demand functions fp will be replaced by $(fr/E - 1)$, and we shall assume that the exogenous variable, E^e, does not alter.

In differential form equations (6.21) – (6.23) can be written as:

$$J\,dy = A\,dx \tag{6.24}$$

where:

$$J = \begin{bmatrix} -(X_c)_1 & -(X_c)_2 & -(X_c)_3 \\ (X_E)_1 & (X_E)_2 & (X_E)_3 \\ (X_{fr})_1 & (X_{fr})_2 & (X_{fr})_3 \end{bmatrix} = \begin{bmatrix} \overset{-}{a}_{11} & \overset{-}{a}_{12} & \overset{+}{a}_{13} \\ \overset{-}{a}_{21} & \overset{-}{a}_{22} & \overset{+}{a}_{23} \\ \overset{+}{a}_{31} & \overset{+}{a}_{32} & a_{33} \end{bmatrix} \tag{6.25}$$

$$dy = [d_{id}\ dE\ dfr]' \tag{6.26}$$

$$A = \begin{bmatrix} (X_c)_4 & 1 & 0 & 0 \\ -(X_c)_4 & 0 & -1 & 0 \\ -(X_{FR})_4 & 0 & 0 & -1 \end{bmatrix} = \begin{bmatrix} \overset{-}{b}_{11} & 1 & 0 & 0 \\ \overset{-}{b}_{21} & 0 & -1 & 0 \\ \overset{-}{b}_{31} & 0 & 0 & -1 \end{bmatrix} \tag{6.27}$$

$$dx = [d_{if}\ d\alpha\ d\theta\ d\beta]' \tag{6.28}$$

The sign on $d\beta$ reflects the supposition that it is positive, i.e. there is a sudden jump in the demand for forward currency; if the opposite occurs, of course, the sign on $d\beta$ would be reversed. The same constraints apply to $d\theta$ (or θ) in the spot market. $(X_c)_i$, for example, is $\partial X_c/\partial i_D$; and, remember that second and third derivatives of all excess demand functions (i.e. with respect to E and fr are 'gross' coefficients, since they incorporate the influences which operate via E and fr through fp. The gross coefficients have the same signs as the 'net' coefficients; and they are, naturally, greater in absolute magnitude. We observe that the Trace of J is uniquely negative. Also, as pointed out in note (7) $|J| < 0$, because it is assumed following Black (1973), of which our model is in a way a derivative, that J has a negative dominant diagonal, such that the absolute value of an 'own rate' response of excess demand exceeds the sum of the absolute values of the response of the other excess demands to that rate: for example, $|a_{11}| > |a_{21}| + |a_{31}|$.

When the Central Bank intervenes in the securities market and disturbs its equilibrium by buying securities we would expect, *a priori*, that the implications would be the following. The domestic interest rate would fall (i.e. would have to fall to persuade the domestic economy to hold the resultant increase in the base money, so enabling an equilibrium to be re-attained) and this would have an immediate impact on the exchange rate, causing it to rise, as domestic residents switched their portfolios from domestic securities into foreign securities. That portfolio switching, assuming that investors cover some of their purchases in the forward market, would mean an excess demand for forward sterling (excess supply of forward dollars) and so the (dollar) forward rate would fall. All these changes would, inevitably, mean that the forward premium and the Eurosterling rate would fall. However, the impact on the forward rate depends upon the net effect of the fall in the domestic rate of interest and of the rise in the spot exchange rate; if the former dominates, the forward rate will fall at the new equilibrium.

The formal analysis of the repercussions of a sudden purchase of domestic securities by the Central Bank is as follows. For $di_f = d\beta = d\theta = 0$ and for $d\alpha > 0$ we deduce from equations (6.24) – (6.28) that:

$$\frac{\partial i_d}{\partial \alpha} = [\overset{-}{a_{22}}\overset{-}{a_{33}} - \overset{+}{a_{32}}\overset{+}{a_{23}}] \, |J|^{-1} < 0 \qquad (6.29)$$

$$\frac{\partial E}{\partial \alpha} = [\overset{+}{a_{31}}\overset{+}{a_{23}} - \overset{-}{a_{21}}\overset{-}{a_{33}}] \, |J|^{-1} \qquad (6.30)$$

$$\frac{\partial fr}{\partial \alpha} = [\overset{-}{a_{21}}\overset{+}{a_{32}} - \overset{+}{a_{31}}\overset{-}{a_{22}}] \, |J|^{-1} \qquad (6.31)$$

Only the own rate response is uniquely signed and then only because of the negative dominant diagonal condition. The sign of $\partial i_d/\partial \alpha$ clearly depends upon the spot market and the forward market (given E); whilst the sign of $\partial fr/\partial \alpha$ depends upon those relative slopes for given forward rate. This model is stable because $|J| < 0$ by the dominant negative diagonal (a_{11}, a_{22}, a_{33}), when J is expanded diagonally. Even so, there exist binding constraints on the relative slopes of the excess demand schedules. The negative dominant diagonal condition limits our degree of freedom; and there exist basically only two sets of signs for the signed minors of J (i.e. for the relative slopes of the schedules) which are consistent sets. We utilize the stronger of those sets, which signs all multiplier effects unambiguously.[8] From note (8) we deduce that:

$$\frac{\partial i_d}{\partial \alpha} < 0; \ \frac{\partial E}{\partial \alpha} > 0; \ \frac{\partial fr}{\partial \alpha} < 0; \ \frac{\partial fp}{\partial \alpha} < 0; \ \frac{\partial i_x}{\partial \alpha} < 0 \tag{6.32}$$

The forward rate impact on the spot exchange market dominates that of the domestic interest rate given the implied assumptions about the relative 'price elasticities' in the various markets. The domestic rate of interest does fall (dominance of our own rate partial-derivatives guarantees this), the forward rate falls, but the spot exchange rate rises.

b. Intervention in the forward exchange market
The Central Bank can attempt to alter the forward rate (and thereby the spot rate/forward premium) by direct intervention in the forward market or by activity in the Euro currency markets. Instead of selling dollars forward to increase the covered return on sterling assets, the authorities can simultaneously borrow Eurodollars and invest the proceeds in Eurosterling deposits. The effects of such a strategy on the endogenous interest and exchange rates would be the opposite of those generated by a purchase of forward dollars by the Central Bank. From equations (6.24) – (6.28), with $d i_f = d\alpha = d\theta = 0$ and $d\beta > 0$ we discover that:

$$\frac{\partial i_d}{\partial \beta} = [a_{22} \, a_{13} - a_{12} \, a_{23}] \, |J|^{-1} \tag{6.33}$$

$$\frac{\partial E}{\partial \beta} = [a_{11} \, a_{23} - a_{21} \, a_{13}] \, |J|^{-1} \tag{6.34}$$

$$\frac{\partial fr}{\partial \beta} = [a_{21} \, a_{12} - a_{22} \, a_{11}] \, |J|^{-1} > 0 \tag{6.35}$$

The increase in the forward rate, consequent upon an increase in excess demand brought about by a Central Bank purchase of forward dollars, is what we expected *a priori*: but the positive 'impact' effect is sustained through 'second round' effects because of the own rate dominance hypothesis. The strong conditions imposed on the relationship between the other 'elasticities' determine that:

$$\frac{\partial i_D}{\partial \beta} < 0; \ \frac{\partial E}{\partial \beta} > 0; \ \frac{\partial fp}{\partial \beta} = ?; \ \frac{\delta i_x}{\delta \beta} = ? \tag{6.36}$$

However, the strong conditions do produce *a priori* acceptable results. The impact effect of a random increase in demand in the forward market must be to increase the forward rate; and that qualitative change is not altered by the subsequent trading between assets/markets which it prompts. It would immediately lead to a fall in the excess demand for domestic credit and hence to a rise in the domestic interest rate. That interest change, given the movement in the forward rate would increase the demand for spot dollars, and consequently the sterling cost of foreign exchange (dollars) would rise.

c.   A change in the Eurodollar interest rate (i_f) or in the foreign (US) interest rate (i_s)

An alteration in the Eurodollar rate disturbs all markets and throws them all out of equilibrium on impact. A higher interest rate on dollars will generate an excess demand for spot foreign exchange and an excess supply of forward foreign exchange, not only brought about by residents in the two countries, but also by the activities of the Eurobanks. There will also be an excess supply of domestic credit. We would anticipate that the final effects of an increase in the dollar rate of interest would be: an increase in the domestic interest rate (necessary to raise demand back to its original level to match the fixed stock of securities); an increase in the spot rate and a lower forward rate (on the supposition that the direct effect of an increase in the foreign interest rate on the exchange markets outweigh the indirect effects which arise because the domestic rate rises in response to the higher foreign interest rate); and, consequently, a lower forward premium, but a higher Eurosterling rate.

The relevant 'price' elasticities, of course, might not be such as to generate such outcomes consequent upon an increase in i_f. The general analysis is provided by the following equations:

$$\frac{\partial i_D}{\partial i_f} = [\bar{b}_{11}\lambda_1 - \bar{b}_{21}\mu_1 + \overset{+}{b}_{31}\epsilon_1] \, |J|^{-1} \tag{6.37}$$

$$\frac{\delta E}{\delta i_f} = [-\bar{b}_{11}\epsilon_2 + \bar{b}_{21}\lambda_2 - \overset{+}{b}_{31}\mu_2] \, |J|^{-1} \tag{6.38}$$

$$\frac{\delta fr}{\delta i_f} = [\bar{b}_{11}\mu_3 - \bar{b}_{21}\epsilon_3 + \overset{+}{b}_{31}\lambda_3] \, |J|^{-1} \tag{6.39}$$

The λ_i are all positive by the dominance postulate, and:

$$\mu_1 > 0; \ \epsilon_1 > 0; \ \epsilon_2 > 0; \ \mu_2 < 0; \ \mu_3 > 0; \ \epsilon_3 > 0 \tag{6.40}$$

λ_1, μ_i and ϵ_i are as defined in note (8).
Hence:

$$\frac{\partial i_d}{\partial i_f} \gtreqless 0; \ \frac{\partial E}{\partial i_f} \gtreqless 0; \ \frac{\partial fr}{\partial i_f} \gtreqless 0; \ \frac{\partial fp}{\partial i_f} \gtreqless 0; \ \frac{\partial i_x}{\partial i_f} \gtreqless 0 \tag{6.41}$$

A mere count of signs in the numerator suggest i_d, E and fr might all increase.

d.   An increase in foreign orders for UK exports
This disturbance, since it relates to *orders*, affects the forward rate; and it will be reflected in an increase in the supply of forward dollars. As a consequence, the impact on interest and exchange rates will be the opposite of those obtained under (6) above; that is, we can envisage ß (or dß) as being negative.

e.   Central Bank intervention in the spot exchange market
Suppose that the Central Bank intervenes in the spot market by increasing its demands for dollars (θ or $d\theta$ is positive). Such a spot purchase would straight away, of course, generate an increase in the spot rate. That would tend to cause (apart from influencing anticipation of further such increases) a shift from foreign to domestic assets by UK residents, pushing down the domestic interest rate and the exchange rate. That would create further movement in the domestic market, persuading foreigners to pull out of the UK market and it would also reverse the UK residents' initial decision to switch to UK assets. The combined effect of such influences could be to raise the domestic rate and to reverse the 'second round' fall in the exchange rate: i_d and E could both rise. The consequent effect on the forward rate would depend upon the relative 'elasticities' of the excess demand for forward dollars with respect to the domestic interest rate and the spot exchange rate.

The actual comparative statics results are:

$$\frac{\partial i_D}{\partial \theta} = [\bar{a}_{12}\bar{a}_{33} - \overset{+}{a}_{32}\overset{+}{a}_{13}] \, |J|^{-1} < 0 \tag{6.42}$$

$$\frac{\partial E}{\partial \theta} = [\overset{+}{a}_{31}\overset{+}{a}_{13} - \bar{a}_{11}\bar{a}_{33}] \, |J|^{-1} > 0 \tag{6.43}$$

$$\frac{\partial E}{\partial \theta} = [\bar{a}_{11}\overset{+}{a}_{32} - \overset{+}{a}_{31}\bar{a}_{12}] \, |J|^{-1} < 0 \tag{6.44}$$

$$\frac{\partial fp}{\partial \theta} < 0; \frac{\partial i_x}{\partial \theta} < 0 \tag{6.45}$$

The final effect on E is positive, being determined by the dominance assumption. The other multiplier effects are signed, as previously, by means of the strong conditions on the relative 'price elasticities' of the excess demand schedules. Hence, the forward premium falls as the Central Bank makes a 'jump' purchase of spot dollars because the E-effect

Table 6.6.   *Predicted effect of Central Bank policy and of exogenous disturbances*

	di_D	dE	dfr	dfp	di_x
Open market purchases of domestic securities	−	+	−	−	−
Forward purchase of dollars by the Central Bank	−	+	+	?	?
Central Bank's purchase of spot dollars	−	+	−	−	−
Simultaneous borrowing of Eurodollars and their investment in Eurosterling deposits by the Central Bank (equivalent to $d\beta < 0$)	+	−	−	?	?
Increased supply of Domestic Securities by the Central Bank	+	+	−	−	−
Increase in the foreign interest rate: likely effect in parentheses	?(+)	?(+)	?(+)	?	?
Increase in orders for domestic exports	+	−	−	?	?

dominates the i_d-effect in the forward market, compared with the domestic securities (credit) market.

A summary of the comparative statics findings is provided in Table 6.6.

We drew attention earlier on to the assumption implicit in the preceding analysis of Central Bank policies that the excess demand or excess supply which its activities generate in a particular market have spill-over excess demand/excess supply effects in the 'exogenous' markets, namely, the Eurocurrency markets and the US domestic financial markets. This, naturally, need not be a true representation of which other markets and market participants are affected directly when, say, the Central Bank intervenes in the spot exchange market. If it initiates an excess demand in that market (for dollars), which is modelled by postulating that θ is positive; the process by which it can engineer, indeed, finance, such an operation, could have direct effects in the endogenous markets. Thus, take the example where the Central Bank does disturb the equilibrium in the market for spot dollars, by purchasing dollars. It will need to finance such a purchase: now, if we imagine that such a purchase is made by its printing money, so that in its balance sheet the holding of foreign currency reserves increases, whilst its liabilities increase, *pari passu*, by the money supply newly printed to cover the purchase of dollars, there will be an *excess supply* of high-powered money, of sterling to the model. It might well be that the dollars are purchased from 'foreigners' in which case our previous analysis holds if they convert the surplus sterling into, say, Eurocurrency deposits. However, it is possible that both residents as well as foreigners will receive the extra sterling and that this (even the additional sterling in the possession of foreigners) will generate a direct, excess demand for domestic securities. We could suppose, in order to analyse such a feasible scenario that this excess demand is equivalent in magnitude to the excess supply of high powered money, which in turn is equivalent to the original disturbance to the spot market. Whether it is, or not, and whether there will be an excess demand for domestic securities consequent upon there being an excess supply of high-powered money, some money could be assumed to find its way into the Domestic Banking Sector: the overall behavioural implications of such an increase in the monetary base, as it were, seen from the Banks' perspective, are problematic as our earlier description of their portfolio indicates. Thus the Banks will wish to increase both loans and other holdings of securities. This will both increase the demand for securities (credit) in this model. However, if non-bank (UK) residents decide to increase the loans they supply by more than the Banks increase the demand, there will be an increase in the *ex ante* supply of securities. Provided the non-bank (UK) residents and/or foreigners do have an excess demand for securities, when there is an excess supply of high-powered money, the increase in demand will outstrip the increase in supply, so that *per* market, there is an excess demand for securities. In these overall conditions, we could model the 'endogeneity' of the excess supply of high powered sterling induced by the purchase of spot dollars by the Central Bank, by assuming that $d\alpha = d\theta > 0$.

There is a policy strategy which the Central Bank might pursue when it purchases spot dollars, and which will absorb the increase in high-powered money, so that it does not, in fact, materialize. Thus, the Central Bank could use the spot dollars to swap them for forward dollars, by selling them for sterling: *ceteris paribus*, this transaction would, in terms of our previous notation, mean that $d\theta = d\beta > 0$.

Let us now investigate, briefly, the impact on asset and exchange markets of $d\alpha = d\theta$ and of the policy swap, $d\theta = d\beta$. We use the symbols Δ and Z to denote the total change in an endogenous interest rate or exchange rate which incorporates $(d\alpha, d\theta)$ and $(d\beta, d\theta)$, respectively.

We discover from our previous findings that:

Table 6.7.

Disturbances/Policies	d_{iD}	d_E	d_{fr}	d_{fp}	d_{ix}
(α,θ)	$-$	$+$	?	?	?
(β,θ)	?	$+$	$+$	?	?

$$\Delta_{id} = [\bar{a}_{33}(\bar{a}_{12} + \bar{a}_{22}) - \bar{a}_{32}(\bar{a}_{13} + \overset{+}{a}_{23})] \, |J|^{-1} \tag{6.42}$$

The negative dominant diagonal (NDD) conditions permit us to deduce $|a_{12} + a_{22}| > |a_{32}|$ and they posit that $|a_{33}| > |a_{13}| + |a_{23}|$, so that the numerator of (6.42) is uniquely positive, hence, $\Delta_{id} < 0$.

$$\Delta_E = [\overset{+}{a}_{31}(\overset{+}{a}_{13} + \overset{+}{a}_{23}) - \bar{a}_{33}(\bar{a}_{11} + \overset{+}{a}_{21})] \, |J|^{-1} \tag{6.43}$$

The NDD conditions themselves allow us to sign this expression uniquely: $\Delta_E > 0$.

$$\Delta_{fr} = [\overset{+}{a}_{32}(\bar{a}_{11} + \overset{+}{a}_{21}) - \bar{a}_{31}(\bar{a}_{12} + \overset{+}{a}_{22})] \, |J|^{-1} \tag{6.44}$$

The NDD enable us to deduce that: $|a_{11} + a_{21}| > |a_{31}|$ and $|a_{22} + a_{12}| > |a_{32}|$, and these two inequalities inform us that the numerator of (6.44) cannot be signed uniquely.

Hence: $\Delta_{fr} \gtreqless 0$.

Now for the results of the swap exchange policy of the Central Bank:

$$Z_{id} = [\bar{a}_{12}(\bar{a}_{31} - \overset{+}{a}_{23}) + a_{13}(\bar{a}_{22} - \overset{+}{a}_{32})] \, |J|^{-1} \tag{6.45}$$

We discover that:

$$Z_{id} \underset{<}{\overset{\geq}{}} 0.$$

$$Z_E = [\overset{+}{a}_{13}(\overset{+}{a}_{31} - \overset{+}{a}_{21}) + \bar{a}_{11}(\overset{+}{a}_{23} - \bar{a}_{33})] \, |J|^{-1} \tag{6.46}$$

We have: $|a_{13}| < |a_{23} - a_{33}|$ and $|a_{31} - a^{21}| < |a_{11}|$, so that the numerator of (6.46) is negative and: $Z_t > 0$.

$$Z_{fr} = [a_{11}(a_{32} - a_{22}) + a_{12}(a_{21} - a_{31})] \, |J|^{-1} \tag{6.47}$$

with $|a_{12}| < |a_{32} - a_{22}|$, we have: $Z_{fr} > 0$.

These results are catalogued in Table 6.7

7.   Capital controls and their consequences for interest rates, exchange rates and the forward premium

a.   The introduction and characteristics of capital controls

During the 1970s major economies such as the United States, Western Germany, Britain and Japan introduced capital controls, at one time or another. It is important to form some view as to the likely repercussions in domestic credit markets, the Eurocurrency markets, and exchange markets of the introduction of such controls. The analysis of those repercussions is the subject of this section; but first we list the possible forms that controls could assume and complete these for the purposes of our analysis. Controls, of course, can be imposed upon Banks or non-banks;[9] we describe these separately.

(i)   Controls on Banks[10]   Financial institutions are almost invariably the first to be subjected to policy measures which are designed by Central Banks and/or Treasuries to regulate financial flows. This is not only because they are the most obvious conduits for internationally mobile funds, but also because the regulatory system for the banking sector is usually well developed; and so the existing instruments only need tailoring to the specific task of reducing the flow of funds out of or into the particular country.

In the category of formal regulations, the traditional tools of reserve requirements, used to control the domestic market, have been used extensively. Special reserve requirements on (1) gross external liabilities, (2) net external liabilities, (3) the level of external liabilities or assets, and on (4) changes in the level of such items have all been used at various times by various countries,[11] to encourage banks to move funds into or out of a national market.

When such measures appear to be ineffective, reserve requirements are 'tightened' in one or more of the following ways:

a)   reserve requirements on external liabilities are increased to 100%;
b)   a prohibition on acceptance of deposits in foreign currency;
c)   a prohibition on acceptance of deposits from non-residents;
d)   imposing ceilings on gross or net external liabilities;
e)   obligatory matching of external assets and liabilities;
f)   control of the term structure of external liabilities; and
g)   a freeze on external liabilities.

(ii)   Controls on Non-banks   The increasing circumvention of controls on banks experienced by Germany and other countries led to experiments with controls on non-banks. The following are some of the more frequently employed methods of restricting the international financial transactions of non-banks:

a)   reserve requirements on external borrowing;
b)   withholding taxes on interest and dividends paid to non-residents;
c)   a prohibition on foreign currency borrowing for internal use;
d)   a prohibition on advanced payments for imports/exports;
e)   control over access of foreign firms to domestic credit markets;
f)   a prohibition of foreign purchases of domestic money market assets, securities and real estate;
g)   restrictions on holding foreign money market investments.

To the extent that it is public or quasi-public entities, such as local authorities, that are involved in undesired foreign borrowing or investing, the government's influence is relatively direct. The private sector proves to be much more difficult to handle, simply because funds can be moved internationally by means of each and every international transaction that, for example, a firm undertakes. If outright foreign borrowing or lending is restricted, funds can be moved through leading or lagging of payments, inventories can be sold to or bought from foreign affiliates, and trade receivables can be carried on the domestic books of foreign 'captive' finance companies or sold to financial institutions abroad. In addition, there are the time-honoured strategies of circumvention through transfer prices, dividend payments or non-payments, and fees for technical services, patents, and overhead allocations.

Obviously, government regulators are aware of these practices, but the authorities face a fundamental dilemma, precisely because funds can be moved by firms in so many ways, a comprehensive system of controls would necessitate scrutinizing each and every transaction that a firm undertakes. This is administratively very difficult to accomplish and prohibitively costly, not only in the sense of enforcement cost but also as a result of damage done to business activity and economic efficiency. However, without being total and comprehensive, all measures regulating the access of non-banks to the external money market remain 'piecemeal'. The end result is usually that the economy incurs the cost of enforcement and suffers the loss of efficiency caused by the controls that have been imposed, and yet the desired effect remains 'elusive' because funds flow through alternative channels.

In our model we could consider controls on banks and non-banks, since we have included those, and other, sectors explicitly. However, since we have telescoped our model to one essentially in three key rates, and to one which is highly aggregative, with its focus the relevant market excess demand function, we shall consider the imposition of controls in a general way, which is consonant with our general framework. We can readily incorporate the different methods of capital controls into our excess demand functions, even though they are an amalgam of the behaviour of divergent market participants.

We might think of capital controls as having two broad objectives, either to reduce capital inflow or to reduce capital outflow. It is not too extravagant a generalization to state that capital controls imposed to meet the one objective will have opposite market implications from those employed to meet the other objective: though it is not a universally true proposition. So, we will only analyse the consequences of the Central Bank's attempt to limit capital outflow.

b.   The effects of capital control
It is self-evident that policies designed to restrict capital inflow into the domestic (UK) economy will influence foreigners' demand for domestic assets, hence their demand for sterling (so, their supply of dollars on the spot market) and their behaviour in the forward market. Referring back to the list (a) – (g) of possible controls on capital movements initiated by non-banks, it is apparent that items such as (b), (e) and (f), if introduced would affect foreigners' attitudes in all three markets.

If (e) and (f) were operative (rather than (b)) it would be valid to model the imposition of capital controls by means of 'shift parameters' in the excess demand functions for all three 'endogenous' markets. In other words, at a given domestic interest rate (and for given values of other factors germane to their portfolio choice) the foreigners' demand schedule for domestic securities (domestic credit) would shift to reveal a lower demand. *Ceteris paribus*, this reduction in the demand for UK assets would cause the (assumed-to-be-in-equilibrium) excess demand in the spot market for dollars to be disturbed: it would increase consequent upon the change in market structure manufactured by the capital controls, because the *ceteris paribus* supply of spot dollars would be reduced. To the extent that foreign investors cover the future income from, or sale of, their purchases of UK assets by buying forward dollars, capital controls will create, on impact, an excess supply of forward dollars.

To the extent that the capital controls are many-faceted and embody a 'tax' element on foreigners investment income in the UK (item (b) in our preceding list), this too could, in part, be modelled, by a lowering of the demand, at any interest rate, for UK securities. But, to that average interest decline, as it were, we could argue that, in Tobinesque fashion (1968, 1969), there is marginal effect on demand, since the degree of substitutability at the margin, as interest rates change, between domestic and foreign assets is likely to decline for foreigners. Accordingly, the partial derivative of the excess demand function with respect to i_d could fall; so too then would the partial derivatives in the excess demand function in the exchange markets. They would all have similar absolute values. The problem with this conceptualization of the behavioural impact of capital controls is that it could be argued that all of the partial derivatives of all of the excess demand functions should change. One escape from the inevitable intractability such a possibility possesses for formal analysis, is to assume that those foreigners who purchase domestic assets have a small share in the volume of activity on both the spot and forward exchange markets; it would be possible, therefore, to argue that either only the partial derivative with respect to the domestic rate of interest changes noticeably in those markets, or that it too changes imperceptibly. In that event, the domestic securities market is the focus of attention; and there, if foreigners play a significant role in it (as they must by virtue of the fact that there is a Central Bank capital control strategy), all partial derivatives of the excess demand function should alter if type (b) capital control is regarded as having a substantial influence on asset substitutability.

Since we do not have sufficient space to carry out a taxonomic exercise we shall have to limit ourselves to two polar cases: (i) capital controls are of type (e) and (f) on foreign residents; and (ii), capital controls embrace type (b) controls and, given market strength, are taken as altering the 'elasticities' of the excess demand function for domestic (UK) securities. As well as the broader consideration of type (b) we have mentioned in the preceding paragraph, (i) and (ii) could, of course, be combined.

(i)   Quantitative controls on foreign holdings of domestic assets   Case (i) can be accorded the short-hand 'quantitative controls'. They can be formalized by the following excess demand functions:

$$-X_c = -X_c(i_d, E, fr, i_f, K_c) \tag{6.48}$$

$$X_E = X_E(i_d, E, fr, i_f, K_E) \tag{6.49}$$

$$X_{fr} = X_{fr}(i_d, E, fr, i_f, K_{fr}) \tag{6.50}$$

The K_i are capital control shift parameters: K_c is negative, as that excess supply rises with capital controls; K_E is positive; and K_{fr} is negative. Again, the effect of these shift parameters is analysed by taking their derivatives (and hence, strictly speaking, assuming that initial $k_i = 0$, hence $dk_i = k_i$). Those effects, self-evidently, have been obtained previously, for Central Banks interventionist strategies in the version of the model where there were no capital controls.

To recapitulate: *ceteris paribus*, when d_{kc} is negative this is the same as an open market sale of securities by the Central Bank ($d\alpha < 0$); $dK_E = d\theta$, i.e. it is equivalent, in principle, to a purchase of spot dollars by the

Central Bank; and $dK_{fr} = -d\beta$, being similar to a Central Bank sale of forward dollars, or to a sudden, once-for-all, fall in the *orders* for home exports.

Combining our earlier findings we see that the forward rate will definitely decline if the impact of the credit market on that rate is relatively small. The spot exchange rate will increase so long as the effect of a *ceteris paribus* sale of forward dollars by the Central Bank (i.e. $-d\beta = dk_{fr}$) is minimal, or is dominated by the impacts on the spot rate produced by the product of the *ceteris paribus* changes emanating from a Central Bank sale of domestic securities ($-d\alpha = dk_c$) and a Central Bank purchase of spot dollars ($d\theta = dK_E$). It is also likely that the domestic interest rate will increase consequent upon the imposition of capital controls. Only if the downward pressure on the domestic rate, which is generated from the excess demand in the spot market, can dominate the upward pressure exerted on that rate by the shifts in excess demand brought about by capital controls in the securities (credit) and forward markets, would the domestic interest fall.

Such outcomes have an *a priori* appeal and admit of an immediate economic rationalization. They will lead to a reduction in the forward premium: we could also conclude, therefore, that the Eurosterling rate would fall. That can only be accomplished, naturally, on the supposition that the capital controls, which, *ex definitione*, divert part of foreign residents' portfolios to the Eurodollar market and to the foreign (US) asset markets, have, at the most, only a marginal impact on those markets.

(ii) 'Price-effect' capital controls Suppose then, by way of contrast, that the net effect of the capital controls, given market behaviour and market concentration, as it were, is felt in the domestic securities market, and manifests itself in lowering the domestic interest sensitivity of excess demand there (and, by symmetry, it must increase the sensitivity of excess demand to alterations in the foreign/Eurodollar interest rate); it will also, *ceteris paribus*, reduce the spot exchange rate 'elasticity' of excess demand, and its forward rate 'elasticity' (i.e. in that case, the *absolute value* of the partial derivative of excess demand with respect to the forward rate will increase).

In deriving the adjustments to the small open economy and its various financial markets of this kind of capital control we are not examining exogenous changes, disturbances or policy changes. Therefore, to draw any conclusions it is necessary to assume that we can obtain a solution to our model for the levels of the interest rates and exchange rates. Hence, we assume that the excess demand function can be expanded in linear form; even so, the comparative statics result which emerges therefrom can only have relevance around the pre-capital control era.

From our now familiar system of equations we deduce that (with all exogenous variables, including i_f taken as constant):

$$J\,dy = N \tag{6.51}$$

Here: J and dy are as defined in (6.25) and (6.26). N is:

$$N = [\; -(i_d da_{11} + E\,da_{12} + fr\,da_{13})\quad 0\quad 0]' \tag{6.52}$$

Recall that: $a_{11}<0;\; a_{12}<0;\; a_{13}>0$. In view of the fact that, given these signs, all three must increase (in the true mathematical sense), the first element in N is negative, and let us label that element I. Then these results are immediate:

$$d_{id} = \bar{I}\,[a_{22}a_{33} \overset{+}{-} a_{32}a_{33}]\,|J|^{-1} > 0 \tag{6.53}$$

The NDD axiom signs the change in the domestic interest rate uniquely.

$$d_E = \bar{I}\,[a_{31}a_{23} \overset{+}{-} a_{21}a_{33}]\,|J|^{-1} > 0 \tag{6.54}$$

and

$$d_{fr} = \bar{I}\,[a_{21}a_{32} \overset{+}{-} a_{31}a_{22}]\,|J|^{-1} > 0 \tag{6.55}$$

All of these adjustments to the interest and the forward exchange rate are as expected; with no compensating adjustments to the interest rate derivatives in the excess demand functions in the exchange markets, the changes in the rates are likely to be different, qualitatively, to the consequences of capital control which can be captured by shift parameters in the three excess demand functions. Here only one market is affected *directly* by capital controls.

The theoretical analysis of capital controls can permit us to advance some propositions, even though we have not here provided a comprehensive, taxonomic analysis of them. On the assumptions we have made about the asymmetry between foreign Eurocurrency markets and the domestic (UK) market we can offer these suggestions to complement the policy conclusions we have provided in Tables 6.6 and 6.7; capital controls (on inflow) will:

(a) increase the domestic interest;
(b) decrease the dollar forward rate;
(c) increase the spot dollar rate;

(d)   lower the forward premium;

(e)   reduce the Eurosterling rate; and,

(f)   if with no capital controls, the UK domestic rate approximated the Eurosterling rate (and, as noted before, arbitrage by Domestic Banks between the Domestic Bankers and the Eurocurrency markets, which we could admit by re-structuring the portfolio balance sheets, could be shown to lead to that outcome), capital controls will raise the UK rate above the Eurosterling rate. In that case, by covered interest parity UK Banks would make sure that the domestic rate of interest equalled the Eurodollar rate plus the forward premium: since covered interest parity obtains in the Eurocurrency/US market, the Eurosterling rate also equals the Eurodollar rate plus the forward premium.

There have, indeed, been recent econometric investigations of the effect of capital controls on domestic interest rates, Eurocurrency currency rates, exchange rates, and foreign interest rates. These have been for West Germany (see Johnston 1979) and Japan (see Ichiro and Siddharth 1983). Eurocurrency markets have been studied by, for example, Johnston (1982). We have also undertaken our own tests for the UK and these as with the empirical work for West Germany and Japan broadly substantiate our boldly-made propositions (see note 11). In addition, we have following the use of Granger Sims causality tests adopted by Kaen and Hachey (1983), conducted an investigation into the relationship between the Eurosterling rate (i_x) and the domestic (UK) interest rate for the period 1972.04 – 1987.09 (i.e. without and with capital controls). Those tests confirm that the exchange controls which were operative until October 1979 did divorce the UK market from the external markets. Removal of exchange control from October 1979 restores the interest parity relationship between the domestic interest rate with Eurodollar interest rate, implying that there is a close relationship between internal and external markets after the abolition. Causality tests indicate that the results for periods 1979.10 – 1985.12 support the view that interest rates in domestic currency markets adjust more quickly to changing conditions than do external markets denominated in the same currency. We suggest that the monetary or economic changes during the period may be originated in the domestic market and this change immediately influences the domestic credit market and exchange markets, then the external market subsequently responds to this change through the arbitrage activities. However, the contemporaneous causality is observed during 1986–1987, denoting that Eurosterling interest rate (i_x) and domestic interest rate (i_d) changes (first differences) move together, or jointly determine one another during this period.

8. Summary

In this paper we have specified a model of the monetary sector of a small open economy integrated with external financial markets, in the foreign country and Eurocurrency markets, and integrated with spot and forward exchange markets, under a system of flexible exchange rates. The framework we have developed is in the spirit of the balance sheet, financial markets, approach of Tobin, taking the real sector activity as given at the time; that is a limitation also of many other studies of interest rates or asset prices. The model we have developed is a derivative in a way of that of Black (1973), using features contained in Briault and Hanson (1982) and Johnston (1979): though we hope we have contributed some mildly original analysis to the investigation of domestic, foreign and Eurocurrency interest rates, determined jointly with spot/forward exchange rates.

We have made a strong behavioural assumption in postulating that as far as the dealings of non-bank agents are concerned, only foreign (US) residents are active in the Eurocurrency market. *Ceteris paribus*, this permits some de-coupling of 'external' asset markets from the domestic (UK) economy: the Eurobanks will act, in maximizing profit, for given transactions costs, to fix the Eurodollar rate to the dollar interest rate (i.e. to the US interest rate). If we normalize transaction costs at zero, for the sake of argument, the Eurobanks will also engage in arbitrage activities that maximize their profits, to the effect that the market will generate a Eurosterling rate that has covered interest policy with the Eurodollar rate: that is, the Eurosterling rate will equal the Eurodollar rate plus the forward premium in the exchange markets (on dollars).

It is then possible to study the domestic financial market and the exchange markets to determine the equilibrium values of the domestic interest, the spot exchange rate and the forward exchange rate. In a sense this means that the US and Eurocurrency market activity is given; so that we have a situation analogous to the conventional one in the context of a small open economy, in that the Eurocurrency market can be envisaged as an extension of the rest of the world's financial markets to include a wider range of assets. However, our model diverges from the conventional one because the increased variety of financial claims does matter: activity in the domestic/exchange markets will affect the markets in the rest of the world because they can, in addition to altering the domestic interest rate *vis-à-vis* the foreign (US domestic) interest rate, produce adjustments in the forward premium, hence, in the Eurosterling rate. This will happen even if we were to argue that under free movement of capital, arbitrage between Domestic Banks and Eurobanks would occur and would produce covered interest parity between the domestic rate and the Eurodollar rate (so that the domestic rate of interest on sterling assets (i_d) was equated with the Eurosterling rate (i_x)).[12] Additionally, the inclusion of the Eurocurrency markets (whether or not Deposit Banks are involved in the activities of the Eurobanks) as an extension of the US market, enables the alternative policy instruments that are at the disposal of the Central Bank in the real world (i.e., it could deal in the Eurocurrency market) to be analysed, and it shows the qualitative effects of various Central Bank policies in a more realistic setting. Whilst those effects are at times similar to those generated from orthodox small country – rest of the world paradigms, they will be different quantitatively (the elements of the Jacobian will change non-proportionately).

Our model has permitted us to investigate the possible implications for asset and exchange markets of capital control. Although we could not cover all manifestations of such controls on the various markets, we did consider two likely ones and their combined pressure. Controls to limit capital inflow (the findings are the reverse of those, of course, for *particular* measures introduced to reduce capital outflow) would tend to reduce the domestic interest rate, because investment in the domestic financial market is reduced in attractiveness compared with investment in the Eurocurrency on foreign asset markets (or investment in the domestic market is actually rationed), and as a consequence, lower the forward rate on dollars, with the effect on the spot rate ambiguous because the on-impact excess demand in the spot market is countered by the change to the domestic interest rate and the forward rate. If the monetary authorities seek for macro-stabilization purposes to lower the domestic rate then 'quantitative' capital controls would be an appropriate strategy: if at the same time it was felt desirable to increase the spot exchange rate this could be feasible, but is a numerical (empirical) question as to whether E would rise. A better way of raising E must be to tax foreigners income from domestic securities: this will limit capital inflow and raise E, as we have seen; however, such a 'price' based form of capital control will reduce capital outflow compared with the case of surfeit capital mobility. So it could be classed as either reducing capital inflow or reducing capital outflow.

The kinds of multiple effects we have suggested might hold for capital controls, with respect to domestic interest rate, the spot exchange rate, the forward rate, the forward premium, and the Eurosterling rate seen to be borne out by the empirical evidence. That evidence shows, as expected, that capital control does insulate the domestic economy to some extent from external financial markets: the domestic interest rate increases and moves away from the Eurosterling interest rate, to which, under perfect capital mobility it will be similar or identical, with arbitrage between Domestic and Eurobanks.

Notes

1. In Marston (1972, 1976), the relationship between Eurocurrency rates and forward premiums is investigated in detail. Over the 7-year period 1965–71 the Eurocurrency rates and forward premiums for the principal Eurocurrencies, the Deutschmark, Swiss franc, and Sterling, are shown to adhere closely to interest parity with respect to the Eurodollar rate. Aliber (1973) also presents evidence that Eurocurrency rates are maintained at parity. It should be noticed that under fixed exchange rate regime, the forward premium can be investigated only by forward exchange rate since spot rate is fixed, while under flexible exchange rates regime, forward premium is determined by both spot rate and forward rate at the same time as spot rate is flexible in this regime.

2. This risk that capital controls might be imposed on financial centres is an important factor limiting arbitrage involving national investments. But the risk of capital controls is of minimal importance in transactions between Eurocurrencies simply because it is unlikely that future capital controls would be applied to one Eurocurrency market and not another. Although governments have compelling reasons to formulate special regulations for transactions in securities denominated in the home currency, there is no incentive for them to formulate regulations which discriminate among securities denominated in different foreign currencies. See Aliber (1973) and Marston (1972, 1976).

3. In practice the Eurobanks also maintain transactions balance with US and British banks. In Section 4 we will consider the case where British domestic banks make transaction with Eurobanks.

4. Since the Eurobanks set i_x equal to $i_f + fp$, covered investment (or borrowing) of Eurosterling by non-banks is generally unprofitable, and therefore can be neglected. Denoting covered investment (borrowing) by $êS^D = êS^L = 0$.

5. The Eurobanks may require some margin between the rate paid on Eurodollar deposits (adjusted for forward cover) and the rate of interest on Eurosterling loans, but that margin is assumed to be constant over the relevant range of net currency positions undertaken by Eurobanks. For convenience, we have assumed the margin to be zero.

6. Wherever exchange markets exist between currencies, then Euro-deposit rates of two Eurocurrencies will equal the cost of conversion spot and reconversion forward. If not, arbitrage operations will bring them back into line.

7. Let us assume that:

$$\dot{i}_d = -\lambda_1(X_c) \tag{i}$$

$$\dot{E} = \lambda_2(X_E) \tag{ii}$$

$$\dot{fr} = \lambda_3(X_{fr}) \tag{iii}$$

A dot over a variable indicates a time derivative; $\lambda_i > 0$ and these are adjustment coefficients.

For given values of the exogenous/policy variables let:

$$-X_c = -X_c(\overset{+}{i_d}, \overset{+}{E}, \overset{-}{fr}) \tag{iv}$$

$$X_E = X_E(\overset{-}{i_d}, \overset{-}{E}, \overset{+}{fr}) \tag{v}$$

$$X_{fr} = X_{fr}(\overset{+}{i_d}, \overset{+}{E}, \overset{-}{fr}) \tag{vi}$$

The impact of fp, the forward premium, on all excess demand function, has been incorporated via E and fr. Write the Jacobian of (iv) – (vi) as:

$$J = \begin{bmatrix} \overset{-}{a_{11}} & \overset{-}{a_{12}} & \overset{+}{a_{13}} \\ \overset{-}{a_{21}} & \overset{-}{a_{22}} & \overset{+}{a_{23}} \\ \overset{+}{a_{31}} & \overset{+}{a_{32}} & \overset{-}{a_{33}} \end{bmatrix} \tag{vii}$$

If, following Black (1973), we assume that J has a negative dominant diagonal (NDD):

$$|a_{11}| > |a_{21}| + |a_{31}|; \quad |a_{22}| > |a_{12}| + |a_{32}|; \quad |a_{33}| > |a_{13}| + |a_{23}| \tag{viii}$$

it will follow that all three Routhian necessary and sufficient conditions for the system (i) – (iii) to be stable will be satisfied unambiguously. We know that Trace $(J) < 0$, but, by *expanding J diagonally*, $|J| < 0$ and:

$$[(a_{11}a_{22} - a_{21}a_{12}) + (a_{11}a_{33} - a_{31}a_{13}) + (a_{22}a_{33} - a_{32}a_{23})] > 0$$

Now, consider Figure 6.3. The slope of $S'E'$ is $-a_{22}/a_{23}$ and the slope of $F'E'$ is $-a_{32}/a_{33}$. If we take the second and third rows of J, the NDD hypothesis tells us that:

$$\overset{-}{a_{22}}\overset{-}{a_{33}} - \overset{+}{a_{32}}\overset{+}{a_{23}} > 0 \tag{ix}$$

Hence:

$$-\frac{a_{22}}{a_{23}} > -\frac{a_{32}}{a_{33}} \tag{x}$$

$S'E'$ does have a greater slope than $F'E'$

8. The numerators in all the multiplier effects, naturally, involve the (three) relative slopes of two of the excess demand equations in two-dimensional space. One of those relative slopes is signed at the outset by the NDD axiom, so only one other can be chosen: the third is implied by that relative slope and NDD. But we have to be careful to avoid contradicting transitivity conditions with respect to relative slopes specified for the three pairs of equations. In fact, we discover that only two sets of signs for the minors of J are internally consistent once NDD is assumed. The stronger of these sets is the one we have used in the text, labelled simply set 1. It is:

   1. $(a_{11}a_{22} - a_{21}a_{12}) > 0$ by NDD
   2. $(a_{12}a_{23} - a_{22}a_{13}) < 0$
   3. $(a_{11}a_{23} - a_{21}a_{13}) < 0$
   4. $(a_{22}a_{33} - a_{32}a_{23}) > 0$ by NDD
   5. $(a_{21}a_{32} - a_{31}a_{22}) > 0$
   6. $(a_{21}a_{33} - a_{31}a_{23}) > 0$
   7. $(a_{11}a_{33} - a_{31}a_{13}) > 0$ by NDD
   8. $(a_{11}a_{32} - a_{31}a_{12}) > 0$
   9. $(a_{12}a_{33} - a_{32}a_{13}) > 0$

   For set 2: 2, 5 and 8 have their signs reversed, and 3 and 9 can be either positive or negative.
   In equations (6.37) – (6.39) later on in the text:

   $$\lambda_1 = 4; \quad \lambda_2 = 7; \quad \lambda_3 = 1;$$

   $$\mu_1 = 9; \quad \mu_2 = 3; \quad \mu_3 = 5;$$

   $$\epsilon_1 = 2; \quad \epsilon_2 = 6; \quad \text{and } \epsilon_3 = 8.$$

9. See G. Dufey and I. H. Giddy (1978), pp198–203.
10. This section follows an outline presented by David T. Llewellyn.
11. Rodney H. Mills (1972).

12. We have mentioned this possibility before, if there is free movement of capital. In reality Domestic Banks assume an active role in the Eurocurrency market. Given sufficient incentive, they may borrow Eurosterling to increase their domestic currency loans or they can borrow Eurodollars, converting them into sterling in order to increase their domestic sterling loans. In the latter case, assuming that transaction costs were zero, such a swap strategy would be engaged in until $i_d = i_f + fp$. In that case, $i_d = i_x$ (again, as Johnston (1979) suggested might be the case).

Appendix
The pseudo-dynamics of the model
Let us assume that:

$$\dot{i}_d = -\mu_1(X_c) \tag{A1}$$
$$\dot{E} = \mu_2(X_E) \tag{A2}$$
$$\dot{fr} = \mu_3(X_{fr}) \tag{A3}$$

Here: a dot over a variable indicates a time derivative; μ_i are (positive) speeds of adjustment. In order that we can consider global solutions for i_d, E and f as a function solely of time, let us further suppose that the excess demand functions (X_j) are linear in their arguments. Accordingly, for changes in exogenous or policy variables we leave the partial derivatives (the a_{ij}) of the excess demand functions undisturbed. Hence, *ceteris paribus*, the solution of the third-order differential equation system will permit us to comment on the *traverse*.

For given values of the exogenous variables $(E^e, i_f$ and policy shift or other exogenous variables) we can write the system (A1) – (A3) as:

$$\begin{bmatrix} \dot{i}_d \\ \dot{E} \\ \dot{fr} \end{bmatrix} = J \begin{bmatrix} i_d \\ E \\ fr \end{bmatrix} \tag{A4}$$

where J is the Jacobian of the main text.

For given values of exogenous variables there will be equilibrium levels for each of the endogenous variables, which we denote by a bar over each one; and we can therefore set out the solution for the third order system (A4) as:

$$\begin{bmatrix} i_d(t) \\ E(t) \\ fr(t) \end{bmatrix} = \begin{bmatrix} \bar{i}_d \\ \bar{E} \\ \bar{fr} \end{bmatrix} + \begin{bmatrix} K_1 A_1 & K_2 A_2 & K_3 A_3 \\ K_1 B_1 & K_2 B_2 & K_3 B_3 \\ K_1 C_1 & K_2 C_2 & K_3 C_3 \end{bmatrix} \begin{bmatrix} e^{\lambda_1 t} \\ e^{\lambda_2 t} \\ e^{\lambda_3 t} \end{bmatrix} \tag{A5}$$

Here: t denotes time; K_i are constants to be determined by the initial conditions in the system; λ_i are the characteristic roots of J; e is the Naperian e; and A_i, B_i, C_i, are constants obtained from the characteristic equation of J, for each λ_i:

$$|J - \lambda I| = 0 \tag{A6}$$

Given the properties of J (it possesses, we recall, the Routhian necessary and sufficient conditions for the system to be dynamically stable) the λ_i all have negative real parts.

In expanded form, equation (A6) is:

$$\lambda^3 + a_1\lambda^3 + a_2\lambda + a_3 = 0 \tag{A7}$$

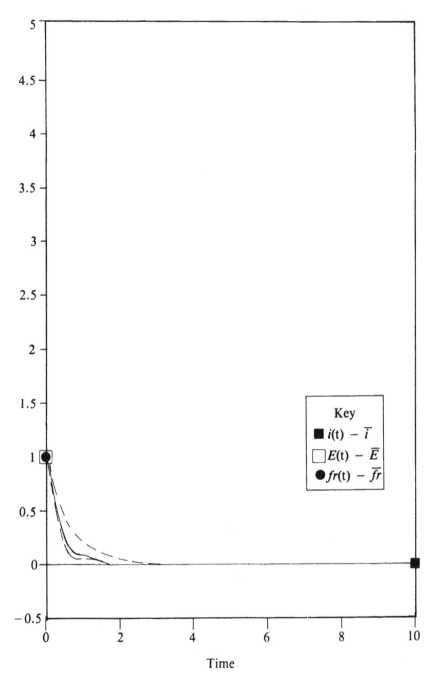

Figure 6.4

Here:

$a_1 = -\text{Trace}(J); \; a_3 = -|J|$ and;
$a_2 = [(a_{11}a_{22} - a_{21}a_{12}) + (a_{11}a_{33} - a_{31}a_{13}) + (a_{22}a_{33} - a_{32}a_{23})]$

To solve (A7) analytically we could resort to Cardan's method, but this yields little of value without some information about the actual values of the a_{ij} or at least of the Trace of J. So, we proceeded straightaway to a numerical solution to the model. We let:

$$J = \begin{bmatrix} -0.8 & -3.0 & 0.25 \\ -0.5 & -4.0 & 0.75 \\ 0.2 & 0.7 & -1.5 \end{bmatrix} \qquad (A8)$$

The resulting solutions for the endogenous variables, with starting values assumed to be $(i_d = 1; E = 1; fr = 1)$ are:

$$i_d(t) - \bar{i}_d = 0.64e^{-4.61t} + 0.445e^{-1.26t} - 0.075e^{-0.42t} \qquad (A9)$$
$$E(t) - \bar{E} = 0.85e^{-4.61t} + 0.133e^{-1.26t} + 0.009e^{-0.42t} \qquad (A10)$$
$$fr(t) - \bar{fr} = 0.227e^{-4.61t} + 0.781e^{-1.26t} - 0.008e^{-0.42t} \qquad (A11)$$

The time paths that these variables will take around their equilibrium level once it has been disturbed by a once-and-for-all disturbance are depicted in Figure 6.4.

These time paths are also the routes which the domestic interest rate, the exchange rate and the forward exchange rate, will follow when they move to a new equilibrium as the old one is shifted because of Central Bank policy intervention in markets, by Central Bank 'quantitative' capital controls, and the other kinds of exogenous disturbances we have analysed in the main text. In this representation of the UK Eurocurrency Exchange and US financial markets, all the interest and exchange rates adjust smoothly to their new equilibrium. There is no question here of Dornbusch overshooting: but, of course, that cannot be ruled out, because the elasticities of the excess demand functions could be such that they continue to produce complex roots from J's characteristic equation. Although we cannot consider the cyclical, and possibly, divergent, cyclical movements of the endogenous variables, we can see from Figure 6.4 which markets adjust the quickest initially and what the form of 'causality' happens to be.

References

Aliber, R. Z. (1973) 'The interest rate parity theorem: a reinterpretation', *Journal of Political Economy*, Nov./Dec., pp1451-1459.

Black, S. W. (1973) 'International money markets and flexible exchange rates', *Princeton Studies in International Finance*, No.32.

Brainard, W. C. and Tobin, J. (1968) 'Pitfalls in financial model-building', *American Economic Review*, vol.58, May, pp 99–122.

Briault, C. B. and Howson, S. K. (1982) 'A portfolio model of domestic and external financial markets', *Discussion Paper No.20*, Bank of England.

Brunner, K. (1973) 'Money supply process and monetary policy in an open economy', in M. B. Conolly and A. K. Sweden, (eds) *International Trade and Money*, London, pp127-166.

Dufey, G. and Giddy, I. H. (1978) *The International Money Market*, Prentice-Hall, Englewood Cliffs, N. J.

Fratianni, M. (1976) 'Domestic bank credit, money and the open economy', in M. Fratianni and K. Tavernier (ed), *Bank Credit, Money and Inflation in Open Economics*, supplement to *Kredit und Kapital*, Berlin, Drucker and Humblot, p142.

Ichiro, O. and Siddhart, T. (1983) 'Capital control and interest rate parity: the Japanese experience, 1978–1981', *IMF Staff Papers*, pp793–815.

Johnston, R. B. (1979) 'Some aspects of the determination of Eurocurrency interest rates', *Bank of England Quarterly Bulletin*, vol.19(1), pp35–46.

Johnston, R. B. (1982) *The Economics of the Euro-market: History, Theory and Policy*, Macmillan, London.

Kaen, F. R. and Hachey, G. A. (1983) 'Eurocurrency and national money market interest rates: an empirical investigation of causality', *Journal of Money, Credit and Banking*, vol.15, August, pp327–338.

Marston, R. C. (1972) *The Structure of the Eurocurrency system*, Unpublished PhD, MIT, Cambridge, Mass.

Marston, R. C. (1976) 'Interest arbitrage in the Eurocurrency market', *European Economic Review*, Jan., pp1–13.

Mills, R. H. (1972) 'Regulation on short-term capital movements: recent techniques in selected industrial countries', *Discussion Paper*, Federal Reserve Board, Washington, D.C., November.

Tobin, J. (1969) 'A general equilibrium approach to monetary theory', *Journal of Money, Credit and Banking*, vol.1, pp15–29.

7. Devaluation, demand and supply disturbances in a macroeconomic model of a mineral exporting LDC

1 Introduction

In the concluding chapter to his seminal work on the macroeconomics of developing nations, Taylor (1983) points out:

> Each economy confronts a special set of structural constraints . . . these restrictions vary greatly from place to place and time to time.
>
> (Taylor 1983, p190)

Not only is he alluding to the heterogeneity of the structural characteristics of developing countries, but also the differing prospects that could emerge from short-run and longer-run analyses. Our purpose, in this paper, is to acknowledge that: we examine the nature of macroeconomic equilibrium for a specific type of economy, over both short and long-run; differing from much of the (known) existing literature in characterization (of the long-run), solution technique (long-run), as well as some results, over both time horizons. In what follows, we look at supply shocks, productivity changes, the wage process and balance of payments considerations.

We believe these variables are of major importance to the type of economy we shall consider; and unlike most of the literature we examine the multiplicity of these exogenous changes in one model, instead of merely considering one or two. We hope to capture the macroeconomic nuances and the heterogeneity of a multi-good economy. Our focus will thus be on the real as opposed to the financial side of the economy.

The economy in question is a small open developing country. It is a major exporter of a mineral, relative to its size. It also imports an important and non-substitutable capital input for its modern (industrial) sector's production process. The export component of the modern sector is so insignificant that it can be considered non-traded. By contrast, part of the output of the traditional sector is exported. Such a characterization, quite obviously conforms to the case of a small semi-industrialized country which exports a mineral and a primary (agricultural) product, pursues an import substitution industrialization (ISI) strategy, but is completely dependent on imported capital equipment; but the model is not applicable to large countries such as Brazil, China or India.

The short-run variant of our model has many features of the models in the Taylor (1983) and Dornbusch (1980) traded/non-traded goods model. But some new results do emerge. Supply shocks or their converse in the traded goods sector and productivity changes in the non-traded goods sector can lead to *counter-intuitive results*. These include an immiserizing effect of rises in the traded good output upon the rest of the economy, and adverse effects emanating from improvements in labour productivity in the non-traded goods sector. There are elements of the Dutch disease which could arise from increases in mineral export revenues. We find, however, the potential for contractionary devaluation as in Krugman and Taylor (1978), *but* the converse could also occur.

The long-run characterization of our model is principally concerned with the dynamic steady-state version of equilibrium in the various markets or sectors of the economy; the Taylor (1983) models focus mainly on the convergence of sectoral growth rates. To meet our objective, for example, we endogenize the exchange rate: it is a state variable bringing about balance of trade equilibrium, which may not occur, or may not be desirable, in the short-run. Our treatment of the wage process also differs in the long-run. Nominal wages are fixed in the short-run but can be varied in the long-run, thus, there is real wage resistance. Here our treatment of the dynamics differs. The wage dynamics in the medium-run can lead to 'steady-state' inflation, as in Cardoso (1981); or cause saddle-path instability, as in Murshed and Sen (1988). In the long-run a 'proper' steady-state could require a *reversal* of the adjustment process of the wage dynamics, as will become apparent in section 4, providing a novel method of closure for models exhibiting real wage resistance and the possibility of structural inflation. The effects of supply shocks and productivity changes are different in the long-run, from the short-run analysis. More interestingly, export biased productivity growth is more welfare enhancing, as in Hicks (1953). One of the innovations of our paper is the use of a numerical solution technique for the long-run steady-state, since an analytical solution is intractable.

The plan of the rest of the paper is as follows: Section 2 contains a sketch of the salient features of the model; Sections 3 and 4 contain the short-run and long-run analysis, respectively; Section 5 presents some conclusions and finally the numerical version of the long-run model is described in an Appendix.

2. The model

As mentioned in the introduction the model outlined below is best suited to describe a small open less developed economy (LDC), which is also a mineral exporter. To this end, we sub-divide the economy into three broad sectors, a traded good (*T*) sector, a non-traded good (*N*) sector and a mineral export (x) sector. Furthermore, we introduce an important imported intermediate input (m), which enters the production process of the non-traded good (N).

We begin by specifying the national income identity for such an economy:

$$Y = EP_x^* \bar{Q}_x + (P_N - EP_m^* m)Q_N + P_T \bar{Q}_T \qquad (7.1)$$

where Y denotes domestic national income (or GDP) in domestic currency units; Q_x is the output of the mineral, which we shall call oil, P_x^* is the given world price of oil, E is the (nominal) exchange rate. Q_N represents output in the non-traded goods sector, P_N is its price; $EP_m^* m$ is the domestic value added of the imported intermediate input in Q_N production where, P_m^* is the exogenous world price of the intermediate input and m its input coefficient. P_T and Q_T are the prices and output of the traded good, respectively.

The traded goods sector corresponds closely to the traditional sector in most LDCs. We postulate that at any point in time, output in that sector, Q_T, is inelastically supplied. This is likely to be the case given the presence of surplus labour in that sector à la Lewis (1954), and other constraining factors such as land and/or capital available for that sector. This allows Q_T to be exogenous in the short-run. Domestic demand for the traded good, D_T, will be a positive function of income, Y, and a negative function of the domestic terms of trade, P_T/P_N. Foreign demand for the domestic traded good, F, is a function of the international terms of trade, P_T/E; foreign demand for Q_T falls as P_T/E rises. Accordingly, the following provides the equilibrium condition for the traded goods sector (after normalizing by P_T):

$$\bar{Q}_T = D_T (Y, P_T/P_N) + F(P_T/E) \qquad (7.2)$$

where $D_{T1} > 0$, $D_{T2} < 0$ and $F_1 < 0$. Following the classification proposed by Hicks we make the traded goods sector a flex-price market. In other words, excess demands will lead to the price, P_T, being bid up and vice versa for excess supply. The nature of the commodity produced in the traded (traditional) sector coupled with its inelastic supply permits us to assume the existence of a Walrasian (classical) price adjustment process. This assumption is also to be found in similar models, such as that of Taylor (1983).

The non-traded goods sector, by contrast, exhibits fix-price characteristics. In other words, excess demands/supplies lead to quantity adjustments. This assumption, is predicated on the presence of spare or underutilized capacity in that sector. We interpret the term fix-price to mean that the price in the non-traded goods sector is determined by cost considerations, as will be outlined below. As such, non-tradeables, Q_N represent the output of manufactures which are substitutes for importables, not for export, arising out of an import substitution industrialization strategy. It is reasonable to assume that they require imported capital inputs. Within the broad category of the non-traded sector, we could also include the production of public services such as housing, communications networks etc. We assume that the demand for non-tradeables, D_N is a positive function of Y and a negative function of P_N (positive function of P_T/P_N). Thus, in equilibrium:

$$Q_N = D_N(Y, P_T/P_N) \tag{7.3}$$

where $D_{N1} > 0$ and $D_{N2} > 0$.

Following the practice in Dornbusch (1980) and Taylor (1983) we make the price of the non-traded good, P_N, a mark-up on wage costs given productivity and imported intermediate input costs:

$$P_N = (1 + g)[\beta W + EP_m{}^*m] \tag{7.4}$$

where g is the desired profit rate of firms in the N sector; ß is the inverse of labour productivity, the labour-output ratio; W the money wage rate in domestic currency units; and $EP_m{}^*m$ the domestic value added of the intermediate input. We let the different parameters in the price equation (7.4) be pre-determined or exogenous in the short run, allowing us to treat P_N as 'given'. In what follows we vary some of these parameters.

We assume the world price of the mineral export, oil, $P_x{}^*$, is given and the quantity to be exported Q_x is a planning decision by the government. Thus we can write oil revenues, $EP_x{}^*\bar{Q}_x = R$. There is no other source of autonomous expenditure.

Lastly, we come to the current account balance, for our small open economy:

$$B = R + P_T F(P_T/E) - EP_m{}^*mQ_N \tag{7.5}$$

We have a fixed exchange rate regime, E, is fixed in the short run. Many LDCs follow a policy of fixing their currency value to the US dollar, say, varying it at discrete intervals, to pursue balance of payments objectives as in a crawling peg. Another policy objective might be to maintain a desired domestic value of imported inputs, so as to keep up buoyant demand for domestic import substitutes which use imported inputs, or to avoid inflation through rising domestic goods prices. Following Taylor (1983) we ignore consumption imports on the grounds that they are negligible or because the domestic non-traded sector is a substitute for them.

If we substitute (7.1) into (7.2) and (7.3); and treat (7.4) as fixed, or substitute it in as needed, the model collapses into (7.2), (7.3) and (7.5) in three unknowns P_T, Q_N and B. Furthermore, once we have obtained P_T, and Q_N, we can solve for B as a residual. This completes the short-run description of the model. The long-run variant will be described in section 4, where E becomes endogenous, the government's policy objective is assumed to be to keep the balance of payments at zero and elements of real wage rigidity are introduced.

3. Short run analysis

In order to proceed we totally differentiate (3) and (2), written in excess demand form, and discover that:

$$\begin{bmatrix} a_{11} & a_{12} \\ a_{21} & a_{22} \end{bmatrix} \begin{bmatrix} dQ_N \\ dP_T \end{bmatrix} = \begin{bmatrix} b_{11} & b_{12} & b_{13} & b_{14} \\ b_{21} & b_{22} & b_{23} & b_{24} \end{bmatrix} \begin{bmatrix} dR \\ dE \\ dQ_T \\ d\beta \end{bmatrix} \quad (7.6)$$

where:
$$a_{11} = D_{N1}(P_N - EP_m{}^*m) - 1$$
$$a_{12} = D_{N1}\bar{Q}_T + D_{N2}/P_N$$
$$a_{21} = D_{T1}(P_N - EP_m{}^*m)$$
$$a_{22} = D_{T1}\bar{Q}_T + D_{T2}/P_N + F_1/E$$
$$b_{11} = - D_{N1}$$
$$b_{21} = - D_{T1}$$
$$b_{12} = D_{N1}mP_m{}^*Q_N$$
$$b_{22} = D_{T1}mP_m{}^*Q_N + F_1P_T/E^2$$
$$b_{13} = -D_{N1}P_T$$
$$b_{23} = 1 - D_{T1}P_T$$
$$b_{14} = -D_{N1}Q_N(1 + g)W + D_{N2}P_T/P_N{}^2(1 + g)W$$
$$b_{24} = -D_{T1}Q_N(1 + g)W + D_{T2}P_T/P_N{}^2(1 + g)W$$

The trace of the Jacobian, J, will be found negative if $D_{N1}(P_N - EP_m{}^*m) < 1$, which is also a necessary condition for $|J| > 0$, i.e. stability.

a.   The effect of an increase in oil revenues, R.
$$\frac{dQ_N}{dR} = \frac{[-D_{N1}(D_{T2}/P_N + F_1/E) + D_{T1}D_{N2}/P_N]}{|J|} \quad (7.7)$$

This is positive.

$$\frac{dP_T}{dR} = \frac{D_{T1}}{|J|} > 0 \tag{7.8}$$

$\frac{dB}{dR}$, we obtain by taking the total derivative of (7.5) with respect to R and use (7.6) and (7.7) to get:

$$\frac{dB}{dR} = 1 + \left[\frac{P_T F_1}{E} + F\right]\frac{dP_T}{dR} - EP_m^* m\frac{dQ_N}{dR}$$

Let $\eta = P_T F_1/FE$, be the elasticity of foreign demand for traded goods with respect to P_T, holding E constant: $\eta < 0$. Thus:

$$\frac{DB}{dR} = 1 + F[1 + \eta]\frac{dP_T}{dR} - EP_m^* m\frac{dQ_N}{dR} \tag{7.9}$$

$|\eta| > 1$, is necessary for $dB/dR < 0$, and vice versa.

These results can be depicted diagrammatically in Q_N, P_T space. We construct an *NN* curve to depict equilibrium in the non-traded goods market.

$$\frac{dP_T}{dQ_N}\bigg|_{NN} = \frac{1 - D_{N1}(P_N - EP_m^* m)}{D_{N1}\bar{Q}_T + D_{N2}/P_N} > 0 \tag{7.10}$$

In the traded goods market:

$$\frac{dP_T}{d\bar{Q}_N}\bigg|_{TT} = \frac{- D_{T1}(P_N - EP_m^* m)}{D_{T1}\bar{Q}_T + D_{T2}/P_N + F_1/E} > 0 \tag{7.11}$$

The slope of *TT* will be positive if the Slutsky condition holds (in the denominator). The slope of the *NN* curve is greater than *TT* by stability. In terms of Figure 7.1, with an increase in R, the *NN* curve shifts right to *NN'* and the *TT* curve left (up) to *TT'*. Final equilibrium is at B with higher Q_N and P_T, than at the initial equilibrium A.

Furthermore, if we wish to look at a change in 'real' income, we would have to deflate nominal income, Y, by some appropriate price index of the form:

$$P = P_T^\alpha P_N^{1-\alpha} \tag{7.12}$$

where P is a weighted average of the price of tradeables, P_T, and non-tradeables P_N; with α and $1 - \alpha$ as their respective weights. This

P_T

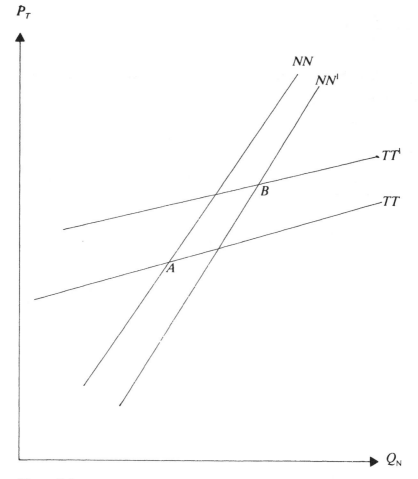

Figure 7.1

corresponds to one feasible ideal cost of living index (Samuelson and Swamy 1974) and is also employed in Dornbusch (1980) and Ford–Sen (1985). Thus the change in real income caused by the rise in oil revenues is:

$$\frac{d(Y/P)}{dR} = \frac{1 + (P_N - EP^*_m m)dQ_N/dR}{P} > 0 \tag{7.13}$$

using the fact that $\alpha = P_T Q_T / Y$, the share of the traded goods sector in income, Y.

A rise in oil revenues can occur for several reasons. A depreciation of the exchange rate can raise the domestic value of oil revenues. Secondly, there could be a governmental decision to increase the quantity of oil production. Lastly, there could be an increase in its world price, P_x^*, caused by increased world demand. We will ignore the first possibility and consider the last two or a combination of them, bearing in mind that the country in question is too insignificant to affect the *world* price of oil. Income rises in our small open economy, in both real and nominal terms, after the increase in oil export revenues. Excess demand pushes up the output of the non-traded goods sector, Q_N, and the price of the traded good, P_T. In at least the former respect, our model differs from that of Taylor (1983) where output of the domestic fix-price sector could fall. Our construction is different from that in Taylor (1983) in several ways. For example, the domestic fix-price sector (non-tradeables in our case) is not exported, rather output of the traded (traditional) sector is the other exportable. In our model, the other exportable falls as the world terms of trade, P_T/E, improve for the domestic economy.

More interestingly, there are *elements* of the 'Dutch disease' present here, provided the rise in R is permanent (long lasting). The real exchange rate (world terms of trade) P_T/E appreciates; there is an increase in non-tradeable production; and a likely deterioration in the balance of trade. In our model the output of the traditional sector cannot decline as its supply is inelastic (exogenously given). Our model differs from the standard models of Dutch disease (Eastwood and Venables 1982, say) in at least two respects; we do not have flexible (nominal) exchange rates, nor do we have full employment output in equilibrium. Thus output, employment and income can increase in our case (over full employment in the Eastwood and Venables analysis). This rise in income in our model could lead to a balance of payments crisis, necessitating devaluation, which in time could have contractionary effects (see below).

Although the increase in oil revenues raises income and employment (the N sector absorbs surplus labour from the T sector at a fixed money wage) it lowers the real wage. Given that the nominal wage, W, is fixed, the real wage, W/P from (7.12) will fall as P_T rises for given P_N.

b. A devaluation

A devaluation (rise in E) might be the response to a payments crisis; or it might be imposed as a requirement for an IMF loan, a common condition of its stabilization programmes.

$$\frac{dQ_N}{dE} = D_{N1} m P^*_m Q_N [D_{T2}/P_N + F_1/E] - D_{T1} m P^*_m Q_N D_{N2}/P_N$$
$$- F_1 P_T/E^2 [D_{N1}\bar{Q}_T + D_{N2}/P_N] \tag{7.14}$$

divided by $|J| > 0$.

$$\frac{dP_T}{dE} = \frac{D_{N1}(P_N - EP^*_m m)F_1 P_T/E^2 - D_{T1} mP^*_m Q_N + F_1 P_T/E^2}{|J|} \tag{7.15}$$

$$\frac{dB}{dE} = F(1+\eta)\frac{dP_t}{dE} - F_1\frac{P_T^2}{E^2} - P^*_m mQ_N(1+\Lambda) \tag{7.16}$$

where $\Lambda = (dQ_N/dE)(E/Q_N)$, the elasticity of the response of the non-traded sector to a devaluation (rise in E). Its sign will depend on the sign of dQ_N/dE in (7.13).

A devaluation will make exports of the traded good cheaper abroad, while at the same time making imports of the intermediate input more expensive in domestic currency units. We will assume that devaluation has no effect on total oil revenues, R, i.e. the authorities adjust quantities supplied so as to keep the domestic value of oil revenues constant. This allows us to concentrate on other, more important issues. Furthermore, as the domestic cost of the intermediate input goes up, the total cost of production in the N sector rises, in (7.4), P_N will tend to rise. For constant P_N, we need a countervailing fall in some other parameter in (7.4). A forced increase in labour productivity (fall in ß) by a reduction in employment, could also maintain a constant P_N. We will assume that it is a fall in money wages, W. This is quite plausible and fits the stylized facts for many LDCs pursuing a policy of 'austerity', devaluation being a part of this policy. Later, we allow P_N to vary in line with the rise in the cost of the imported input.

For constant P_N, the effect of the devaluation on the N and T sectors is ambiguous. But there is a strong possibility of a contractionary devaluation. As far as output in the non-traded sector, Q_N, is concerned it could decline as a result of the devaluation, from two sources. Firstly, the reduction in wages will have an adverse effect on demand for both tradeables and non-tradeables. Thus there is a negative income effect. On the other hand there is a favourable price effect in the export (of tradeables) sector emanating from a depreciated currency, as exports increase. Thus, the deleterious income effect must exceed the favourable price effect for a contractionary devaluation. Secondly, there is a further, unfavourable price effect. As the initial rise in export demand puts upward pressure on the price of the traded good, P_T, this will tend to reduce domestic demand for it from (7.2). If this effect exceeds the expansionary impact of rising exports on P_T, it will tend to decline, reducing income and the demand for both the goods absorbed in the domestic economy. If the devaluation is contractionary both Q_N and P_T will decline in (7.14) and (7.15). The balance of trade will improve in (7.16) as long as both $|\eta|$ and

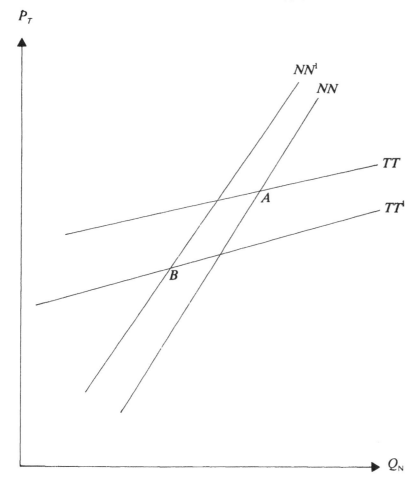

Figure 7.2

$|\Lambda|$ exceed unity. In terms of Figure 7.2, the *NN* curve shifts leftwards to *NN'*, and *TT* downwards to *TT'*. The new equilibrium is at *B* with lower Q_N and P_T.

What of 'real' income?

$$\frac{d(Y/P)}{dE} = \frac{(P_N - EmP^*_m)}{P} \frac{dQ_N}{dE} - \frac{P^*_m m Q_N}{P} \qquad (7.17)$$

Although real income is not necessarily uniquely linked to the direction of the change in Q_N, in this case, real income will decline when $dQ_N/dE < 0$. A decline in Q_N will lead to a reduction in employment in that sector. The real wage, W/P, could fall if the fall in W, mirroring the rise in E (devaluation), exceeded the decline in P_T. This would be also associated with a 'real' depreciation of P_T/E.

c.   A devaluation where P_N is allowed to vary

We retain the assumption that devaluation does not affect oil revenues, R. From (7.4), a change in E will affect P_N, via the cost of imported inputs:

$$dP_N = (1+g)P^*{}_m m dE \tag{7.18}$$

in this case. There will be additional terms for b_{12} and b_{22} above. They will lead to:

$$b'_{12} = D_{N2} P_T (1+g) P^*{}_m m/P_N{}^2 - gP^*{}_m m Q_N D_{N1}$$

$$\text{and} b'_{22} = D_{T2}P_T (1+g)P_m{}^* m/P_N{}^2 - gP^*{}_m m Q_N D_{T1} + F_1 P_T/E^2 \tag{7.19}$$

and

$$
\begin{aligned}
\frac{dQ_N}{dE} = \; & D_{N2}P_T (1+g)P^*{}_m m \,(D_{T1}Q_T + F_1/E)/P_N{}^2 \\
& - D_{T2}P_T(1+g)\,P^*{}_m m D_{N1} \,Q_T/P_N{}^2 \\
& + g\,P^*{}_m \,Q_N \,[D_{T1}D_{N2}/P_N - D_{T2}D_{N1}/P_N - F_1 D_{N1}/E] \\
& - F_1 P_T/E^2 [D_{N1}Q_T + D_{N2}/P_N]
\end{aligned}
\tag{7.20}
$$

divided through by $|J| > 0$.

$$
\begin{aligned}
\frac{dP_T}{dE} = \; & [D'_{T2} P_T (1+g)P^*{}_m m/P_N{}^2 + F_1 \, P_T/E^2] \,[D_{N1} (P_N - EP_m m) - 1] \\
& - D_{T1} (P_N - EP^*{}_m m) \,[D_{N2}P_T(1+g)P^*{}_m m/P_N{}^2] + gP^*{}_m m/Q_N D_{T1}
\end{aligned}
\tag{7.21}
$$

divided by $|J| > 0$.

The sufficient condition for $dQ_N/dE > 0$ in this case is for $b'_{12} > 0$, which will occur if $D_{N1} > D_{T2}$. Also, $dP_T/dE > 0$ if $D_{N1} D_{T2} \geq D_{T1} D_{N2}$. Figure 7.1 describes this outcome. We have an expansionary devaluation, when the price of the non-traded good, P_N, rises after the devaluation! This is the reverse of the result obtained when P_N is held fixed. Here wages do not fall, but as P_N rises, profits increase by a factor of the mark-up rate, g. There is a beneficial income effect. In the case of $dQ_N/dE > 0$, this beneficial income effect (D_{N1}) must exceed the decline in demand for N as P_N rises, the price effect. Output and employment in the N sector rises. The price of the traded good will also increase if the (cross) price effect of falling P_N on demand for tradeables in (7.2) is high. If both P_T, P_N rise the real wage rate will decline. As far as the balance of trade is concerned, referring back to (7.15), the effect on it of an expansionary devaluation is not clear. But it would be expected to improve.

The effect on real income, Y/P is:

$$\frac{d(Y/P)}{dE} = \frac{(P_N - EP^*_m m)}{P}\frac{dQ_N}{dE} - \frac{P^*_m m Q_N}{P} \tag{7.22}$$

This result is ambiguous as both P_T and P_N increase, similar to the Dornbusch (1980), traded/non-traded good model.

In this case with P_N rising after the devaluation, our results differ from Krugman and Taylor (1978), mainly because we have assumed identical spending (or saving) propensities out of wages and profits, whereas in Krugman and Taylor, the propensity to spend out of profits is lower than wages. [Indeed in our case the economy wide spending propensity, would only be indicated by the current account. Net domestic hoarding (saving) would be given by the trade surplus.] Nor do we have an explicit government sector with a savings propensity of unity. In our model, contractionary devaluation arises when P_N does not change through, say, a fall in W; or a rise in productivity (fall in ß) given W; or even a fall in $P_m^* m$. The first two imply a falling real product wage from the firm's point of view. These are often induced and coincide with devaluation, as part of a package to improve competitiveness, by the IMF or less liberal governments in LDCs. A contractionary devaluation would then ensue.

Other, more recent studies of contractionary devaluation include Wijnbergen (1986), whose analysis emphasizes the supply side in the context of a 'classical unemployment' regime. Contractionary effects emanate from three channels, two of which are of interest in our model. First, there is the rising cost of imported intermediate inputs, as is the case in the non-traded sector of our model. However, in our multi-good model, output of the non-traded goods sector is principally demand determined. Secondly, in the Wijnbergen model contractionary effects of devaluation occur via rising real product wage rates, a standard open economy result. The indexation of wages is ruled out in the short-run variant of the type of economy we consider. Furthermore, in our economy consumption imports (including food) are ruled out. The model presented in Buffie (1986) *explicitly* examines net investment and finds that devaluation has a crowding out effect on net investment. These adverse effects persist on to the long-run. However, somewhat unrealistically he assumes the possibility of payments imbalances via sterilization in the steady-state. As will be observed in section 4, in our long-run steady state, the exchange rate is adjusted such that the balance of payments balances, in keeping with the mainstream literature of open economy macroeconomics. The case of the 'structural deficit' described in Arida and Bacha (1987) arises in the context of a disequilibrium rationing approach and (price) inelastic export elasticities. The latter really amounts to the (macroeconomic) Marshall–Lerner conditions not holding. Devaluation cannot cure structural deficits. Our analysis is conducted in an 'equilibrium', demand-determined framework. Structural deficits are ruled out because the economy in question is sufficiently creditworthy and can borrow to finance its short-run deficit. This creditworthiness could diminish in the long-run; which is why we impose balance of payments equilibrium in our (stable) long-run [section 4].

d.   An increase in the output of the traded goods

An exogenous increase in Q_T could be a result of technical progress in that sector or other factors such as a good harvest.

$$\frac{dQ_N}{dQ_T} = \frac{-D_{N1}[Q_T + \Phi D_T + \eta F] - \gamma D_N/P_T + D_T \gamma D_N}{|J|} \tag{7.23}$$

where $\Phi = D_{T2} P_T/P_N D_T$, the price elasticity of home demand for traded goods, $\Phi < 0$; $\gamma = D_{N2} D_T/P_N D_N$, the price elasticity of demand for non-tradeables with respect to P_T, $\gamma > 0$.

$$\frac{dP_T}{dQ_T} = \frac{D_{N1}(P_N - EP^*_m m) - 1 + D_{T1} P_T}{|J|} \tag{7.24}$$

$$\frac{dB}{dQ_T} = (1+\eta) \frac{dP_T}{dQ_T} - EP^*_m m \frac{dQ_N}{dQ_T} \tag{7.25}$$

Thus there is a possibility of *an immiserizing increase* in the output of the traded goods sector. It might lead to a decline in the production of Q_N as demand for it falls. An increase in Q_T will tend to lower its price, P_T. If, $|\Phi|$ and $|\eta|$ are both less than unity, then the increase in demand is less than proportionate to the fall in price, $P_T Q_T$ will fall. The resultant increase in income is dampened and with it Q_N demand. These effects are reinforced if D_{T1} is small, i.e. the marginal propensity to consume tradeables out of the initial rise in income is small. Under these circumstances $dP_T/dQ_T < 0$. The effect on the trade balance is ambiguous. The trade balance will decline when the rise in Q_T is non-immiserizing and $|\eta| > 1$. As far as real income is concerned:

$$\frac{d(Y/P)}{dQ_T} = \frac{P_T}{P} + (P_N - EP^*_m m) \frac{dQ_N}{dQ_T} \tag{7.26}$$

Thus the effect on real income when $dQ_N/dQ_T < 0$ is not clear cut. It will depend on the relative magnitudes of the decline in Q_N as well as the initial values of P_T and P_N. The real wage is likely to rise in the immiserizing case. Thus workers in the non-traded sector benefit, although employment in that sector declines. Unlike the model in Taylor (1983), a supply shock (or its converse, as in our case) may not lead to a fall in Q_N and a rise in P_T in our model, the final outcome depends on the sizes of the relevant price elasticities and income propensities (we do not incorporate Engel's law). Figure 7.2 depicts the immiserizing rise in Q_T.

e. Productivity changes in the non-traded goods sector

Referring back to equation (7.4) and totally differentiating it yields:

$$dP_N = (\beta W + EP^*_m m)dg + (1+g)\,\beta dW + (1+g)\,Wd\beta$$
$$+ (1+g)mP^*_m dE + (1+g)\,Ed(P^*_m m) \tag{7.27}$$

We have already considered a change in E, all the other changes will have similar qualitative results. A rise in any of the other parameters corresponds to a decline a productivity in the N sector. Let us consider a rise in β, a rise in the labour-output ratio, implying a fall in labour productivity.

$$\frac{dQ_N}{d\beta} = (1+g)W[(D_{T2}/P_N + F_1/E)\,(-D_{N1}Q_N) + (D_{T1}\bar{Q}_T$$
$$+ F_1/E)\,(D_{N2})P_T/P_N^{\,2} + D_{T1}Q_N D_{N2}/P_N - D_{T2}D_{N1}\bar{Q}_T P_T/P_N^{\,2}] \tag{7.28}$$

divided through by $|J| > 0$.

$$\frac{dP_T}{d\beta} = (1+g)W[D_{T1}Q_N - D_{T2}P_T/P_N^{\,2} + P_T/P_N^{\,2}(P_N - EP^*_m m) \tag{7.29}$$
$$(D_{N1}\,D_{T2} - D_{T1}\,D_{N2})]$$

divided by $|J| > 0$.

$$\frac{dB}{d\beta} = F(1+\eta)\,\frac{dP_T}{d\beta} - EP^*_m m\,\frac{dQ_N}{d\beta} \tag{7.30}$$

$$\frac{d(Y/P)}{d\beta} = (P_N - EP^*_m m)\,\frac{1}{P}\,\frac{dQ_N}{d\beta} \tag{7.31}$$

Thus real income in this case is uniquely related to movements in Q_N.

A decline in productivity in the N sector can lead to a rise in output there! A decline in productivity for given money wages, profit rates and the price of the intermediate input will raise P_N. This will raise nominal income and earnings from profits and wages in that sector. As long as that income effect, D_{N1}, exceeds the negative price effect of a rise in P_N via D_{N2}, $dQ_N/d\beta > 0$. If that is so real income in (7.31) will also rise. The rise in β, a decline in labour productivity, makes the intermediate input relatively cheaper to the input of labour, as in Taylor (1983), aiding the rise in Q_N. $dP_T/d\beta$ is also likely to be positive if D_{N2} is small. Rising income raises demand for Q_T, pushing up P_T. Figure 7.1 describes the outcome for Q_N andd P_T. If $|\eta| < 1$, then with $dQ_N/d\beta > 0$ and $dP_T/d\beta > 0$, the balance of trade is likely to worsen as more intermediate inputs are imported. The real wage rate in the Q_N sector will decline as P_T and P_N rise. Similar analysis is applicable to rises in the wage rate, profit rate and imported intermediate input price.

4. The long-run analysis

In the long-run if we are, indeed, to find our small mineral-exporting economy in a steady-state, we must assume that the government intervenes to adjust the exchange rate so that balance of payments equilibrium is attained. It will also adjust the volume of oil production (in effect of Px^* Qx; but we can assume that the 'world price' of oil is fixed) to help determine internal balance. In effect, given the behavioural equations in the model described in Section 2, the government will be endeavouring to select those values of R ($= Px^*Qx$) and of E, which will, indeed, produce a steady-state but, we may assume, one wherein *economic welfare is maximized*. We can hypothesize that such a state will occur when real absorption is maximized, which will be achieved when the value of the economy's income, deflated by the price of a basket of consumables, attains a maximum.

To consider the steady-state it is necessary to postulate some dynamic mechanisms by which that condition is attained as the economy endeavours to alter its short-run characterization. This is the subject of the ensuing sub-section, which is followed by a brief analysis of the steady-state properties of the economy once it has reached such a state of 'bliss'. Bliss we shall label it as; since the steady-state will be defined as one determined by the direct aid of government policy, designed to maximize the home economy's real absorption level. The consideration of the steady-state involves a study of the comparative-static (i.e. long-run) effects of certain exogenous changes, essentially of productivity growth in the economy's tradeable and non-tradeable sectors. As we shall see, there is no real possibility of deriving purely *analytical* results even from a model as inherently 'aggregative' as ours is: so that we have solved the model using *numerical* parameter values.

a. The dynamics

The system has three differential equations, in the three prices which are all endogenous once the steady-state is achieved, namely, P_N, P_T and the exchange rate, E. The latter becomes endogenous, of course, in the steady-state, responding to changes in 'truly' exogenous variables, such as labour productivity, (a change in ß or in $\bar{Q}_T$). If full equilibrium is not attained in the short-run then, naturally, prices will adjust, with the government itself altering E, to move the economy towards that steady-state condition.

We make the standard, neo-classical assumption so favoured since its mathematical formulation by Samuelson and Hicks, that prices respond positively to excess demand and negatively to excess supply, except that P_N adjusts also because of changes in the money wage as well as in the, market-responsive, rate of exchange, because of its mark-up specification. In effect, we postulate that:

$$\dot{P}_N = (1+g)\,\text{ß}\,\dot{W} + (1+g)\,(mP^*_m)\dot{E} \tag{7.32}$$

$$\dot{P}_T = \mu\,[D_T\,(Y, \frac{P_T}{P_N}) + F(\frac{P_T}{E}) - \bar{Q}_T] \tag{7.33}$$

$$\dot{E} = \lambda\,[E\,P_x^*\,Q_x + P_T F(\frac{P_T}{E}) - E\,mP_m^*Q_N] \tag{7.34}$$

with $Q_N = D_N\,(Y, \frac{P_T}{P_N})$ *at all times* in the steady-state and:

$$\dot{W} = \epsilon\left[\frac{P_T}{P_N} - (\frac{\bar{P}_T}{P_N})\right] \tag{7.35}$$

Here: μ, λ and ϵ are speeds of adjustment. μ will be positive, whilst λ will be negative; that for ϵ can be either sign. However, in the specific numerical form we have adopted for our model later on, ϵ has to be negative. But what is described by equation (7.35)? It indicates that the money wage (payable to a unit of labour in the non-tradeable sector) will be altered if the price ratio P_T/P_N diverges from a value $(\bar{P}_T/P_N)$: the latter is a 'required' value of the price ratio of 'domestic' goods which the workers in the economy will wish to see in existence so that they can attain a 'desired' real wage (à la Dornbusch 1980 and Cardoso 1981). The manifestation of the 'real wage resistance', will be through P_T/P_N. The *process* of real wage resistance is ruled out in the short-run, as the time period in question is too short for workers to obtain *endogenous* changes in the money wage. Thus, if we revert to the price equation for the non-tradeable sector:

$$P_N = (1+g) [\text{ß}W + mP^*{}_mE] \qquad\qquad (7.4)$$

W, the *money* wage, can be expressed in:

$$w^* = \frac{W}{P} \qquad\qquad (7.36)$$

where

$$P = P_T{}^\alpha P_N{}^{1-\alpha} \qquad\qquad (7.12)$$

so that w^* is the desired *real* wage. Inserting (7.36) and (7.12) into (7.4):

$$P_N = (1+g)\text{ß}w^*P_T{}^\alpha P_N{}^{1-\alpha} + (1+g)\, mP^*{}_mE \qquad\qquad (7.37)$$

Therefore (letting $\theta = P_T/P_N$, domestic relative prices):

$$\left[\frac{P_T}{P_N} \right]^\alpha = \theta^\alpha = \frac{1-(1+g)mPm^*\ E/P_N}{(1+g)\,\text{ß}w^*} \equiv \bar\theta^\alpha \qquad\qquad (7.38)$$

From equations (7.36) and (7.12):

$$w^a = \frac{W}{P_N{}^{\theta^\alpha}} \qquad\qquad (7.39)$$

where w^a is the *actual* real wage. In order that $w^a = w^*$ it must follow that θ^α should equal $\bar\theta{}^\alpha$. Hence, inserting (7.38) into (7.39):

$$w^a = \frac{W(1+g)\,\text{ß}w^*}{P_N - (1+g)mPm^*E} = w^* \qquad\qquad (7.40)$$

Should θ differ from $\bar\theta$ then the real wage actually achieved might diverge from its desired level. Workers are assumed to react to such an eventuality by adjusting their *money* wage demand. It might be thought, *prima facie*, that such an adjustment should be in the upward direction when $\theta > \bar\theta$. However, that kind of adjustment would be self-defeating, and the attainment of the desired terms of trade, i.e. $\bar\theta$, and real wage, w^*, continually frustrated. The increase in the money-wage will feed into an immediate increase in the price of the non-tradeable good, P_N. That price-effect will reduce the demand, *ceteris paribus*, for the non-tradeable good itself, with demand being switched to the tradeable good. The consequence of that will be an increase in the price of the tradeable (P_T) due to the pressure from excess demand. The repercussions on the exchange rate and on income would be such as to aggravate the rise in P_T and halt the rise P_N; the net effect might well be that θ *rises* rather than falls. If this prompts a further rise in the money wage an explosive path will be generated for θ which must take it ever further away from $\bar{\theta}$: the economy will be unstable. Workers acting as *rational economic agents*, or more plausibly, some other agency forcing workers so to act, will realize the impact an increase in the money wage has on the endogenous variables in the economy, and so will have deduced that, to permit θ to confirm to $\bar{\theta}$, and so for them to be in a position where w^* is attained, it is necessary for them to reduce their money wage. Accordingly, the sign of ϵ must depend upon the behavioural structure of the economy. The parameter values we have utilized require ϵ to be negative for stability. This allows us to close the dynamic (long-run) version of the model. *Ergo*, once the government has selected the levels of R and E which produce a maximum level of real absorption, the economy will be resilient: it will return, eventually, to its steady-state (for the optimum levels of R and E) if it is buffeted away from it by a random disturbance to demands or supplies.

There are three key variables in the steady-state, P_N, P_T and E: this latter becomes, *as it were*, an endogenous variable in the steady-state. Thus, if there is a shift in any one of the truly exogenous variables, such as the value of the intermediate input into the price of the non-tradeable good (P_m^*), E will have to alter to generate a new steady-state; this can be accomplished formally by the government, re-calculating the level of E which will now maximize economic welfare, or it could permit the exchange rate to be endogenous in the steady-state. The phase-diagram for the main features of this small open economy is then *three*-dimensional. It is defined over P_N, P_T and E, for $\dot{P}_N = \dot{P}_T = \dot{E} = 0$. The only way by which we can portray the phase-diagram and hence the dynamics/stability of any steady-state is through a two-dimensional diagram, taking allowance of $\dot{E} = 0$.

The three equations describing the complete phase-diagram are the following; which are derived by totally differentiating equations (7.33) – (7.35) with respect to P_N, P_T and E, and setting the resulting expressions equal to zero.

$$\dot{P}_N = 0 \Rightarrow a_{11} \, dP_N + a_{12} \, dP_T + a_{13} \, dE = 0 \qquad (7.41)$$

$$\dot{P}_T = 0 \Rightarrow a_{21} \, dP_N + a_{22} \, dP_T + a_{23} \, dE = 0 \qquad (7.42)$$

$$\dot{E} = 0 \Rightarrow a_{31} \, dP_N + a_{32} \, dP_T + a_{33} \, dE = 0 \qquad (7.43)$$

where:

$$a_{11} = -(1+g)\beta\epsilon\frac{P_T}{(P_N)^2} - \lambda(1+g)(mP^*_m)^2 E\left[D_{N1}D_N(\cdot) - D_{N2}(\frac{P_T}{P_N^2})\right]q^{-1}$$

$$a_{12} = \frac{(1+g)\beta\epsilon}{P_N} + (1+g)(mP^*_m)\lambda\left[P_T\frac{F_1}{E}\bar{E} + F(\cdot)\right]$$
$$- (1+g)(mP^*_m)^2\lambda E[D_{N1}\bar{Q}_T + D_{N2}\frac{1}{P_N}]q^{-1}$$

$$a_{13} = (1+g)mPm^*\lambda\left[R - \left[\frac{P_T}{E}\right]^2 F_1 - (mP^*_m)D_N(\cdot)\right.$$
$$\left. - mP^*_mE[D_{N1}(R - mP^*_mD_N(\cdot))]q^{-1}\right]$$

$$a_{21} = \mu D_{T1}\left[(P_N - mP^*_mE)[D_{N1}D_N(\cdot) - D_{N2}(\frac{P_T}{P_N^2})]q^{-1} + D_N(\cdot)\right]$$
$$- \mu D_{T2}\frac{P_T}{P_N^2}$$

$$a_{22} = \mu D_{T1}[Q_T - (P_N - mP^*_mE)D_{N2}\frac{1}{P_N}]q^{-1} + \mu[\frac{D_{T2}}{P_N} + F(\cdot)\frac{1}{E}]$$

$$a_{23} = \mu D_{T2}[R - mP^*_mD_N(\cdot)]q^{-1} + \mu F(\cdot)\frac{P_T}{E^2}]$$

$$a_{31} = -\lambda EmP^*_m[D_{N1}D_N(\cdot) - D_{N2}\frac{P_T}{P_N^2}]q^{-1}$$

$$a_{32} = \lambda[\frac{P_T}{E}F_1 + F(\cdot)] - \lambda EmP^*_m[D_{N1}\bar{Q}_T + D_{N2}\frac{1}{P_N}]q^{-1}$$

$$a_{33} = \lambda[R - (\frac{P_T^2}{E})F_1 - mP^*_mD_N(\cdot) - P^*_mm E(D_{N1}(R - mP^*_mD_N(\cdot)))]q^{-1}$$

and $q = 1 - D_{N1}(P_N - mP^*_m E)$

The phase-diagram defined over (P_N, P_T) space can be obtained by solving equation (7.43) for dE and substituting the resulting expression into equations (7.41) and (7.42). It is readily seen that the slopes of both $\dot{P}_N = 0$ and if $\dot{P}_T = 0$ are indeterminate since the relevant a_{ij} cannot be signed uniquely. In effect:

$$\frac{dP_N}{dP_T}\bigg|\dot{P}_N = 0 \Rightarrow \frac{a_{13}a_{32} - a_{33}a_{12}}{a_{11}a_{33} - a_{13}a_{31}} \gtrless 0 \tag{7.44}$$

and,

$$\frac{dP_N}{dP_T}\bigg|\dot{P}_T = 0 \Rightarrow \frac{a_{23}a_{32} - a_{33}a_{22}}{a_{21}a_{33} - a_{23}a_{31}} \gtrless 0 \tag{7.45}$$

A purely analytical treatment of the phase-diagram of stability (and of the steady-state comparative statics) is empty: so, as mentioned earlier on, we have resorted to a *numerical* version of the model. On the basis of the parameter values we have selected (see the Appendix) the a_{ij} are as follows:

$$\left. \begin{array}{lll} a_{11} = 1.44593; & a_{12} = -1.43521; & a_{13} = -1.48315 \\ a_{21} = 15.756; & a_{22} = -3.4313; & a_{23} = 0.15948 \\ a_{31} = -0.7877; & a_{32} = 0.80914; & a_{33} = -2.9669 \end{array} \right] \quad (7.46)$$

These figures produce a positive slope of 1 for $\dot{P_N} = 0$ and a positive slope of 0.216 for $\dot{P_T} = 0$, when the steady-state values of R and E are chosen so as to maximize real absorption, given the exogenous variables specified in the Appendix: those steady-state values are $R = 4.484$ and $E = 0.545$ (both rounded-up to three decimal places). Hence, with $\dot{E} = 0$, the phase-diagram over (P_N, P_T) space is as given in Figure 7.3.

The economy is stable on the basis of the a_{ij} given in (7.46) above: thus, the a_{ij} are the elements of the Jacobian (J) of the third-order system contained in equations (7.32) – (7.34), for $P_N(t)$, $P_T(t)$ and $E(t)$, where t denotes time. The Routhian *sufficient* conditions for stability are:

$$|J| < 0, \text{ Trace } J < 0 \text{ and:}$$
$$[(a_{11} a_{22} - a_{21} a_{12}) + (a_{11} a_{33} - a_{31} a_{13}) + (a_{22} a_{33} - a_{32} a_{23})] > 0 \Big] \quad (7.47)$$

An examination of (7.46) reveals that (7.47) holds.

Utilizing the data in (7.46) in equations (7.41) – (7.43) permits us to deduce that a higher value of E than that holding in the steady-state will cause $\dot{P_N} = 0$ to shift to the right (i.e., dP_N/dE given P_T, is positive) and $\dot{P_T} = 0$ also to shift to the right (i.e. dP_N/dE, given P_T, is negative). Hence, a jump in E, brought about by a random disturbance to the steady-state (which latter is epitomized by the point Q in Figure 7.3), which also causes P_N and P_T to be above their steady-state levels, will find the economy at a point such as D in Figure 7.3. The economy will then return to equilibrium via a path such as that arrowed on the diagram. In effect, P_N and P_T will both cycle around their steady-state values (which are equal to the steady-state value of E; hence equilibrium: θ is unity) whilst E (largely) approaches its equilibrium value monotonically.

The determinantal equation of the system:

$$|J - zI| = 0 \quad (7.48)$$

has these three roots as its solution; the pair:

$$Z = -0.587 \pm 4.1789i \quad (7.49)$$

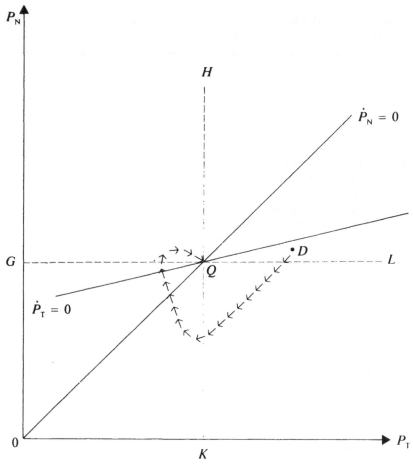

Figure 7.3

and

$$Z_3 = -3.777 \tag{7.50}$$

The complete solutions for: $P_N(t) - \bar{P}_N$; $P_T(t) - \bar{P}_T$; and $E(t) - \bar{E}$ are given in the Appendix. These solutions are graphed in Figure 7.4. We discover that, in view of the impact of $\theta - \bar{\theta}$ on $\dot{W}$, for any adjustment of the exchange rate that the turning points in P_N lead those in P_T as intuition would suggest and since $\dot{W}$ is determined by full knowledge of the workings of the economy, $\dot{W}$ continually falls and rises by ever decreasing amounts in order to ensure a return to the steady-state. The data on P_N, P_T and $\dot{W}$ as they attain that state are provided in Table 7.1.

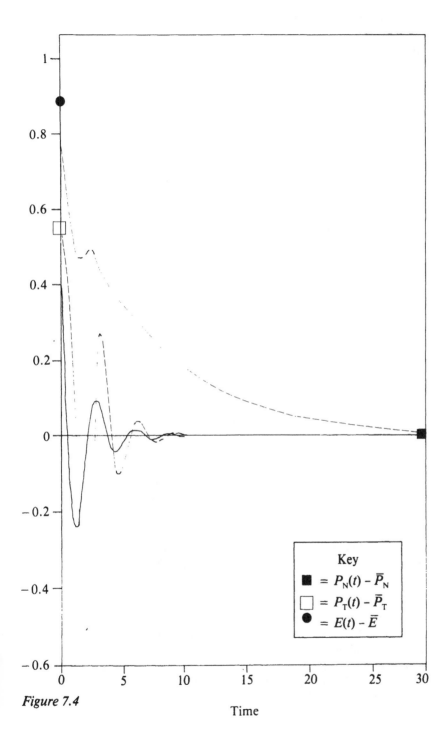

Figure 7.4

Time

Table 7.1.

Obs	P_N	P_T	θ	$\dot{W}$
1	0.598058	1.091345	1.824816	−0.412408
2	0.338895	0.753695	2.223979	−0.611989
3	0.493275	0.038585	0.078222	0.460889
4	0.635295	0.759175	1.194996	−0.097498
5	0.507205	0.577595	1.138780	−0.069390
6	0.535735	0.457635	0.854219	0.072891
7	0.559195	0.581605	1.040076	−0.020038
8	0.537105	0.548585	1.021374	−0.010687
9	0.542345	0.528935	0.975274	0.012363
10	0.546215	0.550255	1.007396	−0.003698
11	0.542405	0.544265	1.003429	−0.001715
12	0.543365	0.541065	0.995767	0.002116
13	0.543995	0.544725	1.001342	−0.000671
14	0.543345	0.543645	1.000552	−0.000276
15	0.543515	0.543125	0.999282	0.000359
16	0.543625	0.543755	1.000239	−0.000120
17	0.543505	0.543555	1.000092	−4.6D−05
18	0.543545	0.543475	0.999871	6.45D−05
19	0.543555	0.543585	1.000055	−2.75D−05
20	0.543535	0.543545	1.000018	−9.00D−06
21	0.543545	0.543535	0.999982	9.21D−06
22	0.543545	0.543555	1.000018	−9.00D−06
23	0.543545	0.543545	1.000000	0.000000
24	0.543545	0.543545	1.000000	0.000000
25	0.543545	0.543545	1.000000	0.000000
26	0.543545	0.543545	1.000000	0.000000
27	0.543545	0.543545	1.000000	0.000000
28	0.543545	0.543545	1.000000	0.000000
29	0.543545	0.543545	1.000000	0.000000
30	0.543545	0.543545	1.000000	0.000000

b.   Comparative statics in the steady-state

In the previous sub-section we have solved for the steady-state and its dynamic stability, for a given set of exogenous variables, with the policy instruments chosen to effect a maximum level of economic welfare. We now turn to consider briefly the comparative statics effects in the steady-state of shifts in the exogenous variables: the *chief* ones of which are, $\bar{\theta}$ (i.e. implicitly w^*), $\bar{Q}_T$, ß and the prices, P_x^* and P_m^* of oil and intermediate inputs, respectively. Since the analysis of the consequences of changes in the prices is almost intractable even in this aggregative model, we shall concentrate on θ, $\bar{Q}_T$ and β. Before we do so, we note that it can be demonstrated that in the numerical version of our model, any change in R, for example, will serve to reduce domestic income and the economy's level of real absorption that must follow, by implication, if we have solved the model initially for those steady-state characteristics, including R, which do maximize real domestic absorption.

(i) A change in $\bar{\theta}$ Analytically:

$$\frac{\partial P_N}{\partial \bar{\theta}} = (1+g)\, \beta\epsilon\, [a_{22}\, a_{33} - a_{32}\, a_{23}]\, |J|^{-1} \tag{7.51}$$

$$\frac{\partial P_T}{\partial \bar{\theta}} = -(1+g)\, \beta\epsilon\, [a_{21}\, a_{33} - a_{31}\, a_{23}]\, |J|^{-1} \tag{7.52}$$

and,

$$\frac{\partial E}{\partial \bar{\theta}} = (1+g)\, \beta\epsilon\, [a_{21}\, a_{32} - a_{31}a_{22}]\, |J|^{-1} \tag{7.53}$$

These effects cannot be uniquely signed, but on the basis of our numerical model (see (7.46) for the a_{ij} and in the Appendix for details of g, β and ϵ), rounded-up:

$$\frac{\partial P_N}{\partial \bar{\theta}} = 0.0747 > 0 \tag{7.54}$$

$$\frac{\partial P_T}{\partial \bar{\theta}} = 0.3465 > 0 \tag{7.55}$$

$$\frac{\delta E}{\delta \bar{\theta}} = 0.747 > 0 \tag{7.56}$$

and the impact upon real domestic absorption, A is:

$$\frac{\delta A}{\delta \bar{\theta}} = 3.02 > 0 \tag{7.57}$$

Thus, an increase in $\bar{\theta}$ in the steady-state will produce an improvement in the economic welfare of the domestic economy. But the new $\bar{\theta}$ could necessitate the government's altering the level of R in order to *maximize A* subject to that new $\bar{\theta}$. However, we leave that issue on one side in considering the comparative statics of the steady-state. Why might $\bar{\theta}$ increase? And why could it lead to increases in domestic prices, the exchange rate and real absorption? Consider first the reasons why $\bar{\theta}$ might rise.

The main *ceteris paribus* reasons can be deduced from equation (7.38). In our case, the emphasis has to rest with a change in w^*, since we are investigating the multiplier effects of just θ in the steady-state, i.e. m, q, . . . are assumed to remain constant. If α, the share of traded goods in absorption is fixed, an increase in θ will be the result of a reduction in w^*; at given P, in the initial steady-state, the fall in w^* clearly requires workers to reduce their money wage demands: so W falls. This leads to an excess demand for the tradeable, so pushing up its price; as a consequence, coupled with the fall in the output of the non-tradeable as its price jumps, the exchange rate will depreciate (i.e. E will rise) because of the concomitant balance of payments deficit. The rise in the exchange rate will begin to lift the price of the non-tradeable, countering the favourable effect brought about by the initial fall in the money wage. With the ultimate effect being to raise P_N, P_T and E, national income in nominal terms will rise: with the rise in E being small we can almost see by inspection of the equation defining nominal internal income (equation (1)) that it will increase. Since real absorption is that income deflated by $P_N\theta^*$, the percentage increase in the latter turns out to be lower (for reasons we cannot deduce in this comparative statics framework) than that in nominal income.

(ii)   A change in $\bar{Q}_T$ Again, analytically, nothing definitive can be deduced about the comparative statics effect on P_N, P_T, E and A of a change in $\bar{Q}_T$; where if the latter were positive, we might envisage this to be the result of a *productivity* improvement in the tradeable sector. The analytical effects are derived from:

$$
\begin{bmatrix}
\dfrac{\partial P_N}{\partial Q_T} \\[2mm]
\dfrac{\partial P_T}{\partial Q_T} \\[2mm]
\dfrac{\partial E}{\partial Q_T}
\end{bmatrix}
= (J)^{-1}
\begin{bmatrix}
\lambda E m P^*_{\ m} D_{N1} P_T q^{-1} \\[2mm]
-\mu [D_{T1} P_T q^{-1} - 1] \\[2mm]
\lambda E m P^*_{\ m} D_{N1} P_T q^{-1}
\end{bmatrix}
\tag{7.58}
$$

where: $q = 1 - (P_N - m P_m^* E) D_{N1}$

In our numerical representation of the economy the multiplier effects for Q_T are:

$$
\begin{aligned}
&\frac{\partial P_N}{\partial Q_T} = 0.0265; \quad \frac{\partial P_T}{\partial Q_T} = 0.0445; \quad \frac{\partial E}{\partial Q_T} = 0.0275; \\[2mm]
&\frac{\partial Y}{\partial Q_T} = 1.26; \quad \frac{\partial A}{\partial Q_T} = 1.227
\end{aligned}
\tag{7.59}
$$

We notice that no matter by how much Q_T does alter, since $P_T = P_N$ in the original steady-state, i.e. $\theta = 1$ at that time, the impact of the increase in Q_T is to alter the steady-state value of θ: hence, w^* must have altered (if the parameter α in the general price index is kept fixed; in general it will alter if it serves to represent the absorption share of tradeables) to permit a steady-state to materialize. The alternative is that when Q_T does alter the government recognizes this and adjusts R simultaneously to attain a steady-state in which θ does equal unity.

On the supposition that a new steady-state is attained the multiplier effects in (7.59) inform us that the dominating force on the economy operates via an income effect. Immediately Q_T is increased as far as heuristic 'dynamic' analysis suggests, the price of the tradeable would be pushed down. The income effect, via earned income generated by the increased production of the tradeable, would operate in tandem with the 'impact' fall in the tradeable's price, to stimulate demand: this would raise the price of the tradeable and, *ceteris paribus*, could take it to beyond its old steady-state level. The increase in disposable income arising from the increased production of the tradeable will stimulate the demand for the non-tradeable. After the price of the tradeable has begun to rise again from its 'impact' fall, the price effect embodied in P_T/P_N which initially militated against the demand for the non-tradeable, might not be strong enough to outweigh the (positive) income effect on the demand for non-tradeables. If this is so, the level of intermediate imports which are imported to support the production of the non-tradeable sector will have to increase. This, bearing in mind the effect of the price of the tradeable upon the level of exports (the level of F), could produce a balance of payments deficit, which would cause E to rise (depreciate), and so leading to a high value of the non-tradeable; an effect which would be amplified by a rise in w^* (and hence in the money wage) which could be required to guarantee the attainment of a (new) steady-state. The increase in the price of the non-tradeable good will, *ceteris paribus*, arrest the rise in the exchange rate; and eventually, we may assume that the economy settles down at a slightly higher level of all prices, and especially at a higher level of nominal income. The increase in domestic prices and in their ratio (θ), will prevent the full benefit of the increased nominal income being translated into real absorption.

This result indicates that a small open economy can derive economic welfare gains for itself if it enjoys a productivity gain in its tradeable sector. This is despite the fact that the 'world terms of trade', P_T/E, worsens, so exports (F) decline marginally. The productivity effect does not, ultimately, get passed on in terms of lower prices.

Of course, the outcome we have described is not a general finding. A glance at equations (7.58), taken in conjunction with merely the signs of the a_{ij} in the *J*-matrix listed in (7.46) will be sufficient for us to declare that even in this numerical version of the economy, our answers have to be approached through calculations of the multiplier effects.

(iii)   A change in ß   The parameter ß is the reciprocal of the average product of labour in the non-tradeable sector: so, as ß is reduced, there is labour-biased productivity growth in that sector. Solving equations (7.32) – (7.34), at the steady-state for changes in ß tells us immediately that any change solely in ß can have *no* impact on the economy.

$$
\begin{bmatrix} \dfrac{\partial P_{\mathrm{N}}}{\partial \text{\ss}} \\[2mm] \dfrac{\partial P_{\mathrm{T}}}{\partial \text{\ss}} \\[2mm] \dfrac{\partial E}{\partial \text{\ss}} \end{bmatrix} = (J)^{-1} \begin{bmatrix} 0 \\ 0 \\ 0 \end{bmatrix} \tag{7.60}
$$

The reason for this is straightforward. Unless the change in ß is accompanied by a change in w^* (hence by a new steady-state value of θ, the economy has to remain at the level of β set at the old steady-state. In that eventuality, β is merely a scalar on the variable $(\theta - \bar{\theta}$: and this difference must be zero in the steady-state). Hence, if w^* does not alter as ß declines, as labour productivity increases in the non-tradeable sector, any such improvement must have a neutral impact on all nominal and real variables in the economy. It is probable that a once-and-for-all increase in labour productivity in the tradeable sector will generate an increase in the w^* and so perhaps in the money wage: this *might* result in an adjustment to $\bar{\theta}$. If, for example, it should lead to the same percentage increase in w^* as occurs in labour productivity, $\bar{\theta}$ is likely to *rise*. In that case, the comparative static result given in sub-section (i) above happens to emerge as the comparative static result from a 'joint increase' in β and $\bar{\theta}$.

It would then be possible to effect a comparison between the impact of productivity growth in the two sectors of the domestic economy. But this comparison depends only upon the numerical model we have adopted and cannot be made on a uniform basis. Thus, to be specific, we have assumed that Q_{T} was set originally at 6 units to obtain a complete solution for the steady-state and its dynamics. A small, essentially, a unit change involved in the comparative statics results for Q_{T} then reflects a 16.6 increase in productivity in the tradeable sector; whilst the implication of an increase in labour productivity in the non-tradeable sector has to be imagined as embodied (as a strictly unknown percentage) in a small increase in $\bar{\theta}$, which with unity in the original steady-state and so now if we want the multiplier effect of $\bar{\theta}$ *per se*, must be taken as exhibiting a 100 percentage increase. An exact comparison, even in the situation where we are allowing the change in $\bar{\theta}$ to be a surrogate for the increase in labour productivity in the non-tradeable sector, requires us, therefore, to suppose that the change in Q_T is of the order of 6 units.

On that basis the impact on economic welfare of a 100 percentage improvement in productivity in the non-tradeable sector is to raise it by 3.02 units, as noted earlier, whilst the effect of a 100 percentage improvement in productivity in the tradeable sector is to advance economic welfare by 7.362 units. The comparative advantage rests, on our assumptions, with encouraging productivity growth in the tradeable sector; in the Hicksian sense (Hicks 1953), export-biased productivity growth not only benefits the economy, but it has a more favourable effect than an equivalent productivity growth in the non-tradeable, 'import-substitution', sector.

4. Conclusions

It is useful at this stage to summarize the main results of the paper.

In the short-run version of our model a sudden increase in oil revenues due to, say a rise in the world price of oil, can present macroeconomic problems, similar to the Dutch disease process. These are reflected in a real exchange rate (P_T/E) or terms of trade appreciation, a rise in non-tradeable production and possible worsening of the trade balance. Our models differ from the standard Dutch disease models, since we do not have flexible exchange rates or full employment in equilibrium. The deterioration in the trade balance may be unsustainable in the long-run, requiring exchange rate depreciation, which raises the price of the non-tradeable, adversely affecting real income and absorption.

Devaluation in the short-run could prove contractionary for the economy, especially if accompanied by a reduction in money wages or a forced increase in labour productivity (via unemployment). There is also the possibility of a devaluation being expansionary, especially if the beneficial income effects of devaluation, if any, are substantial. Thus, our model is ambivalent with regard to the effects of devaluation in the short-run: the contractionary case arising when P_N is fixed; and vice-versa for the expansionary case.

A rise in the output of the traded goods sector, in the short run could result in adverse effects for the entire economy. This is especially true when the price elasticities of demand (domestic and foreign) for tradeables are low. Consequently, a policy induced growth of the traded goods sector would have to be carefully considered in the light of possible contractionary results. However, the contractionary case is clearly ruled out in the long-run. Not only is this so, but a unit growth in tradeable output is found to be more welfare enhancing than a unit rise in labour productivity in the non-traded sector. Thus there could be a policy dilemma presented by differing short and long-run consequences of rises in traded goods production. This would raise the question of time preference, which is likely to be high in LDCs with low (per capita) incomes.

In the short-run, a decline in labour productivity in the non-traded sector would not be contractionary if it is not accompanied by a fall in money wages. An obvious implication is that short-run wage increases not matched by rises in productivity can be beneficial, as they raise aggregate demand. One would expect the balance of trade to deteriorate. In the long-run steady-state changes in labour productivity in non-tradeables are meaningless unless accompanied by changes in the real wage (or the required terms of trade), and they have to be examined in that light.

The major alteration from the short-run into the long-run is that both oil revenues and the exchange rate are employed to attain the twin goals of balance of payments equilibrium and maximum absorption in a *sustainable steady-state*. It is quite reasonable to assume these objectives bearing in mind that if serious indebtedness problems are to be avoided, the balance of payments must balance (see Murshed and Sen 1988). Throughout both the long-run and short-run analysis we look at the effects of exogenous variables on *real* income or absorption, using an appropriate price index, in addition to the usual notions of nominal income and absorption.

We postulate that in the long-run a degree of real wage resistance is possible on the part of workers in the modern, non-traded sector. However, if the actual terms of trade exceed that desired by workers, the money wage demands of workers may have to be lowered, so as to allow for *a sustainable outcome*. In this way, we offer an *alternative* to Cardoso (1981) and Taylor (1983) where unsustainable wage-price spirals are ended by some policy induced action, not by an endogenous process.

Appendix
The numerical version of the model in Section 4
(i) The behavioural equations specified in the short-run model were linearized, such that:

$$D_N = D_{N1} Y + D_{N2}\theta = \frac{24}{62} Y + 4\theta \tag{A1}$$

$$D_T = D_{T1} Y + D_{T2}\theta = \frac{36}{62} Y - 4\theta \tag{A2}$$

$$F = F_0 + F_1 \left[\frac{P_T}{E} \right] = \frac{5}{4} - \frac{1}{4} \left[\frac{P_T}{E} \right] \tag{A3}$$

and the further assumptions made were as follows:

$$P_N = P_T = E; \ mP^*_m = 0.25; \ \epsilon = -1; \ \beta = 0.25; \\ (1+g) = 2; \ \lambda = -1; \ \mu = 1; \ \bar{Q}_T = 6; \text{ and } w^* = 1 \bigg]$$ (A4)

These values imply that $\bar{\theta} = 1$.

(ii) The Steady-State solution was obtained by assuming that the government adopted this procedure:

choose R and E to *max.* $A = \dfrac{Y}{P}$ (A5)

Subject to: $\begin{array}{l} \dot{P}_N = 0 \\ \dot{P}_T = 0 \\ \dot{E} = 0 \\ P = P_T^\alpha P_N^{1-\alpha} \\ D_N = Q_N \end{array} \bigg]$ (A6)

and the data given in (A4).

We should note that w^* and $\bar{\theta}$, given the mark-up equation for P_N and the data on β, $(1 + g)$, and mPm^* determine that $P_N = P_T = E$. The constraint on A provided by P_N, w^* and $\bar{\theta}$ has thus already been accommodated in the solution of the government's optimal policy described by (A5) and (A6).

The maximization process leads to a quartic equation in E, namely:

$$\alpha_0 + \alpha_1 E^1 + \alpha_2 E^2 + \alpha_3 E^3 + \alpha_4 E^4 = 0$$ (A7)

where: $\begin{array}{l} \alpha_0 = 1.00391 \\ \alpha_1 = 8.26501 \\ \alpha_2 = -1.69212 \\ \alpha_3 = -25.611 \\ \alpha_4 = -9.65619 \end{array}$

and to a 'residual' equation for R, namely:

$$R = [3.8306452 - 2.25E]\frac{62}{36}$$ (A8)

The values of E (all other values for E being negative) and R emerge as:

$$E = 0.54535447; \ R = 4.483974$$ (A9)

The consequence is that $D_N = QN = 6.3438256$ and so nominal national income is:

$$Y = 8.3122061$$ (A10)

and real absorption, A is:

$$A = 15.241843$$ (A11)

(iii) *Stability and the Steady-State*

Stability is evaluated by taking the total differentials of the dynamic equations (32)–(34), utilizing equation (35), as described in the text, and taking the Jacobian:

$$\begin{bmatrix} a_{11} & a_{12} & a_{13} \\ a_{21} & a_{22} & a_{23} \\ a_{31} & a_{32} & a_{33} \end{bmatrix} \tag{A12}$$

we have to assess whether the three (in this third-order system) sufficient conditions denoted by Routh for stability are satisfied.

In the numerical version of the economy, J is specified by the a_{ij} in (7.46) and, as noted in the main text, all three sufficient conditions for stability are met. Taking the determinantal equation of (A12).

$$|J - zI| = 0 \tag{A13}$$

with our numerical representation of J permits us to determine *the time paths* of P_N, P_T and E around the steady-state values we have calculated. The aij in J depend upon the level of the endogenous and exogenous variables; these are set at their steady-state values. So, if the economy is stable, after *a purely random disturbance* has caused it to deviate from its long-run equilibrium, its steady-state position, all the variables will eventually return to steady-state values of $P_N = P_T = E = 0.54535447$. In view of the fact that the differential equations in $P_N(t)$, $P_T(t)$ and $E(t)$ do not possess *constant* coefficients we can only use their solutions to describe the pattern of movement of the economy around its initial steady-state.

The solutions for the three prices are:

$$P_N - \bar{P}_N = 0.13232027\,[1.53038507\cos bt + 1.59747947\sin bt]e^{\alpha t}$$
$$+ 0.209719018\,[1.59747947\cos bt + 1.53038507\sin bt]e^{\alpha t}$$
$$+ 0.007831678e^{\beta t} \tag{A14}$$

$$P_T - \bar{P}_T = 0.13232027\,[1.450234633\cos bt - 6.718008\sin bt]e^{\alpha t}$$
$$+ 0.209719018\,[6.718808\cos bt + 1.450234633\sin bt]e^{\alpha t}$$
$$+ 0.67181038e^{\beta t} \tag{A15}$$
$$E - \bar{E} = -0.13232027e^{\alpha t}\cos bt + 0.209719018e^{\alpha t}\sin bt + 0.67767474\,e^{\beta t} \tag{A16}$$

where

$$\alpha = -0.587; \; \beta = -3.777; \text{ and } b = 4.1789$$

References

Arida, P. and E. Bacha (1987) 'Balance of payments. A disequilibrium approach for semi-industrialised countries'. *Journal of Development Economics*, vol.27, pp85–108.

Buffie, E. F. (1986) 'Devaluation, investment and growth in LDCs.' *Journal of Development Economics*, vol.20, pp361–379.

Cardoso, E. A. (1981) 'Food supply and inflation', *Journal of Development Economics*, vol.8, pp269–284.

Dornbusch, R. (1980) *Open Economy Macroeconomics*. Basic Books, New York.

Eastwood, R. K. and A. J. Venables (1982) 'The macroeconomic implications of a resource discovery in an open economy', *Economic Journal*, vol.92, pp285–299.

Ford, J. L. and S. Sen (1985) *Protectionism, Exchange Rates and the Macroeconomy* Blackwell, Oxford.

Hicks, J. R. (1953) 'The long run dollar problem', *Oxford Economic Papers*, vol.5, pp117–135.

Krugman, P. and L. Taylor (1978) 'Contractionary effects of devaluation', *Journal of International Economics*, vol.8, pp 445–456.

Lewis, W. A. (1954) 'Economic development with unlimited supplies of labour', *Manchester School*, vol.22 pp139–191.

Murshed, S. M. and S. Sen (1988) 'Northern monetary policy and the southern debt crisis', *University of Birmingham Discussion Paper no.284.*

Samuelson, P. and S. Swamy (1974) 'Invariant economic index numbers and canonical duality: survey and synthesis', *American Economic Review*, vol.64, pp566–593.

Taylor, L. (1983) *Structuralist Macroeconomics*. Basic Books, New York.

van Wijnbergen, S. (1986) 'Exchange rate management and stabilisation policies in developing countries'. *Journal of Development Economics*, vol.23, pp227–247.

8. A macroeconomic model of East-West interaction: trade, technology, economic welfare, government policies and perestroika

1 Introduction

In this paper we make a limited attempt to model the interaction between Western and Eastern blocs at a very aggregative level. Even at such a level, however, we are not aware of any other analysis of the type of issues with which we shall be concerned. By contrast, after a somewhat late start, as it were, there is now a burgeoning formal macroeconomic literature on North-South models (see, for example, Kanbur and Vines 1986, Murshed 1987, which also contains a North, South, East, model, and the contribution by Taylor 1983, which is the inspiration for all recent work). We shall allow ourselves the liberty, indeed, of drawing on some of its quintessential properties.

As we have noted, our model is very aggregative in nature. The Western countries are seen as a bloc; so too are the centrally planned economies. Production in both regimes consists of an aggregate good, should the composition of total output alter, we assume that relative prices remain fixed so that it is meaningful to refer to 'a' price level for total output. In fact, we shall only be allowing, explicitly, for possible compositional changes in the Eastern regime.

Initially, we shall assume that both production and consumption are planned in the East. On the consumption side we shall characterize this as being epitomized by the fixing of consumption propensities (for domestic and foreign goods) by the planners and of total output; on the production side we shall make the entirely realistic assumption that the Soviet-type economies are, in a way to be explained shortly, constrained by the technological intermediate inputs they can import from the West, which imports are of paramount importance to their production potential. In the West we shall assume that simple Keynesian features appertain in its real sector, whilst in respect of the forces that determine the Western economy's demand for its own (and foreign commodities), we assign key roles to both income and relative prices (essentially the commodity terms of trade effects). As we shall see, the monetary/financial sectors in the two economic blocs are accorded somewhat passive, enabling, roles. The model has no explicit nominal exchange rate; in effect, it is assumed to be fixed and normalized at unity. The constancy ⌐f the nominal exchange rate is, in fact, an apposite one for East-West trade; despite the preponderance of flexible exchange rates nowadays for intra-Western trade. The balance of payments becomes a residual, of course, under fixed exchange rates; and we shall have something particular to say regarding the place of the balance of payments in our model.

We shall investigate East-West *macro*economic interaction, paying special attention to the effect of the technological constraint, East and West demand/supply shocks, and Western fiscal policy on the economic features of the two economies, including their impact on Eastern economic welfare; all this will be for the short-run. We shall also make some comments on the stability and the likely dynamic properties of the model. Furthermore, we shall be in a position to offer some observations on the potential for co-operation and co-ordination between the East and the West.

Thereafter, we shall assume *a regime switch* in the East. In effect, we shall endeavour to develop the model into one which provides a simple, but we hope elemental rather than elementary, characterization of the main economic implications of *perestroika*, inspired by General Secretary, now President, Mikhail Gorbachev, consequent upon his accession to power in March 1985. Clearly, the economic effects of perestroika (literally, 'restructuring', 'transformation') will be manifold; in breadth and depth. However, as far as macro-economic modelling of the most aggregative kind is concerned, there are only a limited number of features which can be influenced. These must relate, initially, to the markets already in existence, and the creation of new markets. In terms of our framework the economic reforms in the East could affect either the production side or the demand side, or both, in the real sector; and/or they could impinge upon the money/financial markets; and/or they could affect the market in foreign exchange. We shall limit ourselves to real sector changes; and we shall attempt in as simple, yet meaningful a way as possible, to encapsulate the macro-economic consequences of reform and their subsequent inter-action with the Western economic bloc. To develop a full-scale monetary/financial sector — within or without interdependence with the West — requires a major study; and the exchange rate regime is not altered because we believe that in the immediate years ahead the Eastern economies will attempt to maintain alignments between their own individual currencies whilst maintaining 'their' exchange rate with Western economies. Naturally, they will, from time to time, be convinced that their currency should be devalued (or revalued). Our model could be amended to incorporate that possibility; but in this first-step analysis we have decided not to pursue this. The model with its perestroikan features is then put through its paces, as it were, in a fashion similar to that utilized for examining the East-West model based on an Eastern planning framework. As far as is feasible, the economic and policy findings from the two types of model are compared.

The remainder of the paper is organized as follows. In Section 2 we summarize the key features of the Western economy; Section 3 does likewise for the case of a planned, pre-perestroika, Eastern economy. There we pay special regard to the role of imported technological inputs from the West into the Eastern production. In effect, because of a saving – balance of payments limit imposed by the West, a kind of Chenery constraint, the East's economic development is restricted.

Section 4 brings together the East and West in a static model of East-West interaction. The comparative statics properties of the model are derived, some consideration is given to its dynamic properties, and to the implications it conveys in regard to co-operation. This is followed in Section 5 by a similar analysis of an East-West model where the possible effects on consumption and production of perestroika are incorporated into the Eastern economy; this regime switch is likely to have implications for money markets in the East and for the foreign exchange market, but, to re-iterate, these are omitted in this paper, where we concentrate on ways of encapsulating real, aggregative, impacts of perestroika. A comparison of the East-West model and the two types of regime, together with some concluding observations on co-operation and co-ordination is contained in Section 6.

2.   The Western Economy

In the West we shall consider explicitly only one market, namely, that for 'the' Western good; that is, its real sector. However, we shall have to refer to the money/financial sector, before we can see that it may be placed on one side without rendering our model inconsistent. Furthermore, we shall have to be open about the part played by the government in the West and about its budget constraint, since we wish to encompass the impact on the East-West model of 'conventional' stabilization policy in the West. We recall that the foreign exchange market *per se* has no direct influence on East-West interaction; and we assume that there are no explicit capital flows between West and East (or vice-versa). Now we must turn to comment on these various issues.

The real sector is postulated to produce 'a' Western good which we label I (to represent 'industrialized'); the quantity of which (Q_I) is demand determined, with the supposition that there is excess capacity in production. Furthermore, the Western real sector exhibits fix-price characteristics in the Hicksian sense; in effect, quantities adjust to clear markets of both excess demand or excess supply, whereas prices respond to *exoge-*

nous cost or supply (e.g. productivity) changes. So we may assume that up to full employment, or up to near- full employment, Western output will increase when there is a positive net excess demand for the Western (composite) good; but that the price of that good will not increase. Naturally, by the customary Keynesian arguments, as full employment is approached, excess demand for labour and intermediate inputs will tend to increase their prices and so the 'exogenous' rise in costs will generate increases in the composite good's price. We simply abstract from that economic scenario; however, we do mention the impact on the Eastern economy of an autonomous change in P_1, the price of the Western composite good. This we can assume, in effect, has occurred because of exogenous disturbances to the Western economy; and is not an endogenous consequence of a Keynesian paradigm.

Aggregate supply (Q_1) in the West will be determined when supply equals demand. That demand, ultimately, will equal the sum of: (total) absorption (A) in the West; Western government expenditure on its own goods (G); Eastern demand for the Western good (ME); and Eastern technological imports, out of the Western composite good; *less* the West's total imports from the East (MW). This total demand is measured in suitable units, naturally; we have chosen to measure it in terms of Western goods. Hence, P_1, 'the' Western price level is our numeraire. We assume that the Western government only purchases Western goods.

As far as the specification of Western expenditure functions is concerned, we assume that:

$$A = A(Q_1(1-t); P_e; W) \tag{8.1}$$

$$MW = MW(Q_1(1-t); P_e; W) \tag{8.2}$$

Here: $P_e = P_E/P_1$, where P_E is the price of the Eastern composite good; W is real wealth in the West, in terms of domestic goods; and t is the marginal rate of income tax in the North. We have no interest rate effects in the Western expenditure functions because we assume that not only are interest payments on government securities small (and, indeed we could assume that the Central Bank issues variable coupon bonds, altering the composition to keep its interest payments fixed, so that for comparative statics analysis the effect of interest rates on consumption expenditure would be zero), but that the interest-sensitivity of the investment expenditure constituent of A can be ignored. Furthermore, we posit that *real money balances* are the elements of real wealth which matter, because we assume that the Ricardian Equivalence Theorem holds in that government bonds/securities are not seen as net wealth.

What about the determination of G and of the nominal stock of money in the West? Consider G first of all: we assume (until stated otherwise) that the government always endeavours to constrain its expenditures to the level of its tax receipts; that if it pursues a balanced budget, to the effect that for purely budgetary purposes, it (or its Central Bank) will not attempt to increase the stock of high-powered money or of government securities, in order to cover government outgoings. Accordingly, we can limit the delineation of the government's budget constraint to:

$$G = tQ_1 \qquad\qquad\qquad (8.3)$$

where t is the marginal (average) income tax rate and both G and tax revenue are in terms of domestic goods; and here we have ignored the fact that G involves interest payments on debt, because if they are made constant they disappear in comparative statics analysis.

The stock of money can alter, potentially, for four reasons; (a) there is a change in high-powered money; (b) there is an alteration to the Western economy's foreign exchange reserves in our East-West framework; there is a balance of payments surplus or deficit with the East; (c) for stabilization purposes; and (d) to accommodate the 'needs of trade', as the Classical economists would have expressed it; that is to satisfy any increased demand for money. In our model, we take it as axiomatic that the East has a deficit with the West. President Gorbachev's revelations to the newly-elected Soviet Parliament on 8 June 1989 substantiates that assumption quite emphatically. We could easily rescind that axiom, but there is little to be gained by our doing so. However, we assume that the Western Central Bank completely sterilizes any increase in its reserves which arise period-by-period consequent upon the continuing Eastern deficit. Accordingly, the stock of money will not be affected by that deficit. To sterilize the change in reserves, naturally, the Central Bank has to increase the stock of government securities. That will affect the stock of real wealth, but we have assumed that wealth effects *per se* are not present in Western expenditure functions. We also recall that the proceeds from the securities' sale are not circulated by the government back into the Western economy.

We also suppose (except where stated explicitly later) that the Central Bank does not adopt any kind of monetary stabilization policy, and that it only expands (or reduces) the stock of nominal money given the change in the money stock is equal to the change in high-powered money, plus the change in foreign exchange reserves, to satisfy changes in the demand for money. Finally, we postulate that the demand for money (L) is such that:

$$\frac{L}{P_1} = \beta \, Q_1 \qquad\qquad (8.4)$$

Hence, the rate of interest, the security rate, is determined in the securities market; but in our model there is no direct role for the security rate so that the security market can be omitted. We have also chosen not to use a consumer price index as our deflator of nominal money behaviour; even though we have argued on other occasions that such a procedure could be inadequate. In a fixed exchange rate world reliance on the domestic price level is less inhibiting.

3. The Eastern (planned) economy

One of the major economic facts about the Eastern, centrally planned, economies is that since the emergence of detente in the 1970s, their trade with the industrialized West has grown as fast as the growth of world trade (see Berrios 1983). It is also revealed that this trade has seen the generation of a massive balance of payments deficit, with its concomitant effect, a burgeoning of the debt burden of Soviet-type economies to the West. Consequently, as we remarked in the Introduction, we model the East's interaction with the West by taking its deficit with the West as axiomatic.

Another major distinguishing feature of the East is the well-known one that it is an 'excess demand' regime in the sense defined by Malinvaud (1977), as Deger's (1985) detailed study of Soviet production makes apparent. The factors responsible for such a regime are, self-evidently, also instrumental in producing the balance of payments problems faced by the Soviet-type economies. In one sense, we could caricature the aggregate supply situation in the East by describing it as one wherein 'supply creates its own demand', in contrast to the way by which we have chosen to describe the supply position prevalent in the West.

The phenomenon of excess demand, essentially, in regard to 'consumption goods' within the composite good, arises, as we know, because of defence production and technological input constraints, so that a Soviet-type economy is frequently simply described as the 'shortage economy'. Thus Kornai (1982), the authority on the theory of planned economies, states that:

> . . . shortage is a consequence of the economic mechanism and of the institutional framework . . . even if household demand is tightly managed . . . the state and firms have also unlimited demand for inputs (Kornai 1982, pp103–104).

The structure of production in the East, and probably the inherent nature of the planned, full-employment, economy, result in a deficiency of manufactured goods, especially of inputs into the production process. Whilst it must be true, as Hanson (1986) has argued, that Eastern productivity will be affected by domestic factors, the predominant constraint on the production possibility frontier in the East appears to be the quantity (and quality, of course) of imported inputs.

In terms of macro production, then, the East is envisaged to be a regime which can be epitomized as one of repressed inflation with full-employment. How we might model this in a purely macro-framework is an issue to which we shall return shortly.

In the meanwhile, we must turn briefly to the demand side in the Eastern bloc; which bears on the way in which production is, in fact, alleged to be planned. We assume that the pre-Gorbachev, planned Soviet-type economies, could be taken to be ones in which the Central Planning Authority determined (or, in principle, *ex ante*, endeavoured to determine) the economy's pattern of consumption and saving. Hence, we postulate that for the East there are fixed, planned, propensities to consume home and foreign goods and to save: these, in effect, are in respect of income, so that there are *no price effects, per se,* on consumption or saving behaviour. The hypothesis about the propensity to save out of income determines the proposed balance of payments position. The latter itself depends upon the view of the West about the sustainable deficit of the East; in essence, it reflects the East's perception of the deficit which the West is prepared to tolerate. It is that deficit, together with the planned level of total output, which influences the technological inputs which can be purchased from the West; and the actual level of output is assumed to be constrained at full employment by the ability to purchase technological imports.

It is not, however, a straightforward procedure to model the production process in a Soviet-type economy especially when it is viewed in the context of an international framework. The conventional view of the method adopted by the Central Planners is described fully in Ward (1967) and Borstein (1979), and is summarized clearly and succinctly by Nuti (1988):

> In the traditional Soviet-type model . . . production is organized as a single giant firm, a monopolistic corporation entirely owned by the state. Individual production units are administrative sub-divisions dependent on branch Ministries and acting exclusively on central instructions. Production tasks are worked out at a central level for the whole economy and stated in a national plan, then broken down by branch and by enterprise as a result of a few (at most half a dozen) iterative rounds of two-way consultations between the centre and the productive units. Workers are employed by state enterprises at a money wage and have a right/duty to work . . . Households' money incomes can be spent freely in state shops at state-fixed prices. (Nuti 1988, pp358–359).

Despite the fact that prices play no allocative role in the Eastern economy and are fixed by the Central Planners, we have to allow for the fact that the price of the corporate good in the East will be influenced by demand in the West; and that an excess demand created by the West for the Eastern good will tend to raise its price. So our East-West interaction can induce an adjustment to the Eastern price level; whilst the East might attempt notionally to set a price, and organize its production around that price, it will have to change with international demand pressures, say, to prevent the deficit of the Eastern bloc from increasing.

It is not easy to characterize the production process described in the conventional paradigm: nor is it a simple matter to see how that paradigm *per se* is supposed to be effected. But we shall assume the Central Planners do, indeed, act as a giant firm endeavouring to minimize the cost of producing any level of output, given the available production function and supplies of the factors of production. Thereafter, the Central Planners produce the greatest level of output (hence, for a given general price index, which is a weighted average of domestic and Western prices, they have maximized real income) using all their available resources in the optimal combination presented by the process of minimizing the costs of any level of output.

As far as technology is concerned, we assume that aggregate output depends upon three broad factors: labour (L), capital (k), and technological inputs (T) from the West. We further assume that there is an input-output, Leontief-type, coefficient for technological inputs that, except where otherwise stated, is unalterable (labelled, μ). The planners also utilize to the full the available labour force; so that the money wage has to be set by the Central Planners to enable them to use labour in the most efficient manner when it is fully employed.

Thus, suppose that the Central Planners have as their objective the minimization of costs for the production of any pre-assigned level of output of the composite good. Then for the sake of illustration suppose that the production function is additive-separable:

$$Q_E = T + f(k ; L) ; T \equiv \mu Q_E \qquad (8.5)$$

That is:

$$Q_E = \frac{f(k ; L)}{1 - \mu} \qquad (8.6)$$

Then, total costs (c) will be:

$$c = (\mu Q_E P_1) + rk + wL \qquad (8.7)$$

Hence, to choose L and k to minimize c subject to $f(\cdot)$, the Central Planners minimize:

$$\Lambda = \frac{\mu}{1-\mu} P_1 f(k \,;\, L) + rk + wL + \frac{\lambda}{1-\bar{\mu}} [f(k \,;\, L) - \bar{Q}_E] \qquad (8.8)$$

where λ is a Lagrange multiplier.

This procedure assumes that a value of T can be selected which is sufficient to produce the output that would ensue from the Central Planners' having made use of the optimal combination of capital and labour. In such a case we have, of course, the standard result that capital and labour should be combined so that the ratio of their marginal physical products equals the ratio of their prices:

$$\frac{f^1_L}{f^1_k} = \frac{w}{r} \qquad (8.9)$$

In order to employ both the available labour force and the capital stock to the full, equation (8.9) will indicate to the Central Planners what factor price ratio they must select to achieve that objective: then the marginal products will depend upon the levels of labour and capital used, and with those set at their maximum values, the required ratio w/r is determined. The full-employment values of labour and capital, naturally, inform us immediately via $f(\cdot)$ what the maximum level of output can be in the East. That level itself then implies the level of T required. The maximum level of output has been produced at minimum cost by the Central Planners choosing the prices of domestic factors of production. The Planners then input the units of T needed to support the maximum level of aggregate output.

If the Central Planners are constrained by the units of T that they can obtain from the West it follows, *ex definitione*, that the maximum level of output the East can produce is below the quantity that could be produced with full employment of *both* labour and capital; and that, as a consequence, there is either unused capital equipment [the Planners, as Nuti (1988) confirmed we remember, always fully employ the labour force] or some capital equipment is used ineffectively so that it can all be absorbed into the production process. In a situation where output is T-constrained, a factor-price ratio, w/r, can never be found, of course, at which any given output is produced at minimum cost if both L and k are fully utilized.

We assume that output is T-constrained and that this is as a consequence of the West imposing a limit on the balance of payments deficit which it is prepared to permit the East to have. How does this limit affect the available level of T and given the Central Planners select Q_E (given T) are the various parameters/economic variables they are alleged to determine mutually compatible? In answering this last question, we need to pay regard to our assumption that the Central Planners choose the level of output together with consumption/saving propensities and to the role of the Eastern price level.

These are, in essence, inter-related issues. But we begin with the notion that the Central Planners determine consumption propensities; *ex definitione*:

$$P_E Q_E = c_e P_E Q_E + s_e P_E Q_E \qquad (8.10)$$

Here; P_E and Q_E are as defined hitherto; and c_e, s_e are, respectively, the (total) propensity to spend and the propensity to save. The Central Planners choose those propensities. They can do so no matter whether they determine P_E or not, as is obvious from equation (8.10). However, $s_e P_E Q_E$, if negative, represents the balance of payments deficit of the East with the West.

We now assume that the East's expectation of the permissible deficit based upon past trading relationships is some number D^*. Hence, we can re-write (8.10) as:

$$P_E(1 - c_e)Q_E = D^* \qquad (8.11)$$

When Q_E, c_e and D^* are chosen/known, this implies a value for P_E. This is what the Central Planners will expect P_E to be consequent upon an expectation that the actual deficit (D) will turn out to be equal to D^*. The actual deficit is:

$$D = c_e(1 - v_1)P_E Q_E + TP_1 - P_E MW(\cdot) \qquad (8.12)$$

The additional parameter here is v_1 which is the propensity to consume own goods in the East, thus $c_e(1-v_1)P_E Q_E$ are the East's consumption imports from the West; also set by the Central Planners (as confirmd by the literature, summarized by Nuti (1988) above). When the expected value of (8.12) is set equal to D^*, this implies that the maximum T (T^*):

$$T^* = [D^* + P_e MW(\cdot)] \Big/ \left(1 + \frac{c_e(1 - v_1)P_e}{\mu}\right) \qquad (8.13)$$

where we have normalized by P_1 to obtain the quantity of T as required. Strictly, the items P_e and $MW(\cdot)$ on the right-hand side of (8.13) are expected values.

Now, when the East is T-constrained in the production of its corporate good, the level of T given by the expression (8.13) is below the level T required to maximize Q_E when both L and k are fully employed in the most efficient manner. Our postulate amounts to one wherein:

$$T^* < \left[\frac{\mu}{1-\mu} \right] f(\bar{k}; \bar{L}) \qquad (8.14)$$

where $\bar{k}$ and $\bar{L}$ denote fully-employed levels of labour and capital in the East, utilized in the optimum fashion. On the basis of their expectations of $MW(\cdot)$, the West's imports from the East, the Central Planners deduce that (8.14) obtains. Then they purchase a quantity of intermediate technological inputs from the West dependent upon T^*. We assume that T^* (and hence D^*) always acts as a constraint on the East; and that any relaxation of D^* is represented by a similar relaxation in T^* so that as the East-West model is constructed T^* determines the actual level of T which appears as an exogenous variable with potential multiplier effects and implications for co-operation between West and East. In effect, this is tantamount to stipulating that the level of T (actual imports) comes close to T^*, but lies just below it for safety-first reasons. The East may wish to make as certain as it can that it does not transgress the D^* limit; so some contingency for this could be to restrict T to below T^*. But, as T^* changes, T also changes; the D^* (or T) constraint is still effective if not fully binding. To make it fully binding implies that the Eastern Planners believe they know the East-West model with certainty and solve it completely, in *Rational Expectations* fashion to set $T = T^* \equiv f(D^*)$. This means, furthermore, that equation (8.13) figures in the complete model and the exogenous variable becomes D^*. Even if our East-West model is solvable in that fashion because it is on a small scale, we do not believe, *a priori*, that such an approach is a useful one. Nevertheless, we have reported results derived from utilizing such a solution technique.

The further implication of our analysis is that the East has an expectation of P_E, but knows that its actual value will be determined in the international market, because it is influenced by the West's demand for Eastern goods. The Central Planners will attempt to set the price level domestically according to their expectation of it; but the interaction with the West determines what this will be in 'equilibrium' in the East-West world.

We have, of necessity, had to devote much space to the real side of the aggregate Eastern economy. But before we proceed to bring together the Eastern and the Western economies we must offer a remark about the money/financial sector in the Eastern bloc. Essentially, the money-generation process in the planned Soviet-type economies is very simple; and it is essentially classical. The money stock is set so that it services the planned production level of the composite good (strictly, of course, so that it accommodates the outputs of the separate commodities determined by the Central Planning exercise). Financial flows are adjusted to planned physical output by a single bank which acts as both commercial and central bank (see Grossman 1968, Berliner 1976). So, the money stock has no independent influence on Eastern output.

4. East-West interaction

The model incorporating both East and West becomes one in which we have just two equations to determine two unknowns, Q_1 and P_e (or P_E, given P_1). Western output is determined by demand for its output. The Eastern price is determined by the demand for the Eastern good in relation to its supply.

In writing the demand by the East for Western goods and in specifying the 'market clearing' equation in the East itself, we shall resort to re-defining Eastern output (Q_E) in net (q_e) terms as suggested by Findlay and Rodriguez (1977); where:

$$q_e = Q_E \left[1 - \frac{\mu}{P_e} \right] \equiv T \left[\frac{1}{\mu} - \frac{1}{P_e} \right] \tag{8.15}$$

and we recall that P_e is P_E/P_1, the terms of trade. The value of this transformation is that the model now incorporates the measure of output which should be employed in every measure of real income used as an indicator of economic welfare or, indeed, of any measure of real absorption constructed for that purpose.

Consequently, we can set out the 'balance' equation in the West, in excess demand form as:

$$\left\{ A(Q_1(1-t); P_e; W) + G + c_e(1-v_1)P_e\, T \left[\frac{1}{\mu} - \frac{1}{P_e} \right] \right.$$
$$\left. - P_e MW(Q_1(1-t); P_e; W) \right\} - Q_1 = 0 \tag{8.16}$$

hence the terms in the ⦃ parentheses represent demand. For the East we can write, in excess demand form:

$$\left[c_e v_1 - 1 - \left[\frac{1}{P_e - \mu} \right] \right] T \left[\frac{1}{\mu} - \frac{1}{P_e} \right]$$
$$+ P_e MW(Q_1(1-t); P_e; W) = 0 \tag{8.17}$$

The total differentiation of equations (8.16) and (8.17) yields this equation:

$$Jdy = Kdx \tag{8.18}$$

where:

$$J = \begin{bmatrix} a_{11} & a_{12} \\ a_{21} & a_{22} \end{bmatrix} ; \quad K = \begin{bmatrix} b_{11} & b_{12} \\ b_{21} & b_{22} \end{bmatrix} ; \quad dy = \begin{bmatrix} dQ_1 \\ dP_e \end{bmatrix}$$

and

$$dx = \begin{bmatrix} dT \\ d\mu \end{bmatrix} \tag{8.19}$$

The coefficients in J and K are:

$$a_{11} = (1-t)(A_1 - 1) - P_e MW_1(1-t) + \beta(A_3 - P_e\, MW_3)$$

$$a_{12} = A_2 + \frac{c_e(1-v_1)T}{\mu} - (MW + P_e\, MW_2)$$

$$a_{21} = P_e[MW_1(1-t) + MW_3\beta] > 0$$

$$a_{22} = MW + P_e\, MW_2 + T\left[c_e v_1 - 1 - \left[\frac{1}{P_{e-\mu}}\right] \right] P_e^{-2}$$

$$\quad + \left[\frac{1}{\mu} - \frac{1}{P_e}\right] \frac{1}{[P_{e-\mu}]^2}$$

$$b_{11} = c_e(1-v_1)\left[\frac{P_e}{\mu} - 1\right] > 0$$

$$b_{12} = \frac{(v_1 - 1)\, c_e\, T P_e}{\mu^2} < 0$$

$$b_{21} = \left[\frac{1}{\mu} - \frac{1}{P_e}\right] \left[c_e v_1 - 1 - \left[\frac{1}{P_{e-\mu}}\right] \right] < 0$$

$$b_{22} = -T\left[\frac{P_e(c_e v_1 - 1) - 1}{\mu^2 P_e} \right]$$

a.   Pseudo-dynamics

In evaluating the *comparative statics* properties of the system we shall need to pay regard first of all, to the *pseudo-dynamics* of the system, in order to invoke the Samuelsonian correspondence principle to enable us to sign the multiplier effects themselves. Recall that we have written the equations for the West and the East which determine the level of output and the price level, respectively, in these blocs, in excess demand form. Therefore, on the Hicksian–Samuelsonian pseudo-dynamic hypothesis that excess demand for output in the West will cause supply to increase, whilst a 'world' excess demand for Eastern output will lead to an upward adjustment of the Eastern price level, the East-West model will definitely be stable if Trace $(J) < 0$ and $|J| > 0$.

Consider, then, Trace (J). The coefficient a_{11} will definitely be negative if, say, the term $A_e\beta$ approaches zero: hence, small wealth or real balance effects on (total) Western absorption will render a_{11} negative. The sign of a_{22} is somewhat more problematical, *prima facie*. But, even if the East has a planned deficit in its balance of payments, which will mean that c_e exceeds one (remember that then s_e is negative; but in our case is defined to be positive because we have defined the balance of payments deficit of the East as being equal to its imports minus its exports), we can assume that $c_e v_1 < 1$; here we recall, v_1 is the propensity to consume home goods in the East out of planned (total) consumption expenditure. Also, $P_e > \mu$, *ex definitione*, otherwise net output in the East is not positive. Hence if P_e is small it is highly probably that without any other side conditions the coefficient on T in a_{22} will be negative. We also note that in a_{22} the first terms can be written as $MW(1 + \epsilon)$; where ϵ, the 'price elasticity' of Western imports, is negative. Hence, if $|\epsilon| \geqslant 1$ and P_e is small, a_{22} will be negative. As a consequence, Trace (J) is automatically negative.

The sign of $|J|$ is indeterminate *a priori*. However, if we invoke the negative dominance diagonal condition $|J| > 0$, uniquely. That condition states, in this two by two model, that: $|a_{11}| > |a_{21}|$ and $|a_{22}| > |a_{12}|$. In effect, 'own effects' dominate in the excess demand equations in either market. We make that supposition; and note that both a_{21} and a_{12} are positive. The coefficient a_{21} is positive because we have assumed that $|\epsilon| \geqslant 1$ and A_2 is positive if the Laursen–Metzler (1950) effect is assumed to hold. Also the b_{ij} coefficients are signed uniquely, except for b_{22}; and that must be positive if the coefficient on T in a_{22} is assumed to be negative, because $P_e > \mu$.

On the phase diagram, Figure 8.1, the curve WW represents 'balance' in the Western goods market; whilst the curve EE portrays 'balance' in the Eastern goods market. The slope of the EE schedule must be lower than that of WW by the stability condition that $|J| > 0$. On WW the time derivative of Q_1 (labelled $\dot{Q}_1$) is zero; likewise, along EE, we have the locus of (Q_1, P_e) which produce a $\dot{P}_e$ of zero. As the terms of trade move in favour of the West, along WW, Western output must rise, because, via the

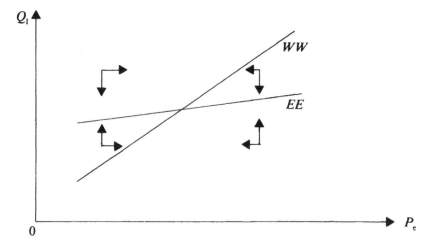

Figure 8.1

Laursen–Metzler effect on its total absorption, the absorption must increase whilst expenditure on imports from the East falls: hence Western demand for Western goods rises (there being no concomitant terms of trade effect on Eastern expenditure on Western goods) and so output must expand, since it is demand determined. In a similar manner, along EE, as the Eastern terms of trade worsen, P_e increases, the level of output (income) has to increase in the West to enable Western consumers to maintain their purchases of Eastern goods; to enable the given level of Eastern output to be absorbed.

When the East-West economy is out of balance, as it were, Western output and the Eastern price level will adjust in the directions indicated on Figure 8.1. If we refer to the EE schedule first of all: below the schedule there is a 'world' excess supply of the Eastern good and its relative price (given P_1, the Western price; Eastern goods absolute price) will fall, as it must to clear the market, and bring $\dot{P}_e = 0$ once more. By contrast, points below the WW schedule indicate situations of excess demand for the Western good; at any given P_e below WW the balance of demand in the West shifts in favour of the relatively cheaper home good (there being no price effect in the East, which would normally reinforce such excess demand for the Western good) and the pseudo-dynamics of our model state that supply will be expanded in the West *pari passu* with the increased demand.

It is not feasible, without a fully-specified numerical version of the model to graph the time-paths which Q_1 and P_e will follow back to the 'equilibrium' point in the system, after they have been displaced from either *WW* and/or *EE* by some one-off exogenous disturbance. In formal terms, we cannot tell whether the two roots of the characteristic equation of the *J*-matrix in equation (8.18) will be complex or real; because it is not possible to evaluate the sign of $\{[\text{Trace } (J)]^2 - 4|J|\}$ *a priori*, of course, because Trace $(J) < 0$ and $|J| > 0$ we know that they must have real parts anyway; and so, as portrayed on the phase diagram, the system is (at least, locally) stable. But, the variables might re-attain their equilibrium levels asymptotically or cyclically.

b. Comparative Statics Analysis

We are now in a position where we can turn to the short-run, comparative statics, of the East-West model. The latter contains two explicitly exogenous variables the way we have chosen to specify it, namely, the level of technological inputs that the Eastern bloc can import for direct use in production of its composite good and the state of technology in that production; as measured by the Leontief input-output coefficient, μ, for the technological inputs that are, indeed, required in Eastern production. We consider the multiplier effects of those two explicitly exogenous variables first of all: the exogenous variable P_1 is subsumed under P_e.

Consider then the consequences for Western output, for the terms of trade, and for both economies in general, of an increase in T which, effectively, means a relaxation of the balance of payments constraint (D^*) by the West. We can write:

$$\begin{bmatrix} dQ_1 \\ dP_e \end{bmatrix} = |J|^{-1} \begin{bmatrix} a_{22} & -a_{12} \\ -a_{21} & a_{22} \end{bmatrix} \begin{bmatrix} b_{11} & b_{12} \\ b_{21} & b_{22} \end{bmatrix} \begin{bmatrix} dT \\ d\mu \end{bmatrix} \tag{8.20}$$

We deduce, therefore, that:

$$\frac{dQ_1}{dT} = \begin{bmatrix} \overset{-}{a_{22}} \overset{+}{b_{11}} - \overset{+}{a_{12}} \overset{-}{b_{21}} \end{bmatrix} |J|^{-1} \tag{8.21}$$

By our negative dominant diagonal assumption, the term in parentheses in (8.21) will be uniquely signed provided that:

$$P_e > \frac{|c_e v_1 - 1|}{c_e(1 - v_1)} + 1 \tag{8.22}$$

We assume that this condition holds, initially, which probably means that P_e would be around a value of two; and so, the stability conditions, the properties of the excess demand functions, that is, almost uniquely determine that $dQ_1/dT < 0$. We shall comment on this in a moment; but we must first look at the related multiplier for the terms of trade.

We discover from (8.20) that:

$$\frac{dP_e}{dT} = \overset{\quad - \quad - \quad\quad + \quad +}{\left[a_{11}b_{21} - a_{21}b_{11} \right]} |J|^{-1}$$

(8.23)

The condition postulated in equation (8.22) means that $|b_{11}| > |b_{21}|$ and, via the negative dominant diagonal assumption, $|a_{11}| > |a_{21}|$. Hence, if the sign of dQ_1/dT is uniquely negative, that for dP_e/dT is, *a priori*, ambiguous. However, if it had happened that Western output responded positively to an increase in T, P_e would also have to have risen or remained constant.

In essence, as can be appreciated from equation (8.19), the impact of an increase in T is to shift both the WW and EE schedules to the right. So, in principle, any outcome is feasible with respect to the influence of the change in T on Western output and the terms of trade; but there is a formal restriction imposed on their relative changes by the negative dominant diagonal assumption and the supposition that $|b_{11}| > |b_{21}|$, as noted in the preceding paragraph.

Suppose that Western output falls after there has been an increase in T. How can this happen? The fact that T has increased requires an increase in D^*; if, say, P_e does remain constant in the new situation, the expansion of the East's deficit will emanate from the stimulus to q_e, Eastern net output, consequent upon the increase in T. That expansion, together with the increase in T itself, will produce an expansion of Eastern imports; this will provoke the required increase in the balance of payments surplus for the West. The 'dynamic' process will lead to an increase in output in the West, which will generate an increase in its imports from the East, and this together with the consequent rise in P_e (in conjunction with an increase in T directly) will generate, will begin to reduce Eastern imports and those of the West. The terms of trade effect will not be large enough (i.e. A_2 will not be sufficiently dominant) to prevent Western output falling and the Eastern price level returning to its pre-expansion (of T) value. These heuristic arguments would be a means of rationalizing the multiplier effects; but, naturally, this is not the only way since we do not have an explicit dynamic model which would permit us to carry out some time, period-by-period, analysis. Of course, the Western equation informs us, quite unequivocally, that if A_3 is small (as we have suggested is guaranteeing that a_{11} in J is negative), any increase in D^* must lead to a fall in Q_1, since:

$$dQ_1 = -dD^*[(1 - \epsilon)(A_1 - 1) + A_3]$$

(8.24)

and the square bracket is negative (with A_3 sufficiently small or zero). All of this the formal mechanics inform us, given the constraints which are contained in the J matrix.

We turn now to the multiplier effects that are likely to emanate from an adjustment to the state (quality) of technology in the Soviet-type economies, as opposed to any alteration in the quantity of T available. Thus, let μ fall; that is, there is technical progress in the East in regard to its use of technological inputs purchased from the West. We find that:

$$\frac{dQ_1}{d\mu} = \left[\overset{-}{a_{22}b_{12}} - \overset{+}{a_{12}b_{22}} \right] |J|^{-1} \tag{8.25}$$

and,

$$\frac{dP_e}{d\mu} = \left[\overset{-}{a_{11}b_{22}} - \overset{+}{a_{21}b_{11}} \right] |J|^{-1} \tag{8.26}$$

The term in parentheses in equation (8.25) will be positive: this is because it can be shown that $|b_{12}| > |b_{22}|$ by the hypothesis that $|b_{11}| > |b_{21}|$, whilst dominance renders $|a_{22}| > |a_{12}|$. Accordingly, as μ falls, the level of Western output also falls; and this is accompanied by an indeterminate effect once again on P_e (hence, on P_E).

When μ *falls*, both the WW and EE schedules on Figure 8.1 shift to the right; and, under the behavioural assumptions of the model (relating to the $a_{ij} \ldots$) the EE schedule shifts further than (or to the same extent as) the WW schedule does. Hence, output in the West falls consequent upon a productivity improvement in the East. The situation is illustrated on Figure 8.2 where it is assumed that P_e remains unaltered.

Should there be an improvement in T-productivity in the Eastern bloc this would necessitate Western output being lower at any given terms of trade in order to preserve balance, *ceteris paribus*, in the Western real sector because, at given Eastern output the demand for Western output would fall (via the fall in T imported by the East); *mutatis mutandis*, Western output must fall to induce a fall in Western imports from the East to match the *ceteris paribus* decline in Western exports to the East: this maintains the balance of payments surplus of the West at D^*. Similar kinds of arguments apply to the shift of EE consequent upon a *ceteris paribus* improvement in the productivity of Eastern technological inputs.

Those arguments provide the intuition as to why, if μ declines, Q_1 might decline (as it must under our behavioural assumptions and the mild extra condition we have imposed on the starting value of P_e) if P_e is, say,

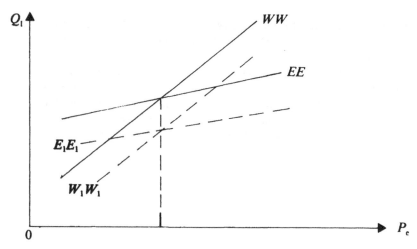

Figure 8.2

constant, as it is on Figure 8.2. They also permit us to deduce, quite readily, that if P_e falls following a reduction in μ, the fall in Q_1 must be greater than would have occurred with a constant terms of trade.

c.   Exogenous changes, economic welfare and policy co-ordination
What about the impact on other aspects of the Eastern bloc of *ceteris paribus* adjustments to T and μ? We know, *ex hypothesi*, that:

$$q_e = T \left[\frac{1}{\mu} - \frac{1}{P_e} \right] \tag{8.27}$$

Hence, any change in q_e is:

$$dq_e = \left[\frac{1}{\mu} - \frac{1}{P_e} \right] dT + T \left[\frac{1}{(P_e)^2} dP_e - \frac{1}{\mu^2} d\mu \right] \tag{8.28}$$

An increase, separately, in T implies that:

$$\frac{dq_e}{dT} = \left[\frac{1}{\mu} - \frac{1}{P_e} \right] + \frac{T}{(P_e)^2} \frac{dP_e}{dT} \tag{8.29}$$

If nothing happens to the terms of trade, any opportunity for increasing T must, *ex definitione*, improve net output in the East. That stimulus to output will be that much the greater the more the relaxation of the D^* constraint and expansion in the East generate at the new 'equilibrium' a higher price of its product: the reason for that needs no elaboration.
    In regard to *ceteris paribus* technical progress in the East:

$$\frac{dq_e}{d\mu} = \left[\frac{1}{\mu} - \frac{1}{P_e}\right] \frac{dT}{d\mu} + T\left[\frac{1}{(P_e)^2} \frac{dP_e}{d\mu} - \frac{1}{\mu^2}\right] \tag{8.30}$$

If, as we have modelled East-West interaction, the improvement in *T*-productivity in the East is not accompanied by an alleviation of the *D** constraint, and it is assumed, as has been done implicitly in our model, that it still constrains the East despite the productivity advance then, obviously, any improvement in q_e consequent upon a fall in μ depends exclusively on the second term on the right-hand side of equation (8.30). If the technical progress does not cause P_e to fall, then a fall in μ unambiguously improves net output in the East. This price effect on output needs no explanation.

In regard to *economic welfare* in the East, we may see that the increase in the quantity of *T* and in its quality, as it were, via the fall in μ, are both definitely welfare-improving if P_e is not reduced; and even in that eventuality they can still be beneficial. We can measure aggregate economic welfare as the real value of real income since it determines real absorption.

Thus, we can define real (net) income (*I*) as:

$$I = \frac{P_E q_e}{C_1} \tag{8.31}$$

C_1 is the consumer price index and so it relates to a basket of Eastern and Western goods:

$$C_1 = P_E{}^{v1}P_1{}^{(1-v1)} \tag{8.32}$$

Hence:

$$I = P_e{}^{1-y1}T\left[\frac{1}{\mu} - \frac{1}{P_e}\right] \tag{8.33}$$

When P_E remains constant an increase in *T* and/or a fall in μ will lead, unambiguously, to an improvement in real income in the East; and, in view of the fact that absorption in the East is positively, proportionally related to real income, it follows immediately that real economic welfare measured by real absorption in the East must also improve.

By way of contrast should P_e remain constant or increase as a result of the increase in *T* or the fall in μ, the West must suffer a decline, unambiguously, in its level of economic welfare. The West, however, can take accommodating action if μ declines by reducing *T*. The interesting question is, given that the West will be aware of this, is it possible for the West *to co-ordinate* its policies with those of the East, in that *both* can benefit from the technical progress in the East? We refer here to co-ordination of policies; to do so, of course, implies that we are imagining that by some policy measures the East has been able to encourage technical progress.

To attempt an answer to this question we must define formally the level of economic welfare in the West, to which we made reference above. Let this be real income (Y) in the West to parallel the measure I for the East. Then:

$$Y = \frac{P_1 Q_1}{P_1^{\alpha} P_E^{1-\alpha}} = P_e^{\alpha-1} Q_1 \tag{8.34}$$

where α denotes the share of expenditure on domestic goods by Western residents.

Therefore:

$$dY = (\alpha-1)P_e^{\alpha-2} Q_1 dP_e + P_e^{\alpha-1} dQ_1 \tag{8.35}$$

$$
\begin{aligned}
dI &= T \left[\frac{1}{\mu} - \frac{1}{P_e} \right] (1 - v_1) P_e^{-v_1} dP_e \\
&+ P_e^{1-v_1} \left[\frac{T}{(P_e)^2} dP_e - \frac{1}{\mu^2} d\mu \right] + P_e^{1-v_1} \left[\frac{1}{\mu} - \frac{1}{P_e} \right] dT
\end{aligned} \tag{8.36}
$$

In general, on the supposition that the policy makers in each economic bloc have as their objective a target value of real economic welfare and, hence, a target value for the change in economic welfare they are trying to bring about at any time (with each change assumed to be positive, i.e. $d\bar{Y}>0$, $d\bar{I}>0$) we can deduce from equations (8.35) and (8.36) that:

$$
\begin{bmatrix} dT \\ d\mu \end{bmatrix} = \Delta^{-1} \begin{bmatrix} c_{22} & -c_{12} \\ -c_{21} & c_{11} \end{bmatrix} \begin{bmatrix} d\bar{Y} \\ d\bar{I} \end{bmatrix} \tag{8.37}
$$

In (8.37):

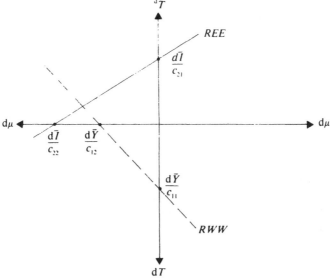

Figure 8.3

$$c_{11} = \left[(\alpha - 1)P_e^{(\alpha - 2)} Q_1 \frac{\partial P_e}{\partial T} + P_e^{(\alpha - 1)} \frac{\partial Q_1}{\partial T} \right]$$

$$c_{12} = \left[(\alpha - 1)P_e^{(\alpha - 2)} Q_1 \frac{\partial P_e}{\partial T} + P_e^{(\alpha - 1)} \frac{\partial Q_1}{\partial \mu} \right]$$

$$c_{21} = \left[\left[\frac{1}{\mu} - \frac{1}{P_e} \right] (1 - v_1)P_e^{-v_1} + P_e^{-(1+v_1)} \right] T \frac{\partial P_e}{\partial T}$$
$$+ P_e^{(1-v_1)} \left[\frac{1}{\mu} - \frac{1}{P_e} \right]$$

$$c_{22} = \left[\left[\frac{1}{\mu} - \frac{1}{P_e} \right] (1 - v_1)P_e^{-v_1} + P_e^{-(1+v_1)} \right] T \frac{\partial P_e}{\partial \mu} \qquad \frac{- P_e^{(1-v_1)}}{\mu^2}$$

and: $\Delta = c_{11}c_{22} - c_{21}c_{12}$

Assume that $\partial P_e / \partial T = \partial P_e / \partial \mu = 0$ and that $\Delta > 0$: then $c_{11} < 0$; $c_{12} < 0$; $c_{21} > 0$; and $c_{22} < 0$. The optimum change in μ is negative; and this should be met by a fall in T, as our previous results have indicated. In terms of policy co-ordination this finding informs us that it *can* be beneficial to both countries if when μ falls the West responds by increasing T (and, hence, D^*). Productivity improvement will still occur in the East, but some of its gain will now be distributed to the West.

The optimum reaction-curve for the Western economy, in respect of a (positive) change in economic welfare, since we cannot detail the reaction curve for levels of all variables without imposing additional assumptions on the system, is *RWW* on Figure 8.3. *REE* is that curve for the Eastern economy. Of course, these reaction curves are constrained on the supposition that we are omniscient 'Martian' observers of the East-West interdependence.

d.   *The impact of demand disturbances and government activity in the West*

The East-West model is capable of incorporating several random, that is, one-off, shifts in demand/supply. One such major disturbance would be to demand in the West. To be precise, we could posit (say) an autonomous strengthening of demand in the West for Western goods. This could most easily be modelled by our introducing a random error term, U, to the absorption function in the West, with no such term being embodied in the Western demand for imports; so that U would reflect an increased preference for home goods. Such a change in preference could also be envisaged as having arisen from Keynesian *stabilization policies* which have been implemented by the Western government. Since we have specified our East-West model with a 'balance-by-tax-budget' for the West, this strengthening of demand would be tantamount to our writing the Western government's budget constraint so that it contains a component U which is added to government expenditure, G. Hence, $G + U$ is spent on home goods in the West. Consequently, when the 'balance' equation for the West is differentiated it contains the extra item dU, which is transferred to the right-hand side of equation (8.18) and added to the set of exogenous variables in equation (8.19). We can think of that dU as simply 'a U', a random shift variable if we so wish.

This government deficit in the West has no other direct implications for our model, since we will assume that the deficit is financed by a sale of government bonds, which do not count as net wealth. Its impacts will be:

$$\frac{dQ_l}{dU} = -\bar{a}_{22} \, |J|^{-1} > 0 \tag{8.38}$$

and,

$$\frac{dP_e}{dU} = \overset{+}{a}_{21} \, |J|^{-1} > 0 \tag{8.39}$$

As must be the case, *ex hypothesi*, fiscal deficits in the West, when used to increase, directly, just demand for home goods, must be expansionary in the West. Furthermore, they must also benefit the East because the 'equilibrium' level of its price level will increase, so improving its *terms of trade* and its level of economic welfare (since q_e increases, even though the

West has not relaxed D^*). P_e must increase to preserve the level of balance of payments deficit, given that Q_I has increased. Fiscal expansion, in the form of a deficit, is welfare-improving for both the East and the West. In such a circumstance there is no obvious need for the East to adjust its policy in regard to Q_E, to consumption propensities or to technical progress (affecting μ). The question of co-ordination of policies is not a meaningful one. This does not mean, naturally, that for the attainment of designated levels (or changes in) economic welfare in the East and the West there can be no need for co-operation and co-ordination over Western policies of, say, fiscal deficit expansion and Eastern policies of, say, altering μ or consumption propensities.

We can mention at this juncture that *supply* side disturbances occurring in the West could be modelled in a similar fashion. However, one direct way to model them is through a change in P_I. So, if the latter falls because of productivity improvements in Western production, by noting that $P_e = P_E/P_I$ we can readily discover from equations (8.18) and (8.19), given the a_{ij}, b_{ij} that, as must happen *ex hypothesi*, Western output remains unaltered; but, as we would anticipate, *a priori*, the Eastern price level also falls. This is because Western output is entirely demand determined. Thus, if Q_I is to be unchanged, P_e must remain constant, as demands are only price sensitive in the West.

5. East-West interaction with perestroika: regime-switching in the Eastern bloc

We will consider now the *short-run* effects of perestroika. To attempt to model their likely long-run consequences would require a complete re-specification of the preceding framework.

As we have intimated previously, we shall also limit the type of short-run considerations we shall discuss. These exclude any reference to the development of the monetary/financial system and the possible changes that will be effected to the operation of the foreign exchange market. They only include likely manifestations of perestroika in the real sector. These, again by the very nature of our macro-model, can only embrace such changes in an aggregative fashion. We indicated previously, that we would encapsulate the possible impact of change, on demand and supply; and on demand especially.

As the Eastern block begins to dismantle some of its planning machinery to encourage an enterprise culture, the demand side of the economy will be permitted more flexibility: there will already be expectations by the policy-makers of the broad outline of the economy, in regard to overall and sectoral demand. But this will have to be a set of defined expectations more dependent than hitherto on the preferences of purchasers; these are now allowed a freer role in the market where demands are assumed to depend upon relative prices and income. In essence, the assumption is advanced that Eastern absorption depends upon the same type of economic variables as does Western absorption; so that in the East an effective terms of trade, or Laursen–Metzler, effect helps determine the level of expenditure and also its composition between home and foreign goods. One of the several objectives of perestroika is to promote an economic regime in which supply is more responsive to market forces so, *ceteris paribus*, leading to a more efficient use of resources, and, ultimately, to an economic system from which excess demand, repressed inflation, has been removed. As the constraints on demand are being lifted, accompanied by the introduction of more autonomy for business enterprises, it is inevitable that in the short-term (maybe even up to the medium-term) some overall constraints will have to be imposed upon *total* output; and even the looked-for responses of sectoral output to the wishes of the consumer will have to be limited for some time as resources are more likely than not to have been allocated sub-optimally as far as consumers are concerned. The high proportion of national output spent on defence will be just one of many factors contributing to such a production imbalance.

We may suppose, therefore, that those responsible for economic strategy in the rejuvenated Eastern regime will, on lines similar to Central Bank, Treasury, monitoring or control in the West, determine the level of the composite good that should be produced at any point; and that the mechanism for determining what that level might be is inherently the same as that outlined in Section 3. The difference is that expectations are formed by the policy-makers of private absorption in the East: this is used, along with the balance of payments constraint (D^*) which we assume at the start of perestroika is maintained by the West, to determine just the level of aggregate output. The *distribution* of production across commodities/sectors is left to demand, in contrast to what happens in the fully-planned economic regime.

The two new behavioural functions for the East which relate to total expenditure (E) and expenditure on imports (ME), which imply the expenditure function for home goods, are assumed to be:

$$E = E(q_E; P_e) \tag{8.40}$$

$$ME = ME(q_e; P_e) \tag{8.41}$$

Potential wealth effects arising in the East are ignored. The Laursen–Metzler effect postulates that E_2 will be negative (remember that this will be the opposite sign to that of A_2 because of the definition of P_e as P_E/P_1).

The Eastern 'balance' equation becomes:

$$E(\cdot) - P_e q_e - ME(\cdot) + P_e MW(\cdot) = 0 \qquad (8.42)$$

Making use of the 'balance' equation for the West and the definition of q_e, given in equation (8.15), the counterparts to (J) and (K) in equation (8.19) are:

$$a_{11} = (1-t)(A_1 - 1) - [MW_1(1-t) + \beta MW_3]P_e + A_3 B < 0$$

$$a_{12} = A_2 - ME_2 - \frac{ME_1 T}{P_e^2} - MW[1 + \epsilon]$$

$$a_{21} = P_e[MW_1(1-t) + \beta MW_3] > 0$$

$$a_{22} = E_2 + T\left[\frac{(E_1 - P_e - ME_1)}{P_e^2} - \left[\frac{1}{\mu} - \frac{1}{P_e}\right]\right] + MW(1 + \epsilon)$$

$$b_{11} = ME_1\left[\frac{1}{\mu} - \frac{1}{P_e}\right] < 0$$

$$b_{12} = \frac{-ME_1 T}{\mu^2} < 0$$

$$b_{21} = (ME_1 - E_1 + P_e)\left[\frac{1}{\mu} - \frac{1}{P_e}\right]$$

$$b_{22} = (E_1 - ME_1 - P_e)T/\mu^2$$

The coefficients a_{11} and a_{21} are identical with those for equations (8.18) and (8.19). The coefficients b_{11} and b_{12} are also signed uniquely. It is possible to sign a_{12} unambiguously: it is positive because $A_2 > 0$, and the rest of a_{12} must be positive for the Marshall–Lerner condition to hold. Then, if the equivalent of a *ceteris paribus* devaluation (i.e. a fall in P_E) were to improve the East's balance of payments $-[ME_2 + ME_1 T/ P_e^2 - MW(1 + \epsilon)]$ must be positive. The coefficient a_{22} will definitely be negative if $(E_1 - P_e - ME_1) < 0$. We shall assume that this is so; and, consequently, $b_{21} > 0$, $b_{22} < 0$. Hence the trace (J) and $|J| > 0$ conditions for stability are satisfied. We have:

$$\begin{bmatrix} dQ_1 \\ dP_e \end{bmatrix} = |J|^{-1} \begin{bmatrix} \overset{-}{a_{22}} & \overset{+}{-a_{12}} \\ \overset{+}{-a_{21}} & \overset{-}{a_{11}} \end{bmatrix} \begin{bmatrix} \overset{+}{b_{11}} & \overset{-}{b_{12}} \\ \overset{+}{b_{21}} & \overset{-}{b_{22}} \end{bmatrix} \begin{bmatrix} dT \\ d\mu \end{bmatrix} \qquad (8.43)$$

For the 'planned version' of the East-West model, to recapitulate we had, in terms of *qualitative* effects:

$$\begin{bmatrix} dQ_1 \\ dP_e \end{bmatrix} = |J|^{-1} \begin{bmatrix} \overset{-}{a_{22}} & \overset{+}{-a_{12}} \\ \overset{+}{-a_{21}} & \overset{\cdot}{a_{11}} \end{bmatrix} \begin{bmatrix} \overset{+}{b_{11}} & \overset{-}{b_{12}} \\ \overset{-}{b_{21}} & \overset{+}{b_{22}} \end{bmatrix} \begin{bmatrix} dT \\ d\mu \end{bmatrix} \qquad (8.44)$$

The signs of the impacts of T and of μ on the Eastern economy *per se* have altered; and so have the multiplier effects for both economies in the context of the East-West model.

The multiplier effects for the West from (8.43) are:

$$\frac{dQ_1}{dT} = \overset{-\ +}{(a_{22}b_{11}} - \overset{+\ +}{a_{12}b_{21})} \, |J|^{-1} < 0 \tag{8.45}$$

$$\frac{dQ_1}{d\mu} = \overset{-\ -}{(a_{22}b_{12}} - \overset{+\ -}{a_{12}b_{22})} \, |J|^{-1} > 0 \tag{8.46}$$

They are signed unambiguously. As previously, a relaxation of D^*, *ceteris paribus*, reduces Western output; and a fall in μ reduces Western output.

The multiplier effects for the Eastern regime are:

$$\frac{dP_e}{dT} = \overset{-\ +}{(a_{11}b_{21}} - \overset{+\ +}{a_{21}b_{11})} \, |J|^{-1} < 0 \tag{8.47}$$

$$\frac{dP_e}{d\mu} = \overset{-\ -}{(a_{11}b_{22}} - \overset{+\ -}{a_{21}b_{12})} \, |J|^{-1} > 0 \tag{8.48}$$

An expansion of T must now lead to a fall in P_E. This arises through the need for the East's deficit to increase; whilst the fall in output in the new 'equilibrium' in the West requires that P_E has to fall to induce a sufficiently strong counter-effect in the West to prevent its imports from the East falling. When technical progress occurs in the East, with no change in the D^*-constraint, the price of the Eastern good has to fall since, *ceteris paribus*, supply is too great.

As far as the West is concerned, the multiplier effects in a qualitative (but not in a quantitative) sense are identical in the two East-West regimes. However, for the East, on similar restrictions as those imposed upon the East-West model with a planned Eastern economy, definitive findings are obtained in regard to the multiplier effects on its own general price level. Previously, those effects were ambiguous and, for the most part, we imagined them to be zero. How can the notion that expenditures in the East, on home and foreign goods, are price sensitive, contribute to these strong results?

The model contains, implicitly, an equation for the balance of payments deficit which the East can incur towards the West. For the East-West model when the Soviet-type planners are assumed to determine consumption and saving propensities in the East, the relevant specification of the equation which contains the balance of payments deficit to be $D*$ is this:

$$\left[1 + c_e(1 - v_1)P_e\left[\frac{1}{\mu} - \frac{1}{P_e}\right]\right] T - P_eMW(\cdot) = D* \tag{8.49}$$

This provides a limit on *T per se*. When the Eastern residents are accorded more freedom in the choice of expenditure:

$$T + P_eME(\cdot) - P_eMW(\cdot) = D* \tag{8.50}$$

We have not incorporated these constraints into our explicit framework, because we have assumed that the policy-makers in the East know that (8.49) or (8.50) holds and that they approach the constraint $D*$. We have said that it is effective on the East but we can regard this as being operational in a slightly looser sense than would be implied in the sense of Kuhn–Tucker. As the constraint is slackened the East always expands *T*-imports. To use (8.49) or (8.50) explicitly, obviously, requires us to postulate that, in making expectations of their deficit, and limiting it to near $D*$, as we have suggested would happen, planners go further than we would think sensible; that is, we would have to assume *rational expectations* on behalf of the Eastern planners. They know with certainty the nature of the East–West model; they can solve it for the balance of payments and they then select *T* by taking the rational expectation of (8.49) or (8.50): the model of East–West interaction, as a consequence, would solve for the *three* endogenous variables, Q_1, P_e and *T*; or for Q_1 and P_e given $T = T(D*)$ as specified in (8.49) or (8.50). We have, for what we regard as acceptable intuitive reasons, deviated from solving the model in that fashion for this paper. We note, however, that the *J*- and *K*-matrices obtainable from that procedure produce the multiplier effects and policy conclusions that we have described here.[1]

Having made these observations we must return to equations (8.49) and (8.50). Our task in specifying them was to see if any simple intuitive reasons could be advanced for the different terms of trade multipliers in the two types of East-West models. Now, let us write both equations for a unit change in *T*; they become, respectively:

$$(1 + Z) - P_edMW(\cdot) = dD* \tag{8.51}$$

$$1 - P_edMW(\cdot) + P_edME(\cdot) = dD* \tag{8.52}$$

where:

$$Z \equiv c_e(1 - v_1) \left[\frac{P_e}{\mu} - 1 \right]$$

(8.53)

Thus, suppose that P_e remains constant as it could do in the planning variant of the model, whilst simultaneously therein Western output (Q_1) must fall. For any designated change in the 'permitted' balance of payments deficit a reduction in Q_1 with P_e fixed could be feasible; for, in equation (8.51), we observe that dMW would fall consequent upon the fall in Q_1; the East's deficit would rise. If we consider equation (8.52), we can deduce that if P_e were to remain unaltered, the allowable change in the deficit might not be achieved merely by a fall in Q_1. This is because q_e increases consequent upon the expansion in T and ME increases. Since this effect is likely to exceed the relatively small 'parameter' Z, the value of P_e will have to fall to reduce ME and its value, whilst also reducing the Western income effect on $-P_e dMW(\cdot)$, even though partially increasing it through the fall in P_e increasing MW. The consequent changes in P_e will, quite clearly, reflect the terms of trade elasticities of both Eastern and Western expenditures on foreign goods.

What are the economic welfare implications of the changes to demand in the East? We repeat the definitions of real income in the East (I) and in the West (Y) used previously:

$$I = P_e^{1 - v_1} T \left[\frac{1}{\mu} - \frac{1}{P_e} \right]$$

(8.54)

$$Y = P_e^{\alpha - 1} Q_1$$

(8.55)

Recall that v_1 denotes the proportion of total expenditure which is allocated to Eastern goods by Eastern residents. This is likely to fall under perestroika; but we have to assume that the policy-makers do not restrict foreign exchange dealings too much and/or D^* is relaxed. However, let us assume, *ceteris paribus*, that $(1 - v_1)$ remains constant.

Consider equations (8.35) and (8.36) which are the total differentials of equations (8.54) and (8.55). We discover that:

$$\frac{dy}{dT} = \frac{(\alpha - 1)}{P_e} Y \frac{dP_e}{dT} + P_e^{\alpha - 1} \frac{dQ_1}{dT}$$

(8.56)

An expansion of T, and so a relaxation of D^* by the West, has now become potentially welfare-improving because of the reduction in the East's terms of trade.

It would require specific values to be assigned to all relevant parameters before we could decide on the actual sign of (8.56). Likewise, because technical progress implies that μ declines, this eventuality could produce

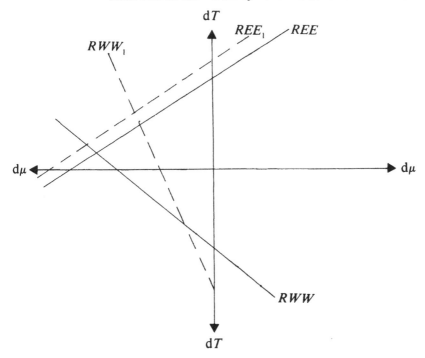

Figure 8.4

an increase in Western economic welfare, since it too, causes a deterioration in the East's terms of trade. Equation (8.35) informs us that the impact of changes in T and in μ on Eastern economic welfare are also ambiguous.

To justify that contention we need to glance back again at equations (8.35) – (8.37) and consider the c_{ij}. We recall that, in determining the signs of the latter coefficients, we assumed that on balance the impact on the terms of trade of movements in either T or μ would be negligible enough for us to ignore them. But we know that the terms of trade could alter in either direction; suppose that they were to increase when T increased, but stayed constant, for the sake of argument, when μ altered. Then c_{11} could be positive, so that the RWW curve had a positive slope and no coordination or co-operation would indeed be feasible. After perestroika, we have unique impacts of T and μ on the terms of trade. We may assume that the c_{ij} retain the signs we assigned to them in constructing Figure 8.3, for we find now, for example, that c_{11} *is* unambiguously negative; the REE schedule shifts upward, whilst the RWW schedule has a steeper slope, which is definitely negative. The situation is depicted in Figure 8.4, where the perestroikan schedules are represented by the dotted lines.

The emphasis in the preceding has been on characterizing (in a way 'caricaturing') the demand changes in the East consequent upon the liberalization of markets. The supply side is not easily re-modelled even at the aggregative level upon which we are focusing. One way in which the shift towards the production of more consumer goods, with a concomitant fall in μ will represent not only an increase in consumer goods but an Leontief input-output coefficient, μ. We may be permitted to argue that a fall in μ will represent not only an increase in consumer goods by an increase in global production as production resources are re-distributed directly and indirectly via the market, in the Eastern bloc. The global resources in the economy become more productive. The possible aggregative consequences of production-shifts have been considered for the very short-run wherein perhaps consumption propensities have not changed, in Section 4; whilst in this Section they have been analysed for the situation where consumers are permitted to express their preferences. Supply side changes in the former case (Section 4) are likely to be wholly beneficial to Eastern economic welfare and output; in the latter case (Section 5), benefits can still be derived from them, but the likelihood is that the shift to greater freedom of choice in consumption will dissipate some of the gains from supply-side strategies. That much could be expected *a priori*. But the chances for co-operation are that much greater when demand-side and supply-side changes are effected hand-in-hand. The message of this type of macro model, as simplified and as aggregative as it is, is that both demand-side and supply-side reforms should be instigated in the East; and the West should co-operate with the economic transformation in the Eastern regime by direct and indirect technological aid. A 'Marshall Plan' is required; it would be to the mutual advantage of East and of West. That Plan could incorporate more Keynesian fiscal expansion in the West because in both types of East–West models such expansion is of direct economic benefit to both regimes.

6. Summary and conclusions

We are all well aware that the aggregative model which we have utilized in this paper has certain limitations. The most obvious ones of which are: it *is* a model which functions at the highest feasible level of aggregation, so that we do not have the real sector separated out into tradeables and non-tradeables; consequently the role of defence expenditure cannot be high-lighted explicitly; and the existence of COMECON, together with bilateral trading-agreements between sections of the East and the West, is not acknowledged.

Nevertheless, the framework we have developed does embody government activity, the government budgetary position, the nature of money/

financial markets, the money supply process, and, hopefully, it epitomizes the Soviet-type economies (certainly) before and after the effects of perestroika have changed the macro-economy. We also like to think that the Chenery-type balance of payments deficit-limit imposed by the West on the East broadly captures, with a fixed exchange rate, the essence of the trading relationship between them, even if it ignores bilateral agreements. In that trading relationship it is essential to draw out the crucial role played by the technologial imports upon which the Eastern bloc depends. Our framework also makes it feasible for us to encapsulate the broad implications for the real sector of the economic transformation which the Soviet-type economies are trying to effect. Further analysis of the economic consequences of that transformation process would require the formulation of a model which was slightly less aggregative than the current model; in the medium-term this model also would need to be extended, to encompass a more sophisticated money/financial system than the one currently operative in Soviet-type economic systems.

What are the implications which we can extract from our two models of East-West interaction? Let us take the two variants of the model *seriatim*. We begin, then, with the one based on a planning model in the Eastern economy. Our findings are: (1) a fiscal deficit in the West will expand Western output, improve the terms of trade of the East, and increase economic welfare in both countries; (2) *mutatis mutandis*, even though we have not analysed this formally, a monetary expansion designed to raise output in the West will generate similar results; (3) a slackening of the balance of payments constraint imposed on the East by the West will almost certainly improve the terms of trade of the East and, via the increase in technological imports (hence, q_e will be increased), the level of Eastern economic welfare; whilst probably having a detrimental effect on Western economic welfare; (4) technical progress in the East will generate similar findings; and, hence, if we could imagine such progress was engineered by the Central Planners, such a policy stance is likely to be unwelcome to the West; (5) however, since only the output effects in the East and the West, consequent upon the expansion of T and the fall in μ, are certain, the terms of trade effects being ambiguous, the impacts on economic welfare are also uncertain; and it is possible for policy co-ordination to take place between East and West to the effect that a particular increase in T with a specified reduction in μ, will lead to an improvement in the economic welfare of both regimes.

In respect of the perestroikan variant of our East-West model our findings on fiscal and monetary policy are unaltered (though we have not formally provided these results in the text). If the West permits the Eastern deficit to expand, the output effects are the same as those first detailed;

and the terms of trade response is still uncertain. The presence of technical progress in the East can provide different impacts on the two economies when Eastern demand is permitted to respond to relative price (terms of trade) effects from those given by our first model. Since we may think of a fall in μ as either a shift in the structure of production in the East following on from perestroika or as arising out of *technical co-operation* by the West, we can again deduce optimal values for changes in (T,μ) which the governments of the two economic blocs should implement together in order to permit *both* levels of economic welfare to be enhanced. The potential benefits will probably be higher than they were before perestroika; and the scope for co-operation will in general be larger (equations (8.35) – (8.37) indicate that both reaction curves have a greater likelihood of being in the top left-hand quadrant of Figure 8.3). Such co-operation would be true co-ordination of policies if μ were a reflection of the conscious re-structuring of production in the East; whilst, if it were to be taken as a variable which the West could alter via technological aid, coupled with 'quantitative aid', as it were, through the expansion of D^*, the choice of $(dT, d\mu)$ might best, indeed, be thought of as *co-operation* by the West with the East.

Notes

1. The a_{ij} and b_{ij} are:

$$a_{11} = (1-t)(A_1 - 1) + \frac{P_e}{1+a}[MW_1(1-t) + \beta MW_3] + \beta A_3$$

$$a_{12} = A_2 - \left[\frac{1}{1+a}\right]MW[1+\epsilon]$$

$$a_{21} = \left[\frac{b}{1+a} + 1\right]P_e[MW_1(1-t) + \beta MW_3]$$

$$a_{22} = \left[\frac{b}{1+a} + 1\right] + MW(1+\epsilon)$$

$$b_{11} = \left[\frac{a}{1+a}\right](P_e - 1)$$

$$b_{12} = (D^* + P_eMW)\left[\frac{1}{(1+a)^2}c_e(1-v_1)\right]\frac{P_e}{\mu^2}$$

$$b_{21} = \left[\frac{b}{1+a}\right] - \left[\frac{b}{1+a} + 1\right]\beta P_eMW_3$$

$$b_{22} = -(D^* + P_eMW)\left[\frac{bc_e(1-v_1)P_e}{(1+a)^2\mu^2} - \frac{P_e}{(\mu - P_e)^2(1+a)}\right]$$

with:

$$a \equiv c_e(1-v_1)P_e\left[\frac{1}{\mu} - \frac{1}{P_e}\right] > 0$$

$$b \equiv c_e v_1 - 1 - \left[\frac{P_e}{P_e - \mu} \right] < 0$$

The signs of a_{ij} are: $a_{11} < 0$ (on the same assumption we have made concerning the low value of βA_3); $a_{12} > 0$, because we made the assumption that $|\epsilon| \geqslant 1$; $a_{21} > 0$; and $a_{22} < 0$. These signs are identical with those where the presence of the constraint D^* is modelled in a somewhat weaker fashion. Under the negative-dominance diagonal condition we must have $|J| > 0$.

Turning now to the b_{ij}, we see that it is in this respect that the qualitative properties of the model could alter when D^* is entered as a binding constraint along rational expectations lines. However, since $P_e > 1$, $b_{11} > 0$; $b_{12} > 0$, so that its sign alters; $b_{21} < 0$; and now we will have $b_{22} > 0$ with $|b_{22}| > |b_{12}|$. The only changes to b_{ij}, therefore, relate to the impact of changes in μ; but the changed signs and the reversal of the dominance condition relating $|b_{21}|$ and $|b_{12}|$ means that the multiplier effects all have the same signs as those in the text; and quantitatively also they could be identical. We note that dT is now replaced, of course, by the variable dD^*.

References

Berliner, J. (1976) *The Innovation Decision in Soviety Industry*, MIT Press, Cambridge, Mass.

Berrios, R. (1983) 'The political economy of East-South relations', *Journal of Peace Research*, vol. 20, pp 239–252.

Bornstein, M. (1979) *Comparative Economic Systems: Models and Cases*, Irwin, Homewood, Illinois.

Deger, S. (1985) 'Soviet arms sales to developing countries: the economic forces', in R. Cassen (ed.), *Soviet Interests in the Third World*, Royal Institute for International Affairs, Sage Publications Ltd., London, pp 159–176.

Findlay, R. and Rodriguez, C. (1977) 'Intermediate inputs and macroeconomic policy under flexible exchange rates', *Canadian Journal of Economics*, vol. 10, pp 208–17.

Grossman, C. (1968) *Money and Planning*, University of California Press, Berkeley and Los Angeles.

Hanson, P. (1986) 'Soviet foreign trade policies in the 1980s', *Bericht des BIOst*, no. 41.

Kanbur, R. and Vines, D. (1986) 'North-South interaction and commodity control', *Journal of Development Economics*, vol. 23, pp 371–387.

Kornai, J. (1982) 'Shortage as a fundamental problem of centrally planned economies and Hungarian reform. An interview with A. Jutta-Pietsch in *Economics of Planning*, vol. 18, pp 103–113.

Laursen, S. and Metzler, L. A. (1950) 'Flexible exchange rates and the theory of employment', *Review of Economics and Statistics*, vol. 32, pp 281–299.

Malinvaud, E. (1977) *The Theory of Unemployment Reconsidered*, Blackwell, Oxford.

Murshed, S. M. (1987) *Analytical Models of North-South Interaction*, Unpublished Ph.D. dissertation, University of Birmingham.

Nuti, D. M. (1988) 'Perestroika: transition from central planning to market socialism', *Economic Policy*, October 1988, pp355–389.

Taylor, L. (1983) *Structuralist Macroeconomics*, Basic Books, New York.

Ward, B. (1967) *The Socialist Economy: A Study of Organizational Alternatives*, Random House, New York.

Index